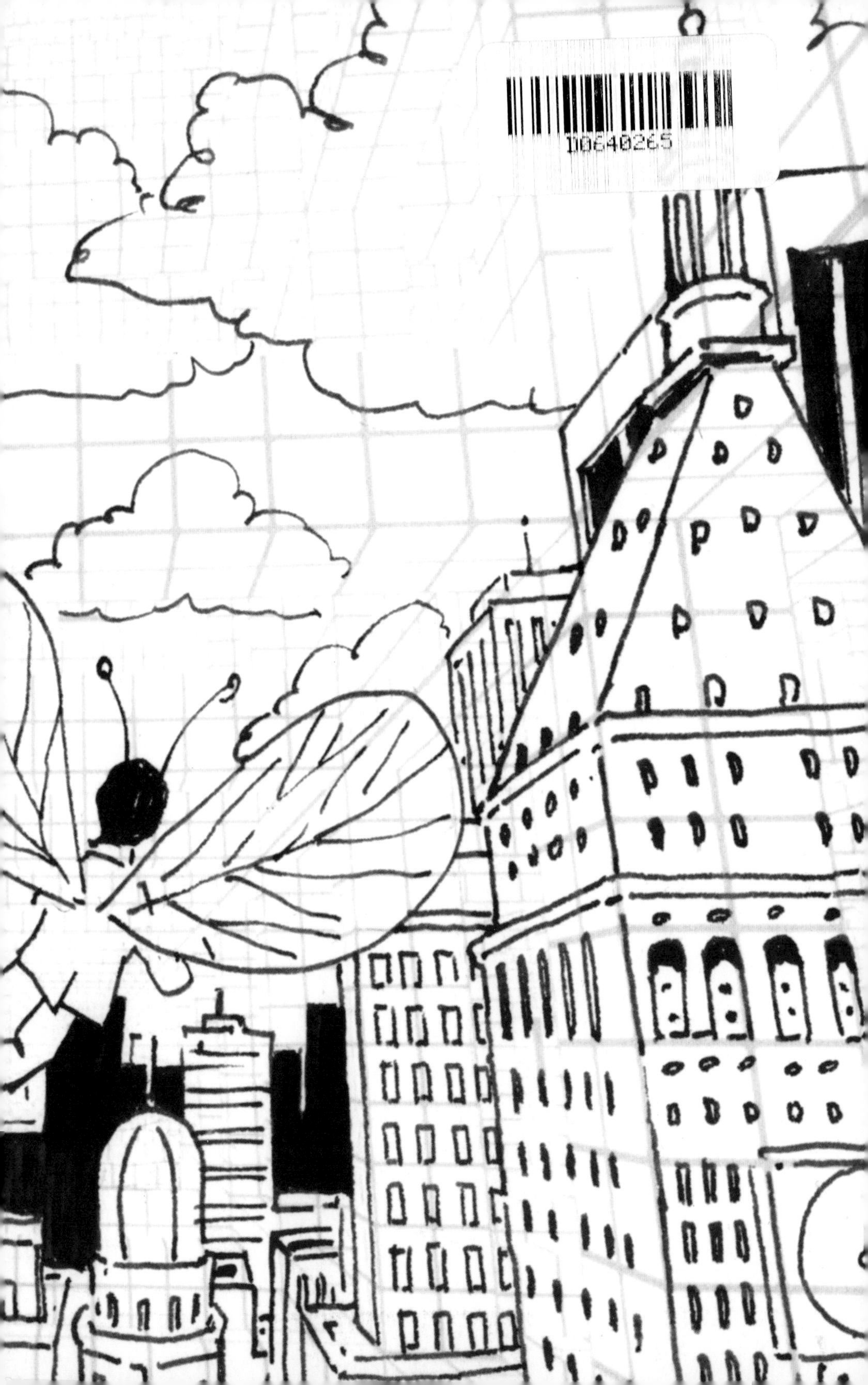

EVERYBODY GETS IT WRONG! (AND OTHER STORIES)

DAVID CHELSEA'S 24-HOUR COMICS VOLUME 1

HARVEY
PEKAR
GETS IT
WRONG!

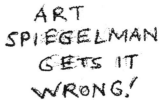

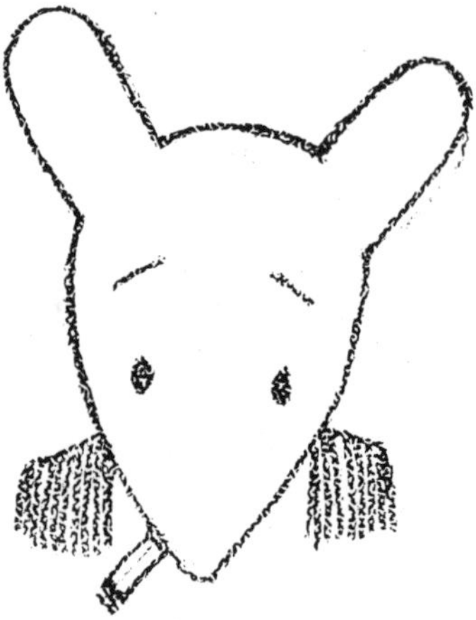

ART
SPIEGELMAN
GETS IT
WRONG!

NINA
PALEY
GETS IT
WRONG!

EVEN THE
GREAT CRUMB!
WRONG!
WRONG!
WRONG!

EVERYBODY GETS IT WR⊘NG!

(AND OTHER STORIES)

  DAVID CHELSEA'S
24-HOUR COMICS™
VOLUME 1

ALL STORIES WRITTEN AND DRAWN BY
DAVID CHELSEA, WITHIN TWENTY-FOUR HOURS.

FOREWORD BY NAT GERTLER

DARK HORSE BOOKS

President and Publisher
MIKE RICHARDSON

Editor
PHILIP R. SIMON

Designer
ADAM GRANO

Digital Production and Retouch
CHRIS HORN and CHRISTINA McKENZIE

Special thanks to EVE HARRIS CELSI, NAT GERTLER, TOM LECHNER, and MIKE RUSSELL.

Published by Dark Horse Books
A division of Dark Horse Comics, Inc.
10956 SE Main Street
Milwaukie, OR 97222

DarkHorse.com
DChelsea.com

International Licensing: (503) 905-2377
To find a comics shop in your area, call the Comic Shop Locator Service toll-free at 1-888-266-4226.

First edition: June 2013
ISBN 978-1-61655-155-1

10 9 8 7 6 5 4 3 2 1

Printed in China

FOREWORD
BY NAT GERTLER

Look, if you want a comics collection that's like a perfect studio album, all recorded instrument by instrument and polished and remixed and refined by a team of top engineers, put this book down and grab the next one on the shelf. This ain't the book you're looking for. This is 24-hour comics. This is live jazz.

And it's not just any live jazz, either. For many comics creators, making a 24-hour comic is a rite of passage. For others, it's a challenge. But for David Chelsea, it's a method, a process that allows him to achieve an impressive range of creative results. He's the king of this breed of jazz.

The 24-hour comic is the brainchild of comics theoretician Scott McCloud. The goal is for a single cartoonist to create in 24 hours a 24-page comic. That may be simple, but it is by no means easy, because creating a comic of that length is normally months of work. And there are rules to the 24-hour comic, but those rules merely enforce the simplicity. Can you prepare for the 24 hours of comics creation by doing character designs or writing out a plot? Nope. You can have your tools and your reference, but for a pure 24-hour comic, you must have put nothing down on paper (or computer, or other medium) before the 24 hours begin. Can you take time to catch a nap, eat a meal, or make love to George Clooney? Yes, yes, and if you can get his permission, sure . . . but while you're doing these things, the clock doesn't stop, and you still have to finish page 24 of your comic within 24 hours of having begun.

Some people create a 24-hour comic simply to prove (to themselves or the world) that they can do it. They may need multiple attempts to succeed, as many folks who set out to make a 24-hour comic find themselves finishing page 6 after thirteen hours and trade in their drawing tools and good intentions for a comfy bed. Others tackle it a few times for what they have to learn from the experience, for the confidence it gives them, and the timesaving techniques they add to their creative toolbox.

Chelsea has created more 24-hour comics than anyone, and by the time you've created even as many as are in this first volume, you've gained whatever you have to gain by the process. You've proven yourself, and you've gained your tools. The only reason to keep doing it, then, is for the product, for the comic that results. Read these stories, and you'll understand why he finds it worthwhile.

Creating a 24-hour comic is liberating in terms of content. A cartoonist can try wild and creative things; an idea for which a month's work would be a foolhardy investment can certainly justify the spending of two turns of the clock. You'll see in these pages that Chelsea has used those days well, trying a wide variety of things— wordy political tales, dialogue-free animal adventures, a one-man anthology, explanations of uncommon creative techniques, and more.

The constantly ticking clock leaves little time to plan, and one can hardly afford to go back, rework, and adjust what one has already done, whatever its imperfections. Even the talented and attentive Mr. Chelsea generates slight inconsistencies, story lines that disappear, and unintentionally creative spelling. You will see moments that arise from the process—the page that suggests that the artist needed a change of pace after hours of drawing similar shots, or that he had fallen behind the clock and needed a page that could be drawn quickly to catch up, or that he just got in the mood to draw some famous characters. These are not flaws; they are texture, texture that reveals the artist and his process. A 24-hour comic is almost always personally revealing in some form, because there is no time to hide yourself behind layers of creative polish.

So in these pages, you will see plenty. Not just of Chelsea's work, but of the man behind it. His jazz is about to begin playing. Listen.

—Nat Gertler, founder, 24-Hour Comics Day

Nat Gertler is the publisher of About Comics *and founder of 24-Hour Comics Day. He has edited four books of 24-hour comics, and in doing so published the first works of Fiona Staples and Faith Erin Hicks, among others. An Eisner Award–nominated comic book creator in his own right, Nat spends his days sequestered among far more* Peanuts *books than any small nation needs.*

For more information about 24-Hour Comics Day, the annual worldwide event of comics creation, go to 24HourComicsDay.com!

THE HAROLD PROJECT

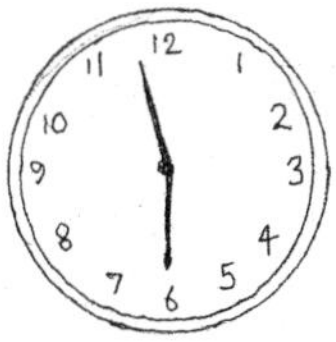
12
1
2
3
4
5
6
7
8
9
10
11

NOTES ON "THE HAROLD PROJECT"

I drew my first 24-hour comic mostly as a vacation from artist's block. I had been wrestling for some time with my own monster in a box, an ambitious graphic novel about Portland in the 1970s, basically getting nowhere. I had never been happy enough with the script to work up a finished version, or even send a proposal to a publisher. Eventually, I decided it was time to do something drastic to prove to myself that I could actually complete something, so I invited some cartoonist friends over for a "24-Hour Comics" session in May 2004.

This challenge was devised by Scott McCloud—your objective is to draw an entire 24-page comic in a single daylong session. All in all, my first experience worked out far better than I would have expected. Work began at nine in the morning, and I wrapped page 24 up at six a.m., three hours short of deadline—I then went back and added some blacks and extra details, but was basically done by seven a.m. Rather than utterly winging it, I'd decided to adopt two variations to lend a bit of structure to the proceedings—setting aside a sack of unsorted reference photos, which I picked from randomly every time I began a page, and drawing over my own CGI perspective grids, which I had previously printed out onto Bristol in nonrepro blue (versions of these were eventually included as a companion disk with my instructional book *Extreme Perspective!*). The square columns of my perspective grids suggested the girders of a building, and Harold Lloyd has always been a favorite of mine (hence the glasses), so I decided to basically remake *Safety Last!*, stealing all the gags I could half remember. The end result was goofy and insubstantial but not more so than a lot of other things I spent more time on. It probably helps that the story I chose to tell had nothing to do with the project I was blocked on, and in the end my newfound momentum didn't carry over to further work on that. Still, I had found a way to rack up the pages without thinking too hard about it, and in the years since I have taken the plunge thirteen more times, trying to meet a self-imposed quota of one or two a year.

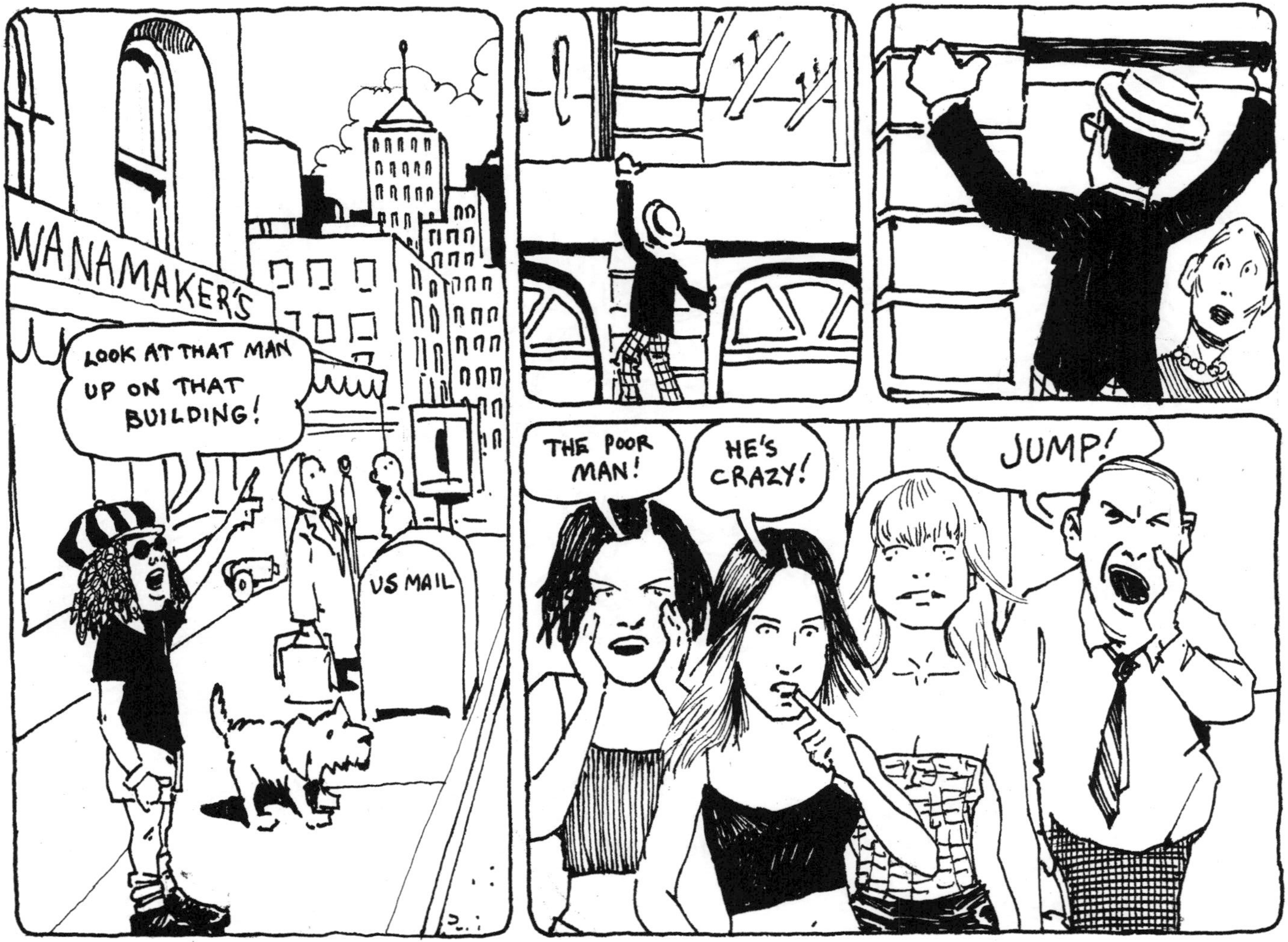
WANAMAKER'S
LOOK AT THAT MAN UP ON THAT BUILDING!
US MAIL
THE POOR MAN!
HE'S CRAZY!
JUMP!

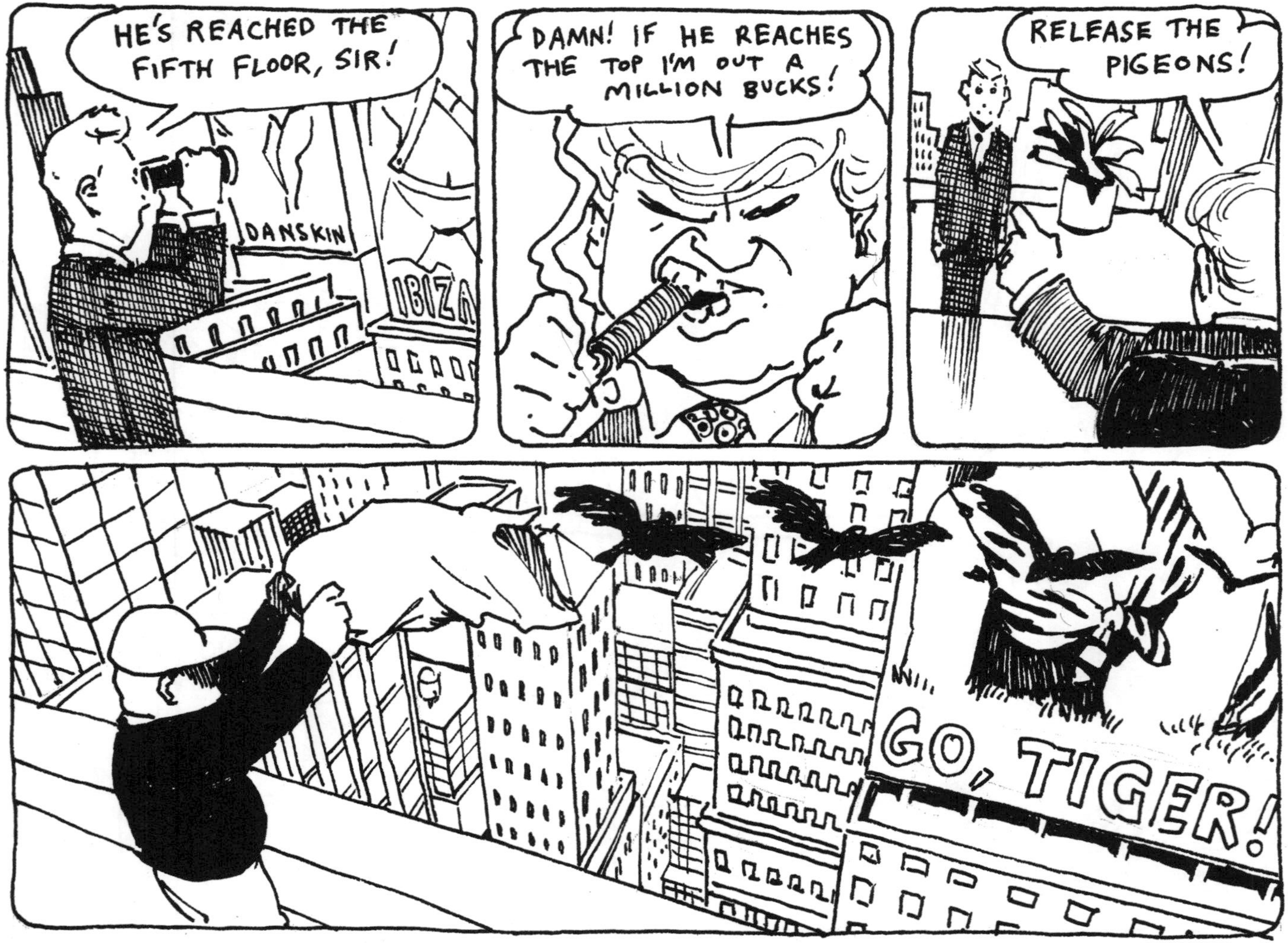
HE'S REACHED THE FIFTH FLOOR, SIR!
DANSKIN
IBIZA
DAMN! IF HE REACHES THE TOP I'M OUT A MILLION BUCKS!
RELEASE THE PIGEONS!
GO, TIGER!

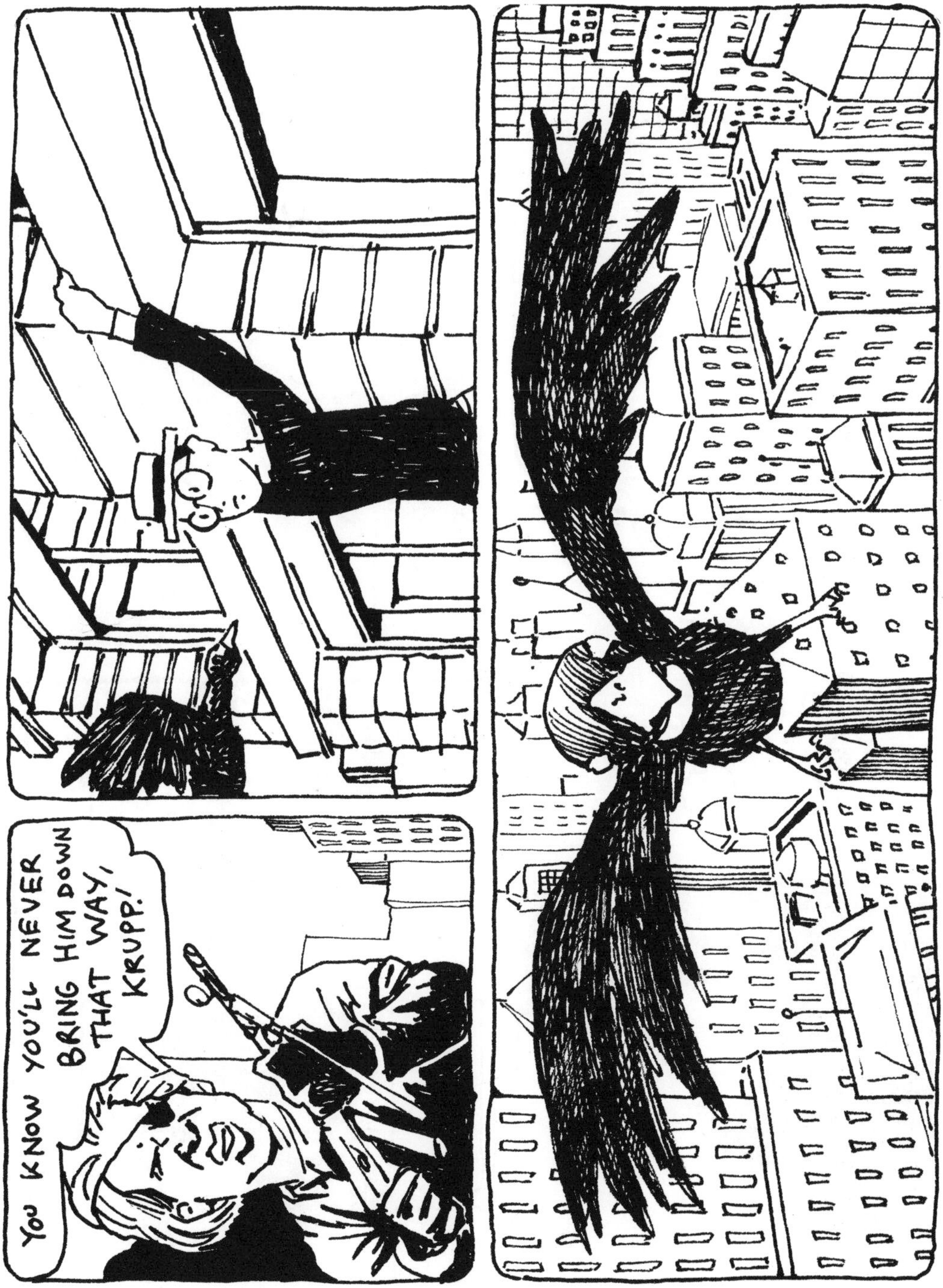
YOU KNOW YOU'LL NEVER BRING HIM DOWN THAT WAY, KRUPP!

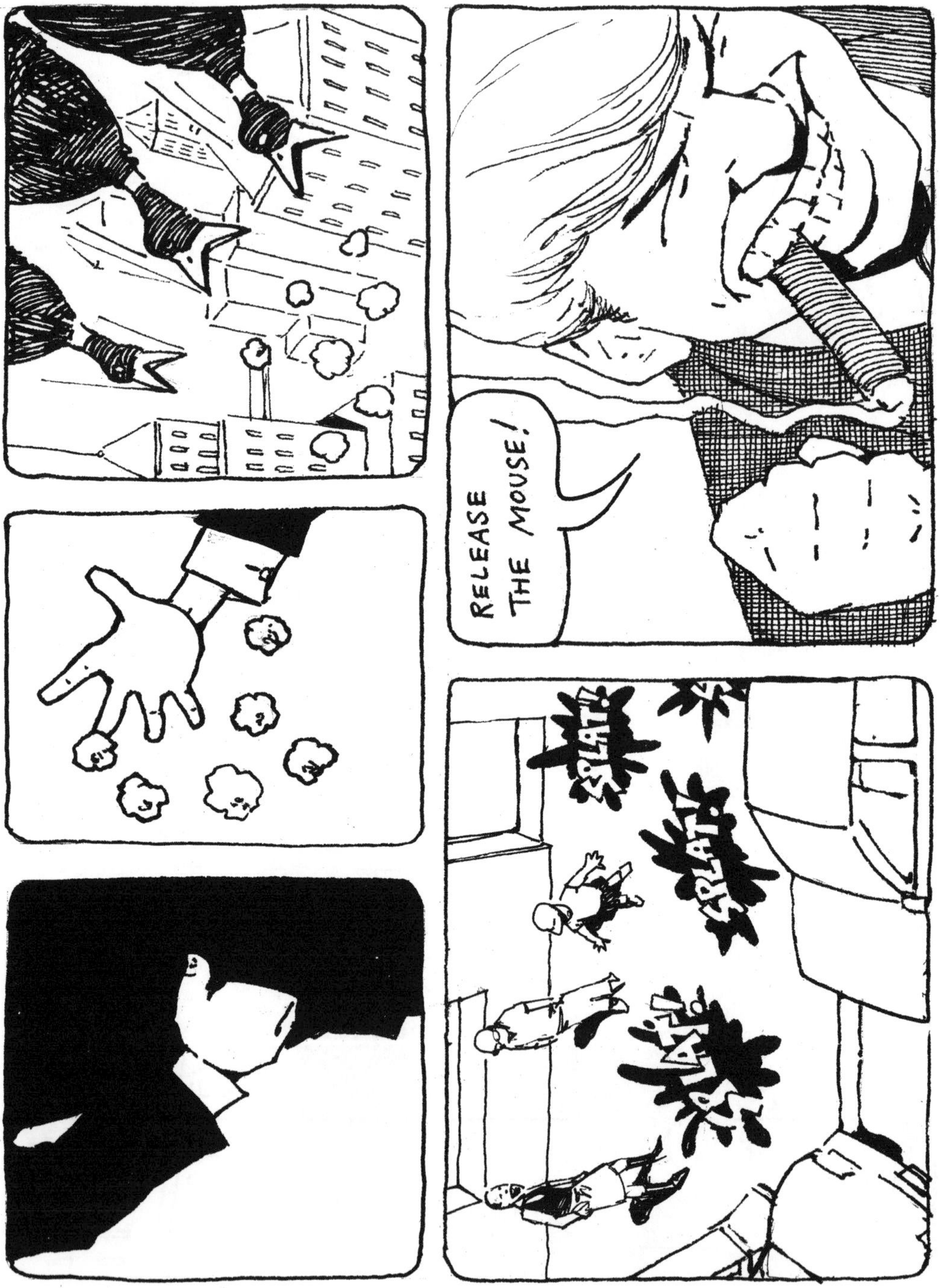
RELEASE THE MOUSE!
SPLAT!
SPLAT!
SPLAT!

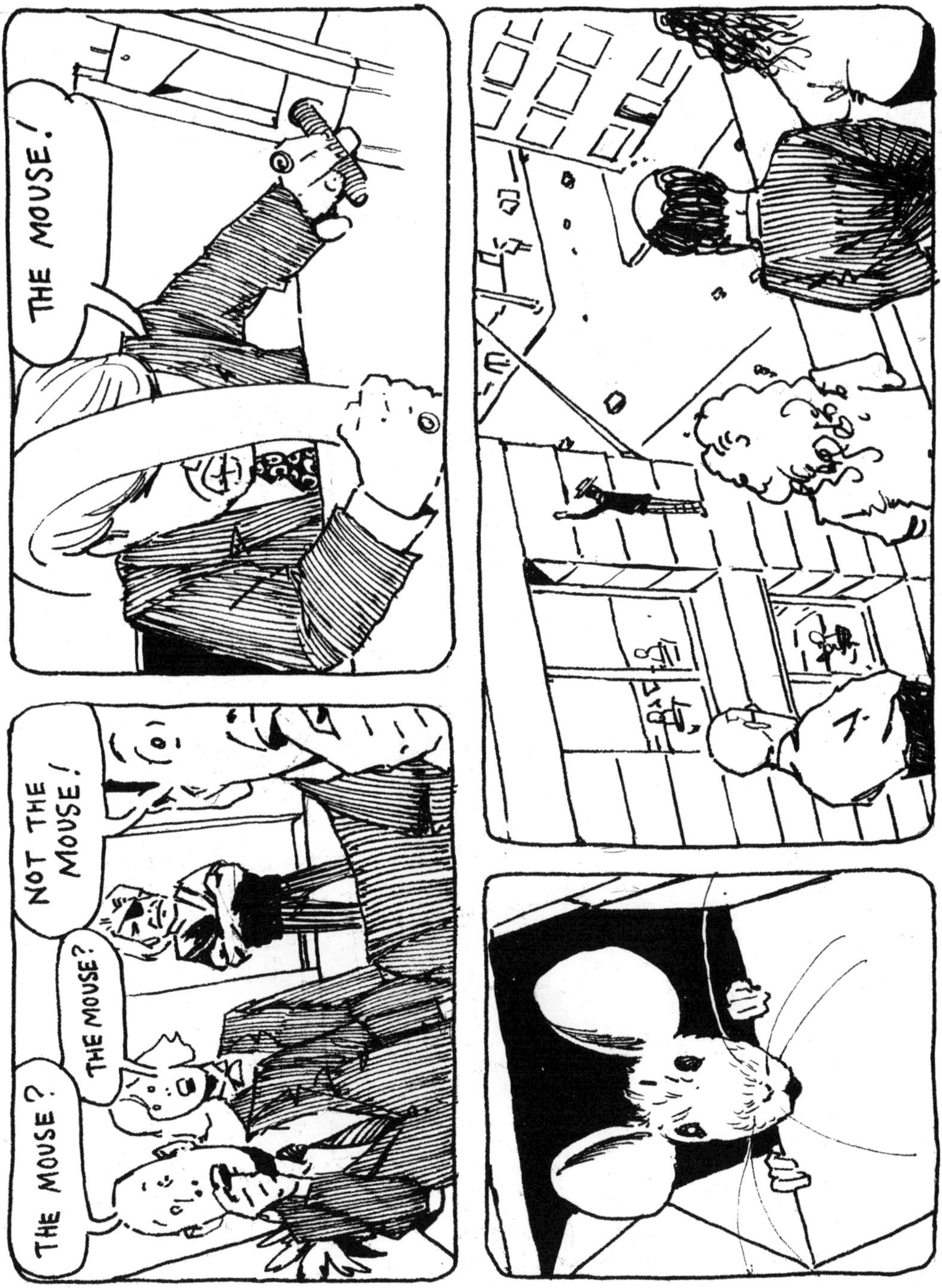
THE MOUSE?
THE MOUSE?
NOT THE MOUSE!
THE MOUSE!

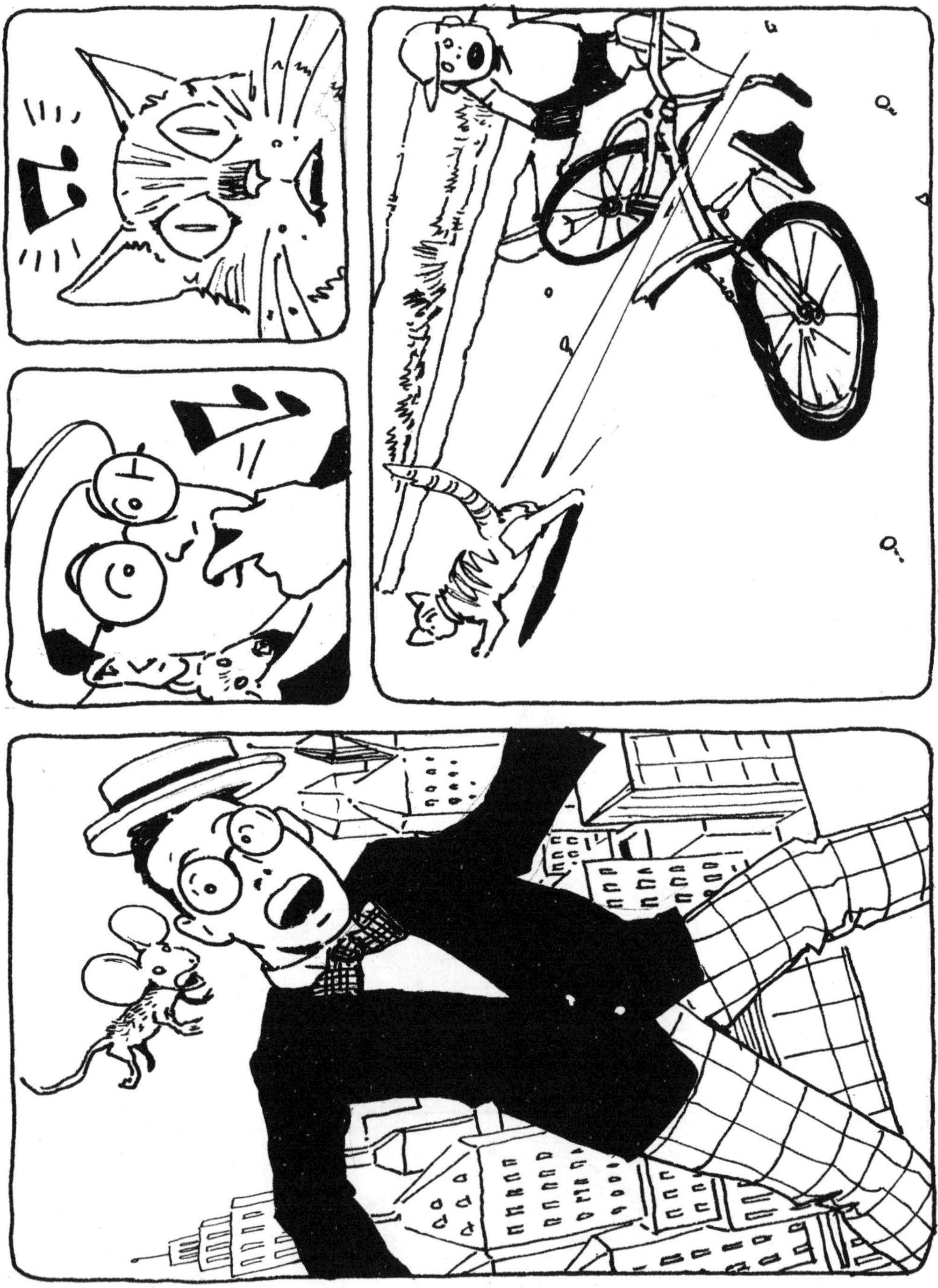

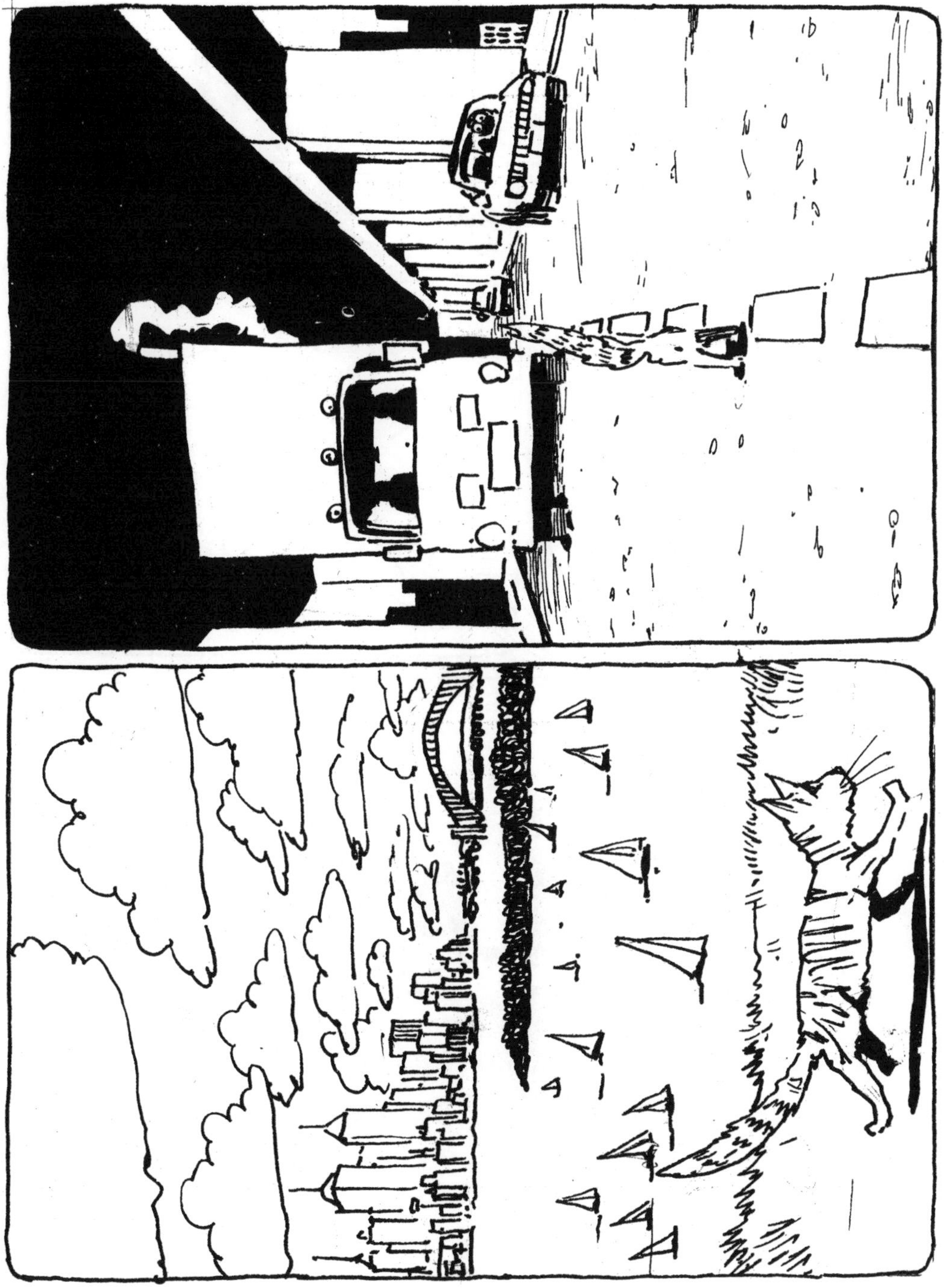

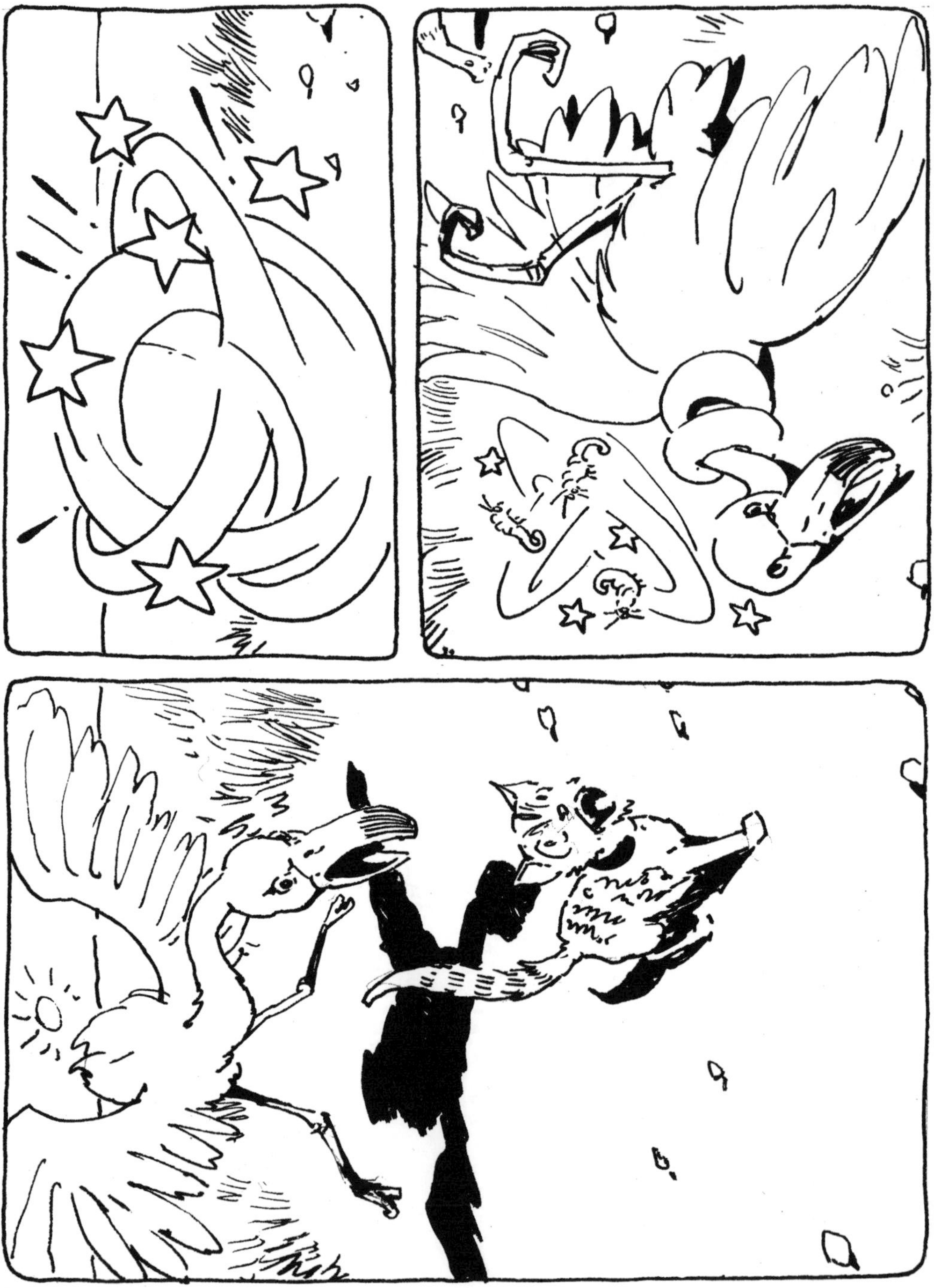

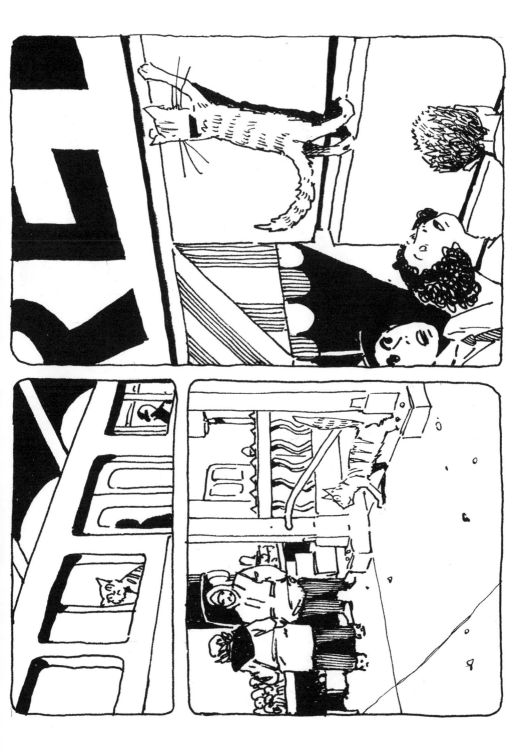

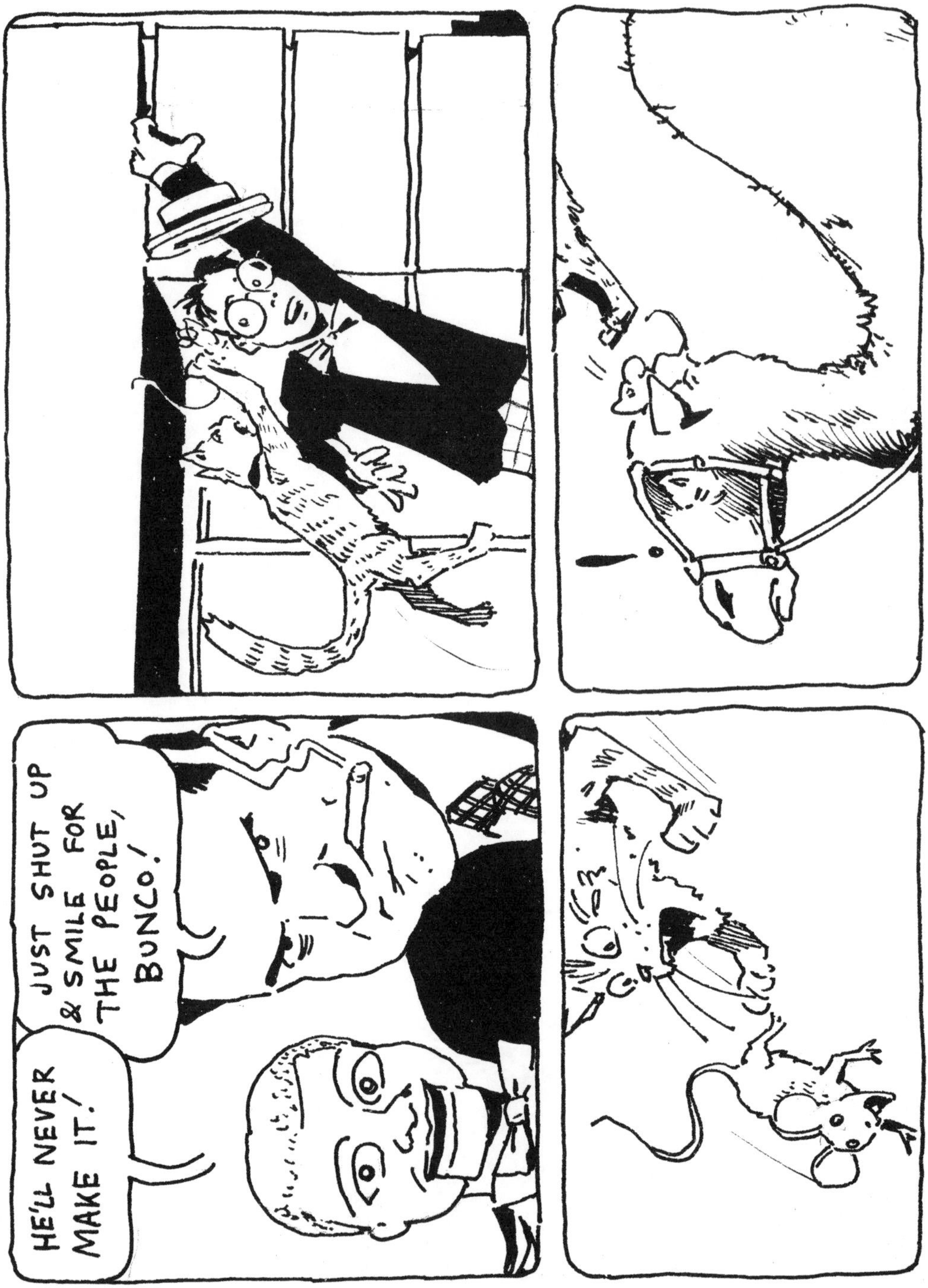
HE'LL NEVER MAKE IT!
JUST SHUT UP & SMILE FOR THE PEOPLE, BUNCO!

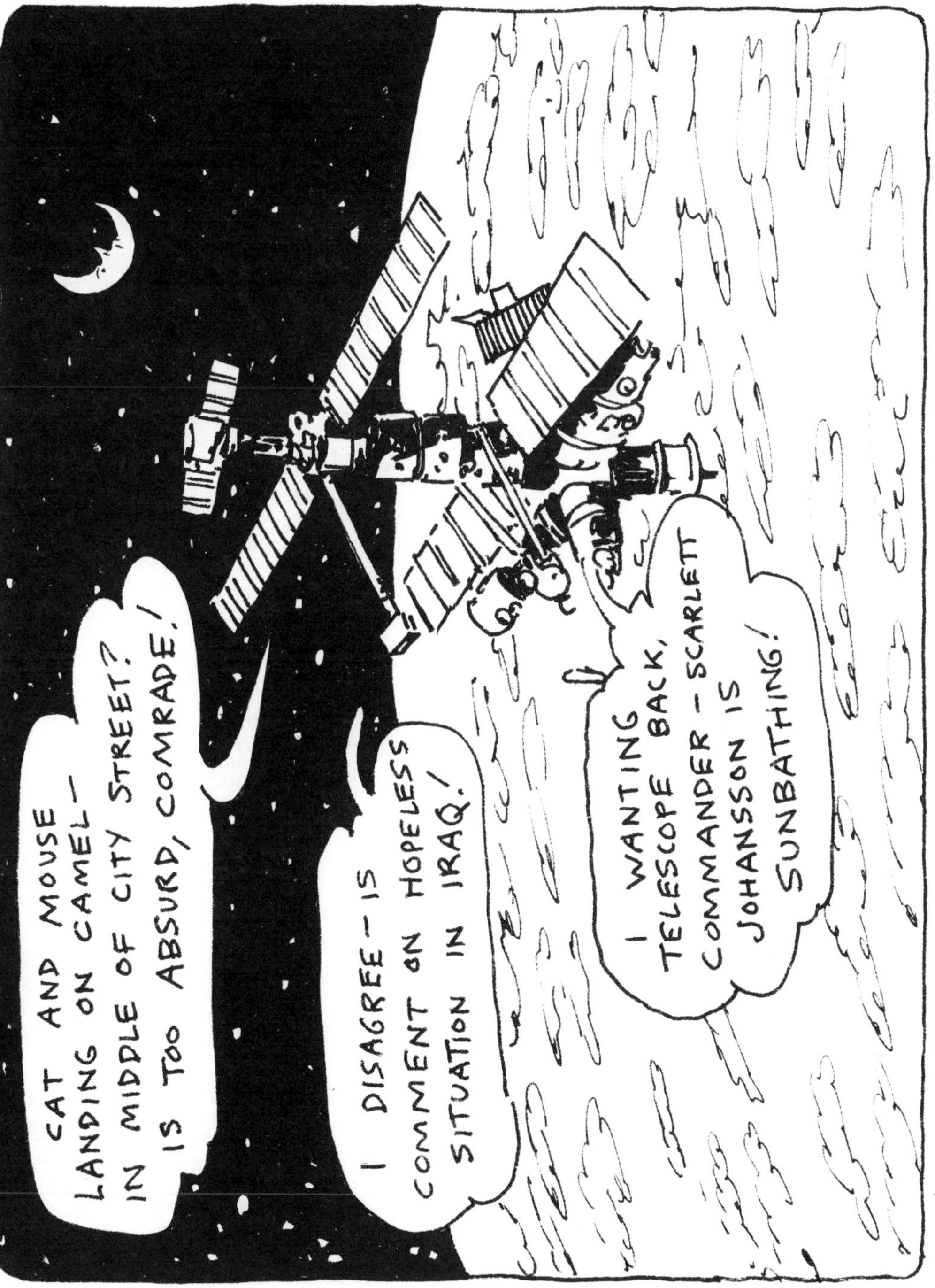
CAT AND MOUSE LANDING ON CAMEL— IN MIDDLE OF CITY STREET? IS TOO ABSURD, COMRADE!
I DISAGREE—IS COMMENT ON HOPELESS SITUATION IN IRAQ!
I WANTING TELESCOPE BACK, COMMANDER—SCARLETT JOHANSSON IS SUNBATHING!

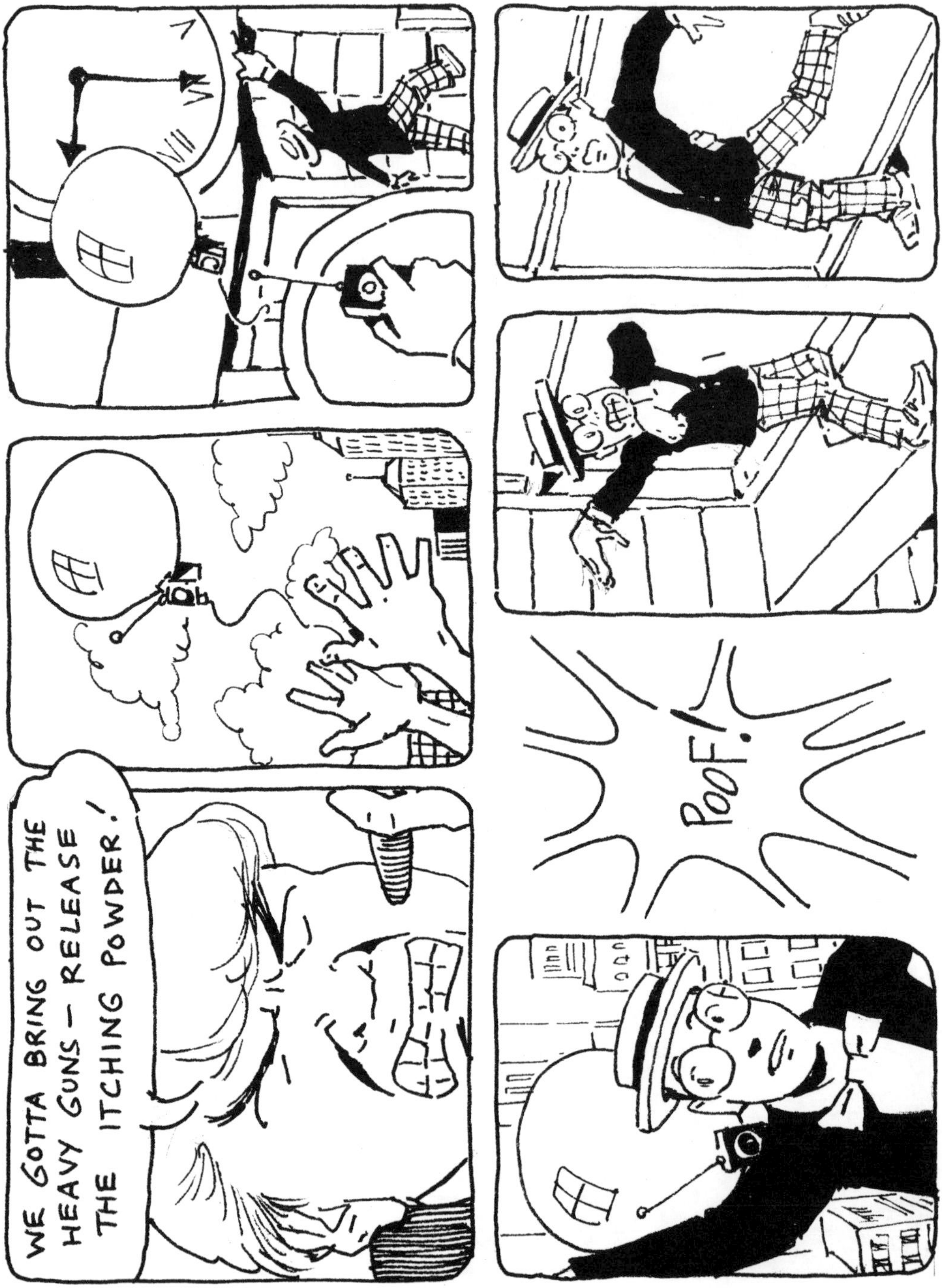
WE GOTTA BRING OUT THE HEAVY GUNS — RELEASE THE ITCHING POWDER!
POOF!

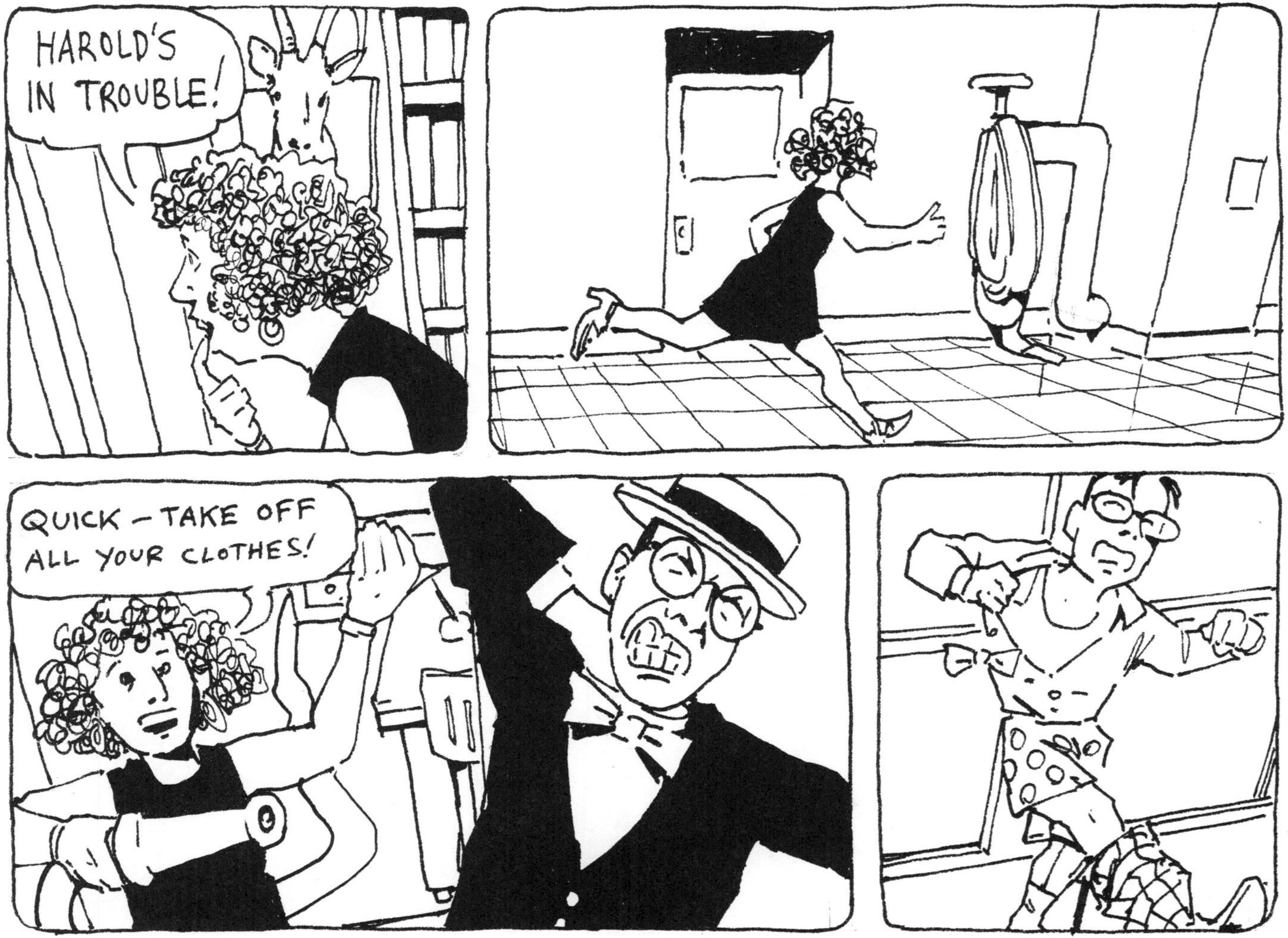
HAROLD'S IN TROUBLE!
QUICK – TAKE OFF ALL YOUR CLOTHES!

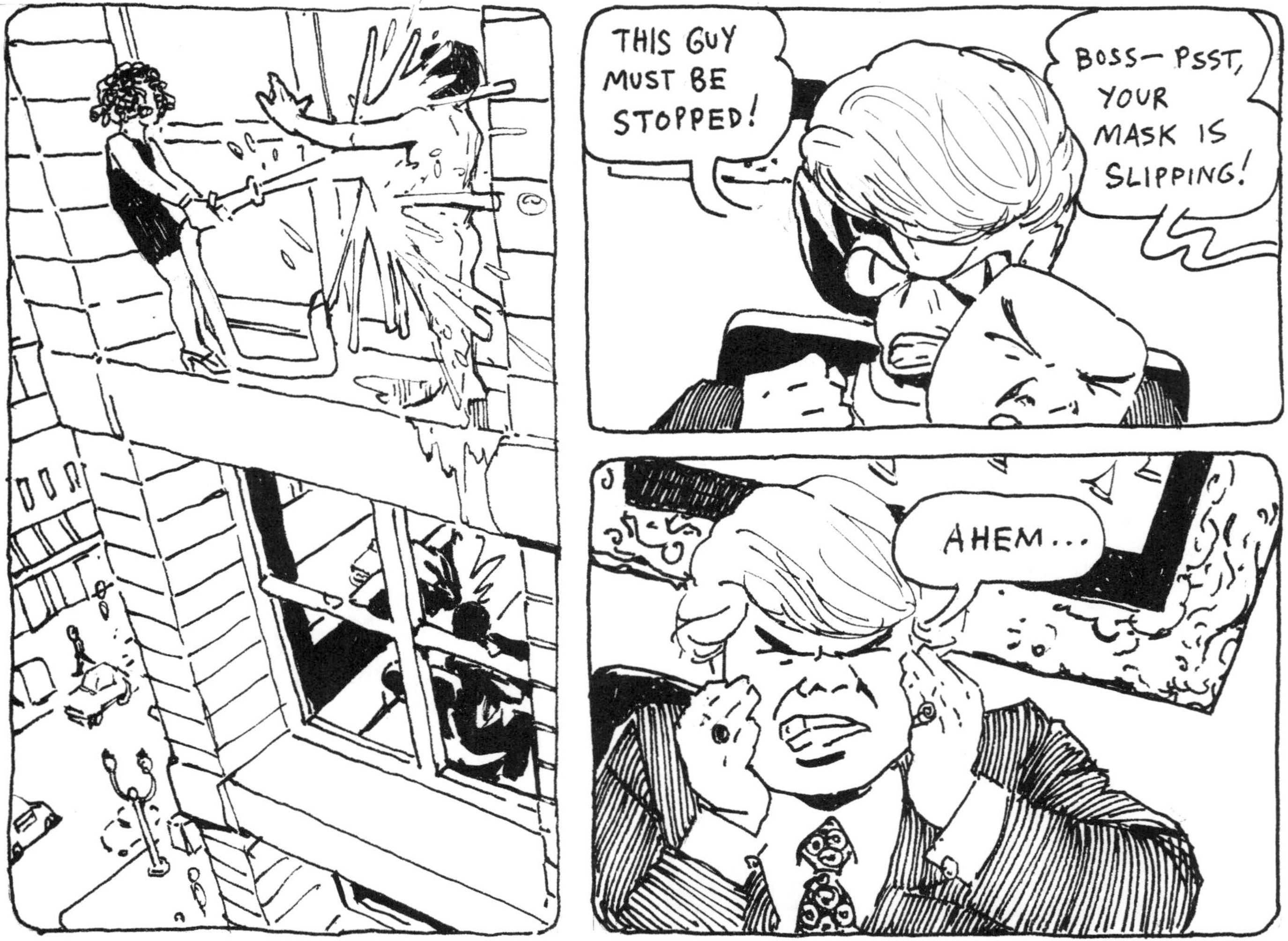
THIS GUY MUST BE STOPPED!
BOSS— PSST, YOUR MASK IS SLIPPING!
AHEM...

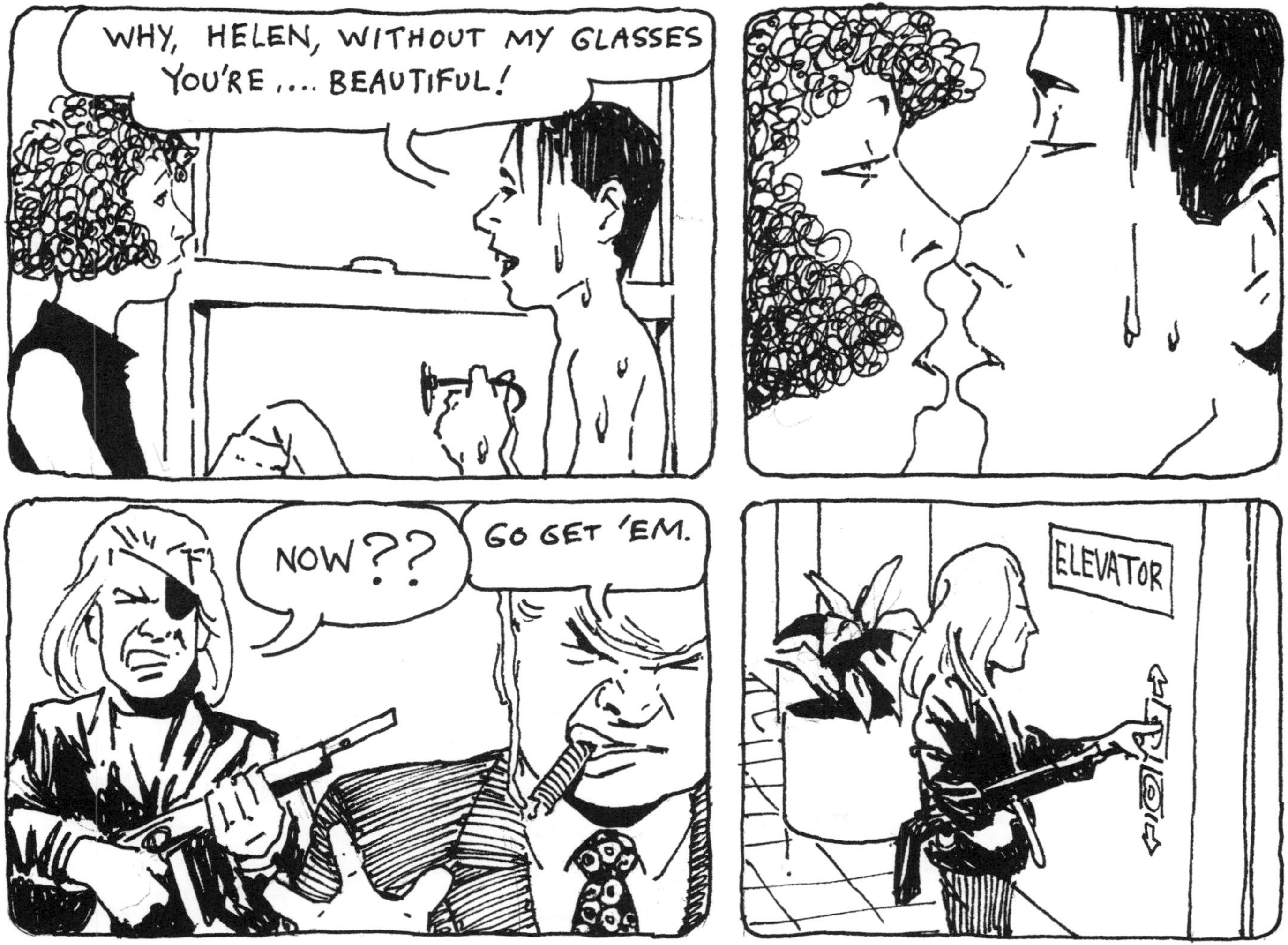
WHY, HELEN, WITHOUT MY GLASSES YOU'RE .... BEAUTIFUL!
NOW??
GO GET 'EM.
ELEVATOR

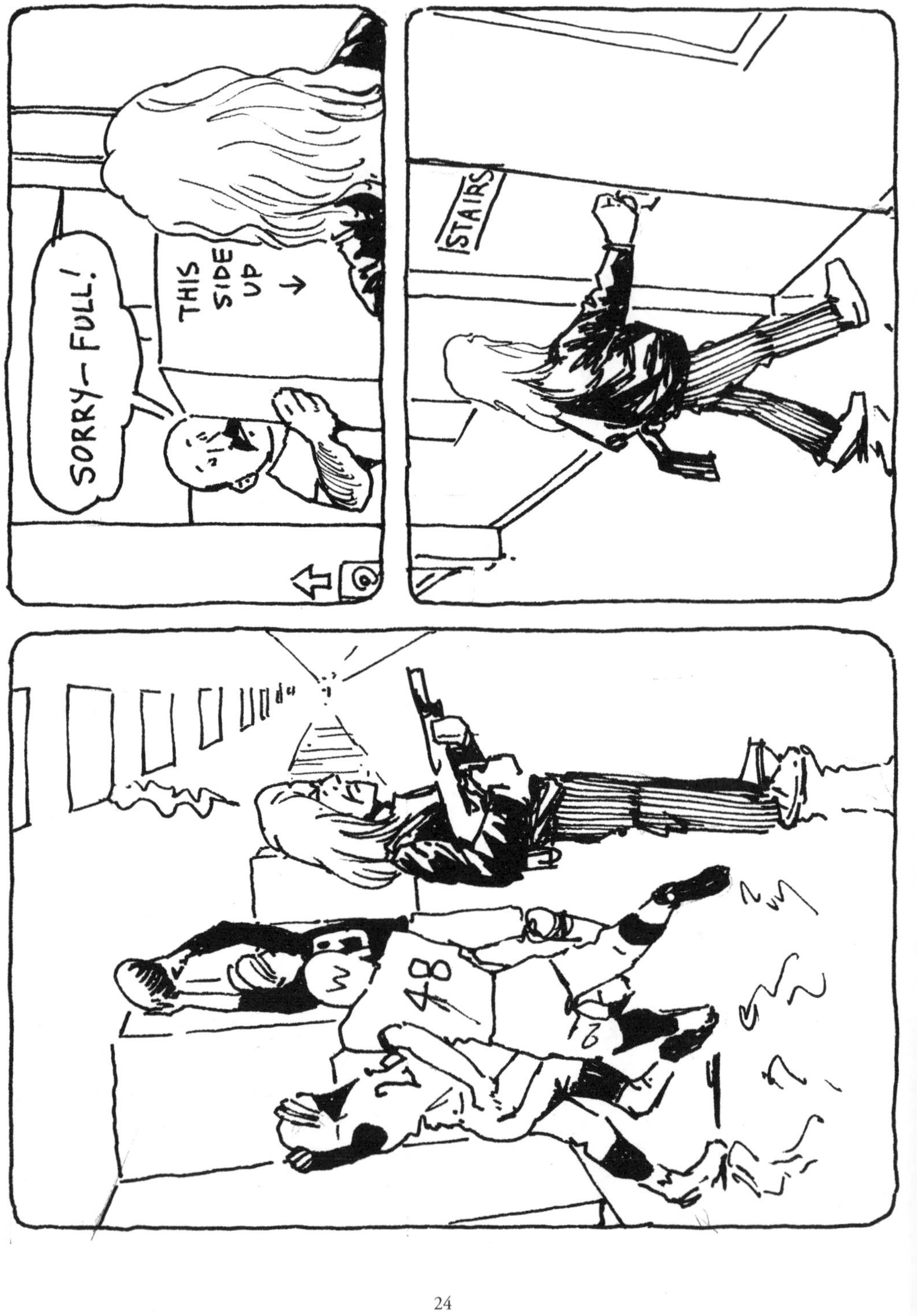
SORRY—FULL!
THIS SIDE UP
STAIRS
48

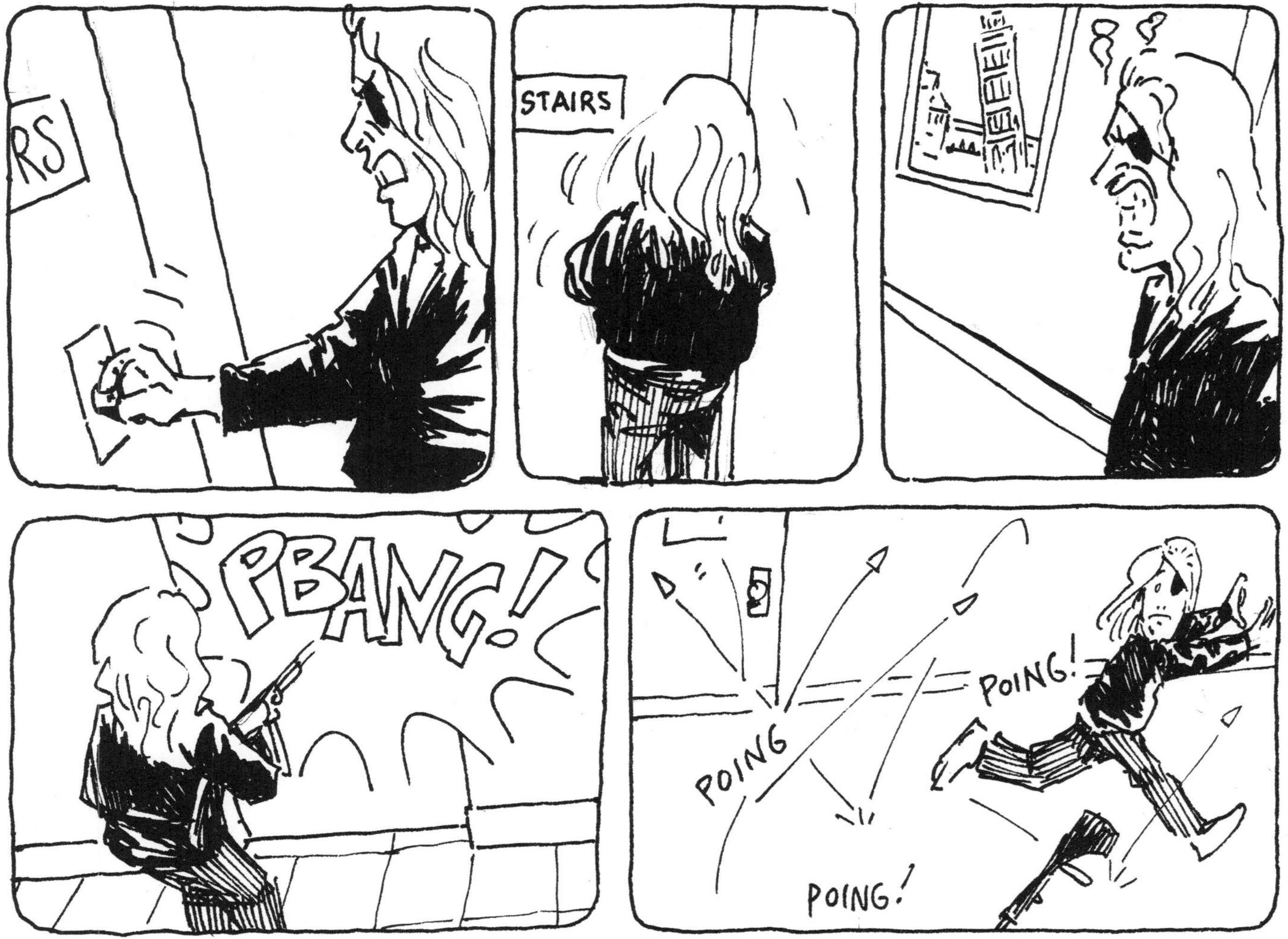
RS
STAIRS
PBANG!
POING
POING!
POING!

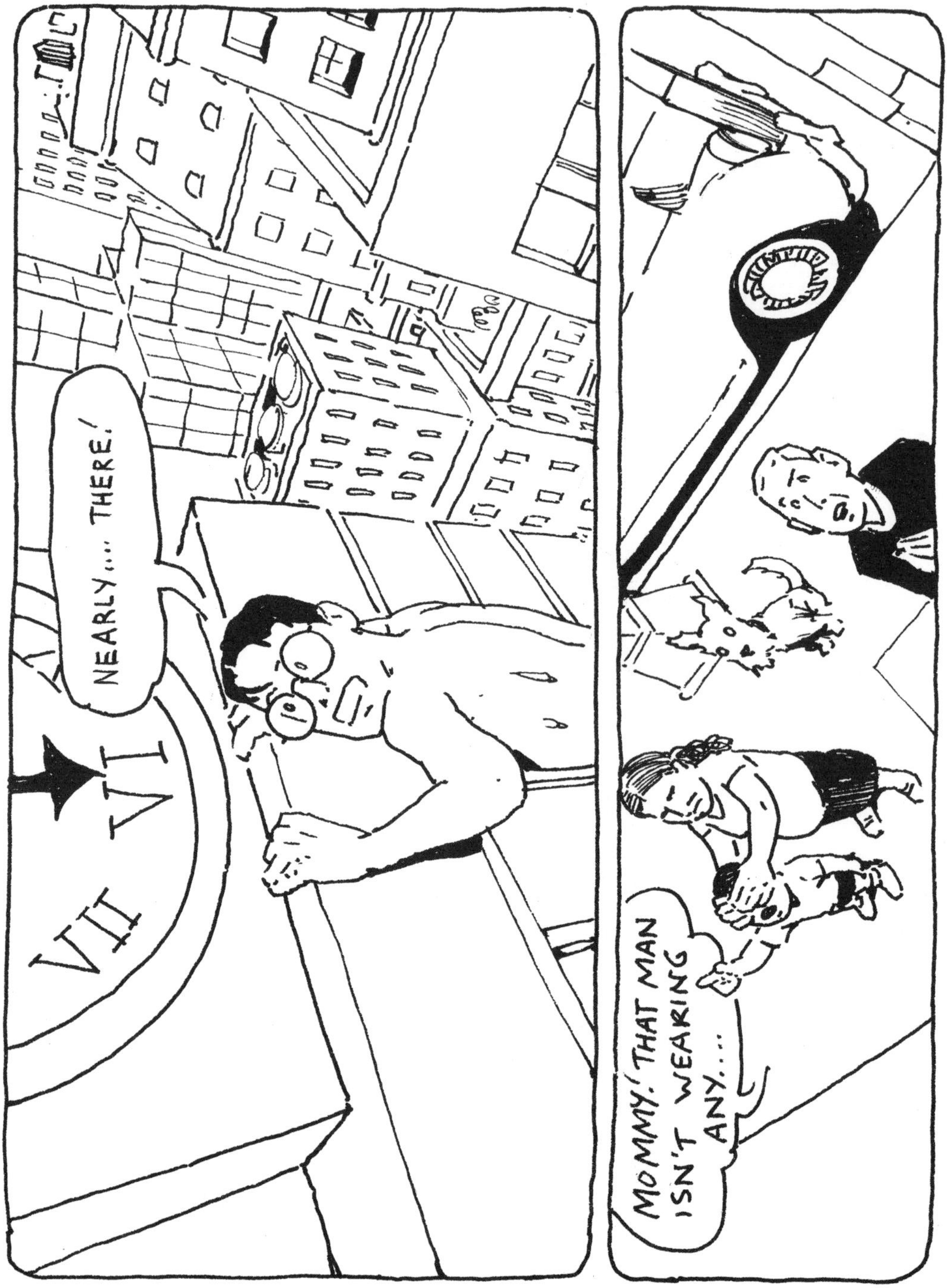
NEARLY.... THERE!
MOMMY! THAT MAN ISN'T WEARING ANY....

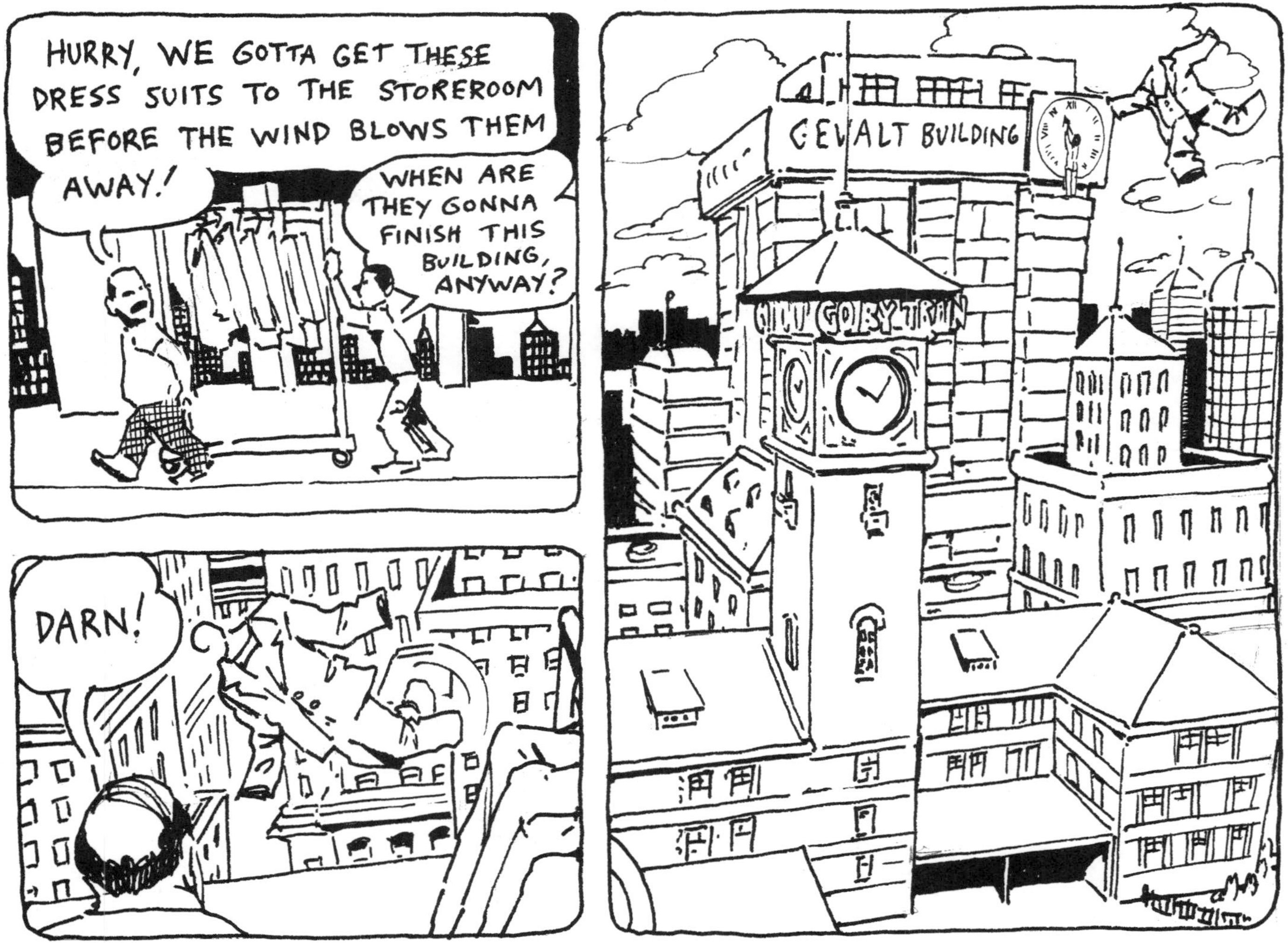
HURRY, WE GOTTA GET THESE DRESS SUITS TO THE STOREROOM BEFORE THE WIND BLOWS THEM AWAY!
WHEN ARE THEY GONNA FINISH THIS BUILDING, ANYWAY?
DARN!
GEVALT BUILDING

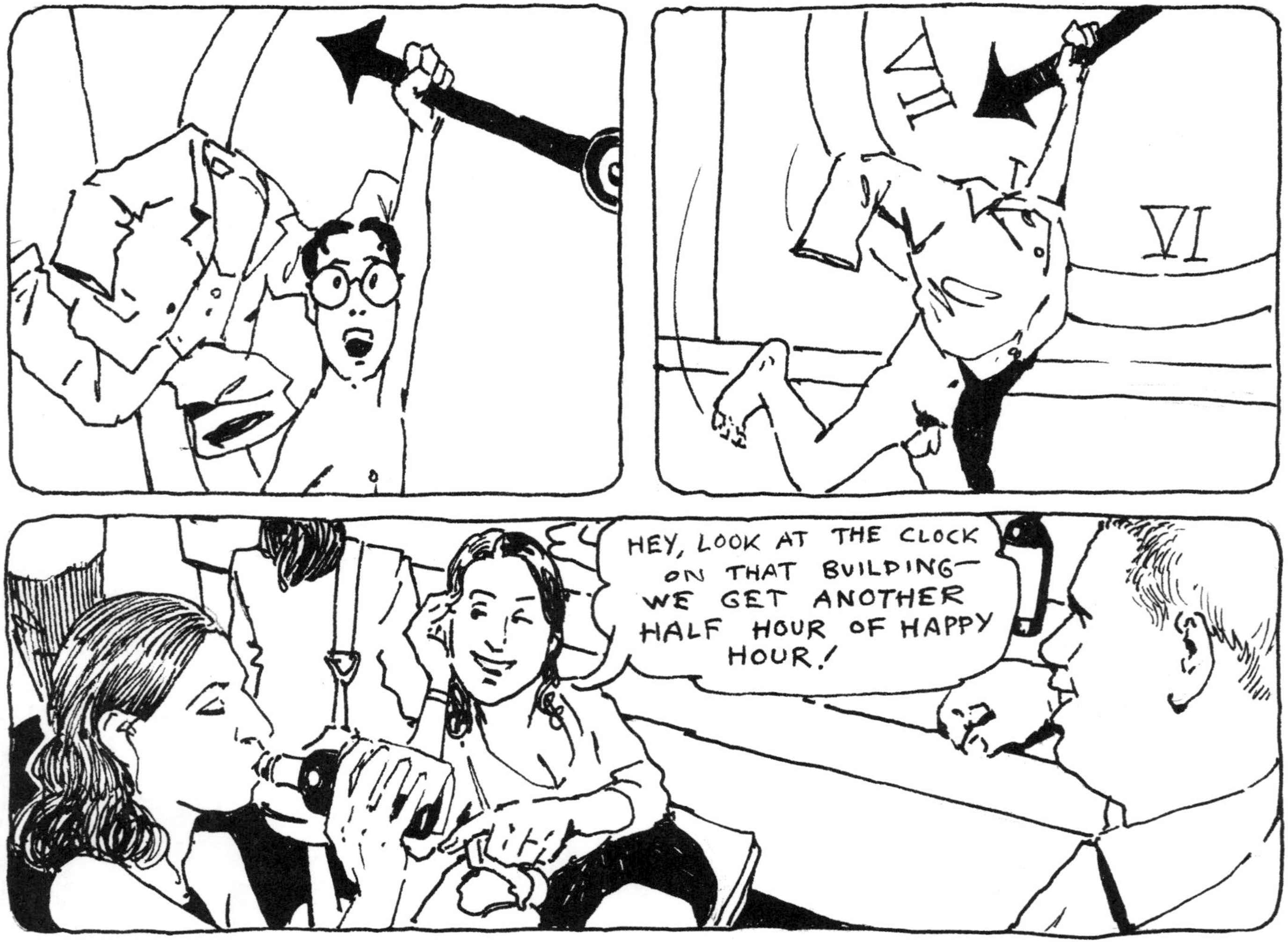
VII
VI
HEY, LOOK AT THE CLOCK ON THAT BUILDING— WE GET ANOTHER HALF HOUR OF HAPPY HOUR!

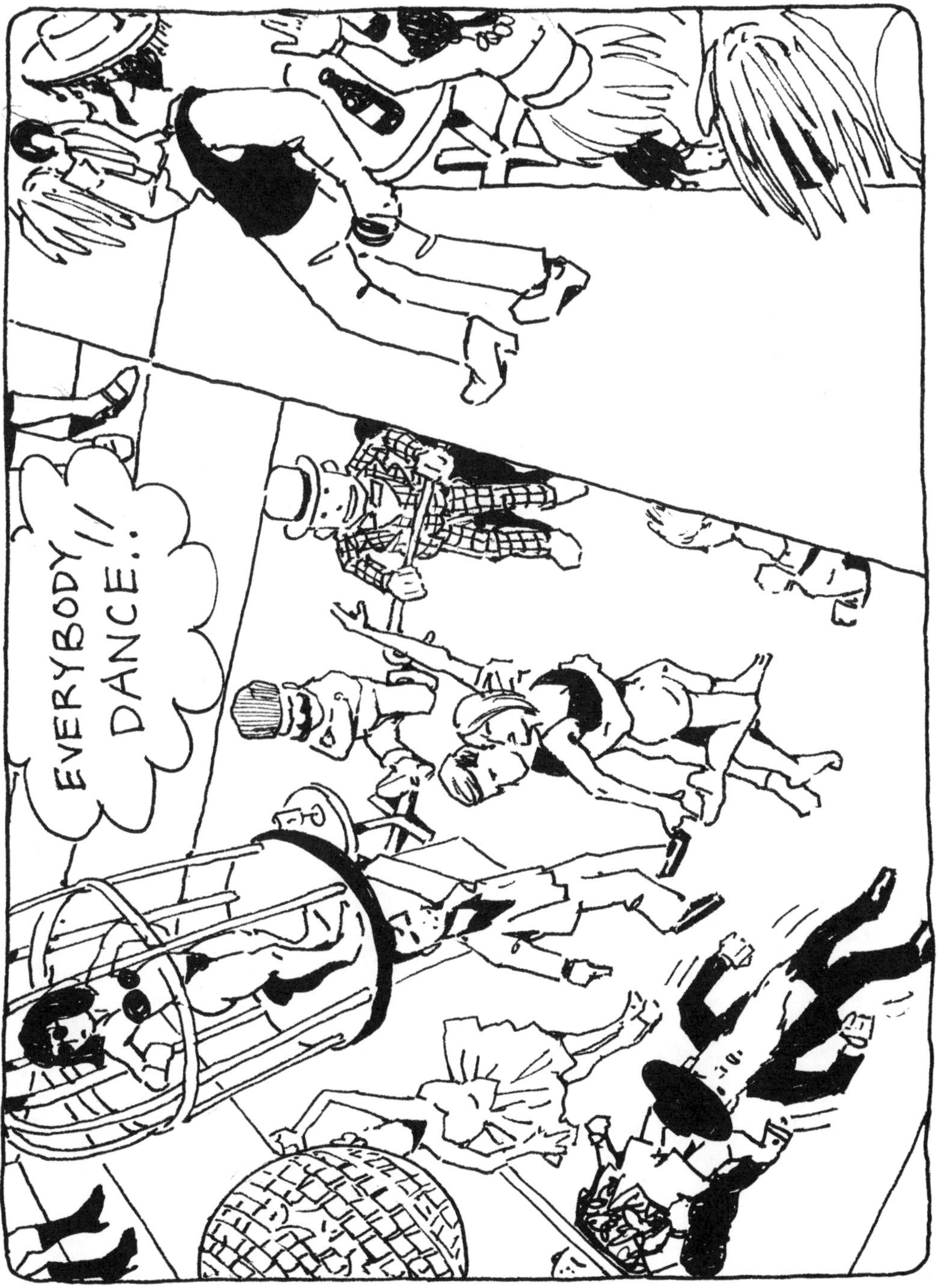
EVERYBODY DANCE!!

MADE IT!
YAY!!
KONNG!

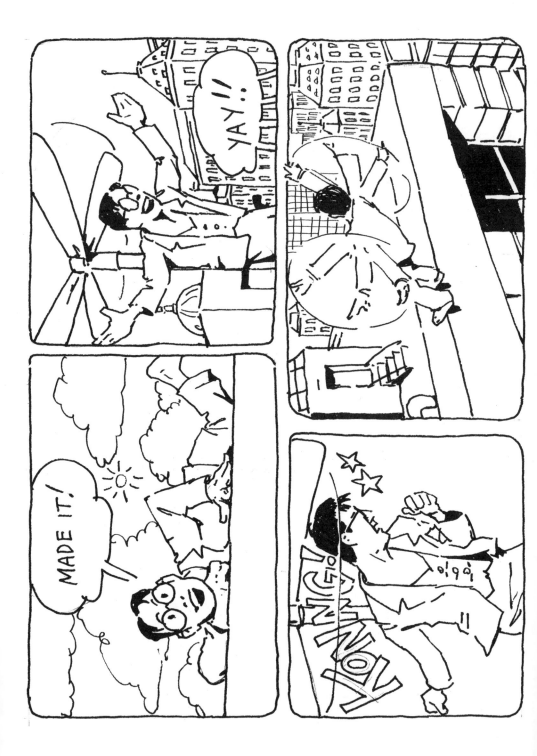

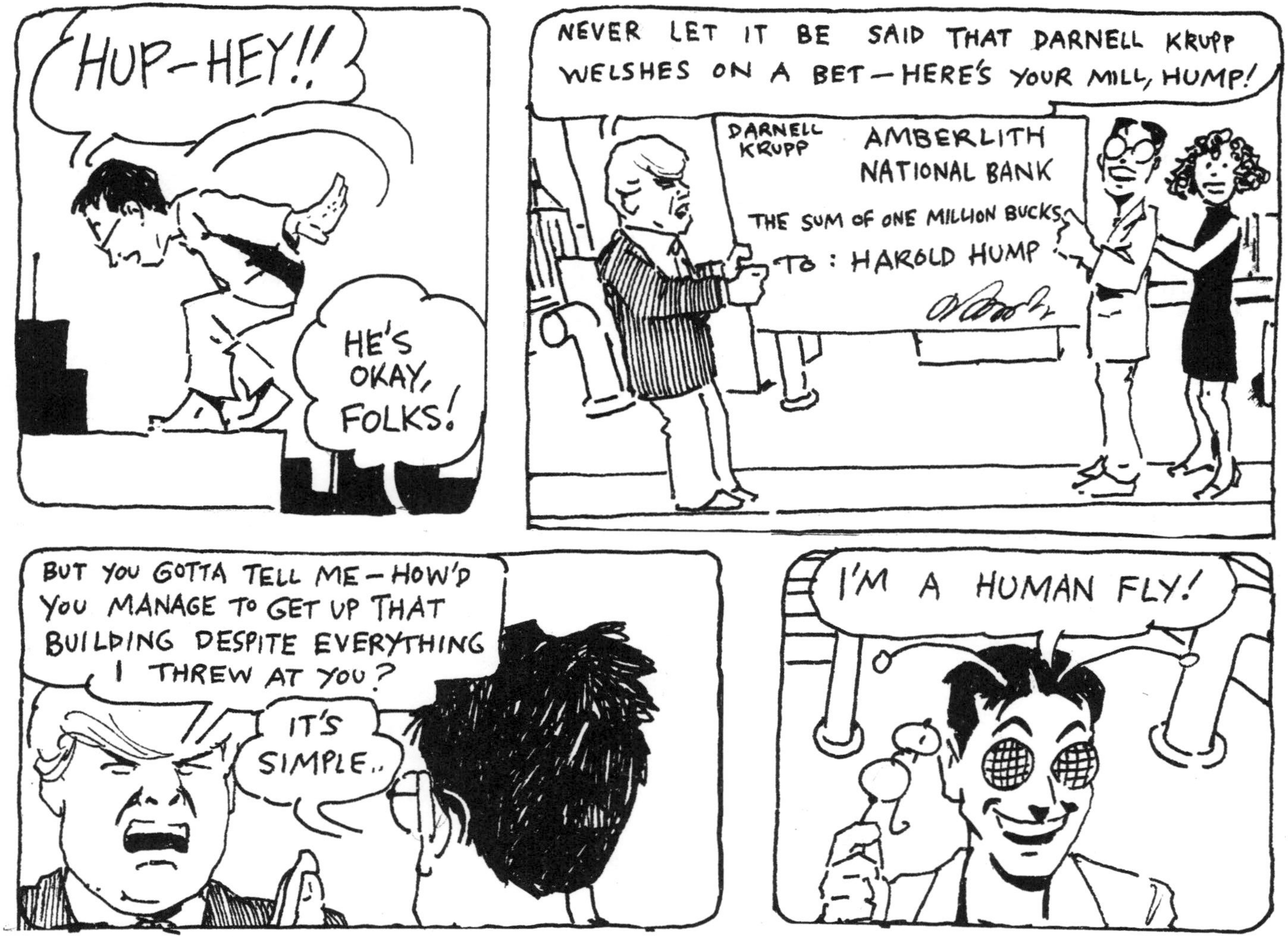
HUP-HEY!!
HE'S OKAY, FOLKS!
NEVER LET IT BE SAID THAT DARNELL KRUPP WELSHES ON A BET—HERE'S YOUR MILL, HUMP!
DARNELL KRUPP
AMBERLITH NATIONAL BANK
THE SUM OF ONE MILLION BUCKS
TO: HAROLD HUMP
BUT YOU GOTTA TELL ME—HOW'D YOU MANAGE TO GET UP THAT BUILDING DESPITE EVERYTHING I THREW AT YOU?
IT'S SIMPLE..
I'M A HUMAN FLY!

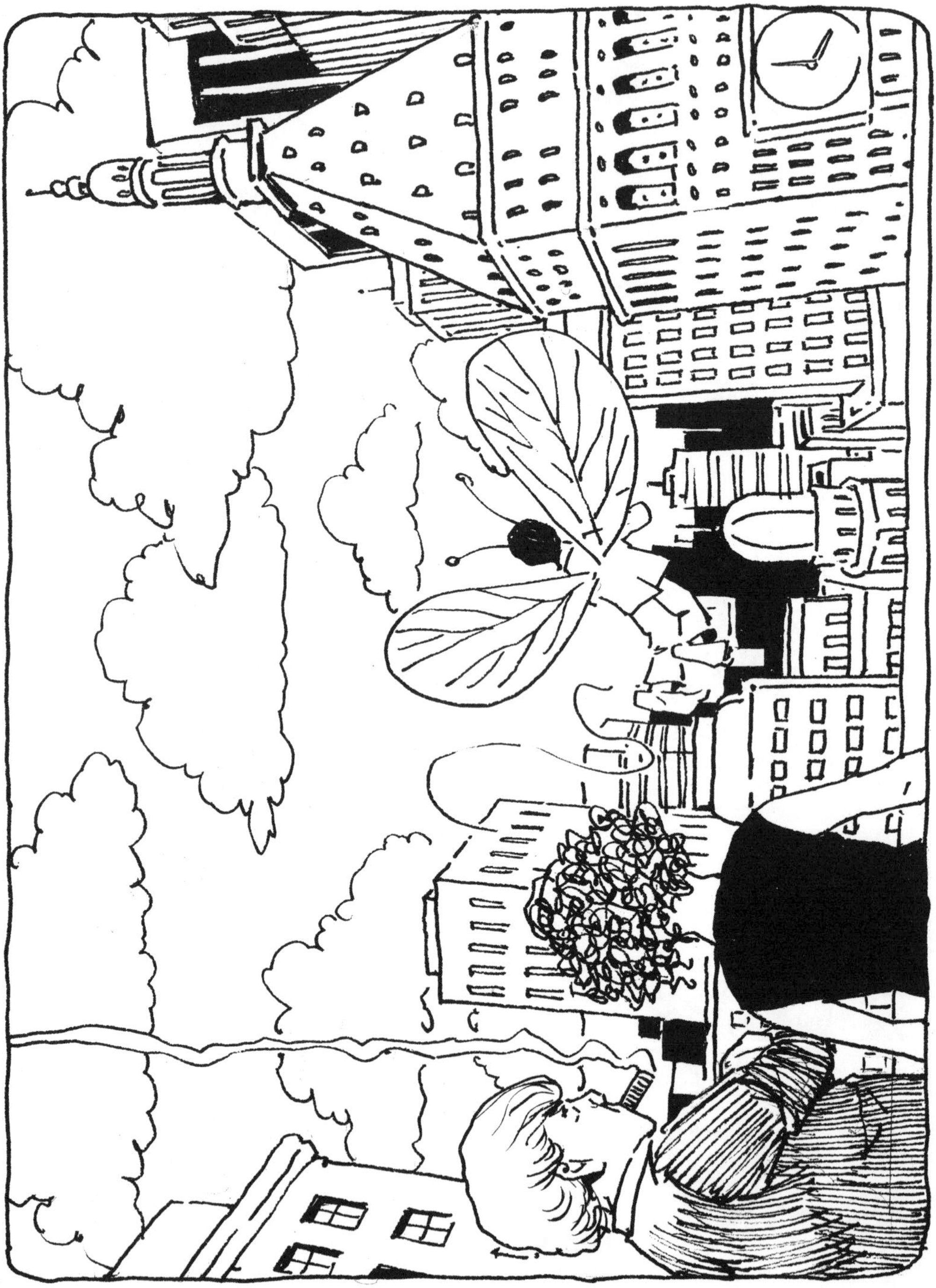

AUGUST 29, 2004

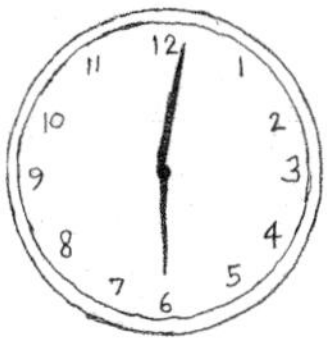

NOTES ON "AUGUST 29, 2004"

Instead of devoting all of my pages to one story, I did four shorter pieces this time: one playing out a twenty-questions-like game I play with Ben, one story featuring Singar and Mingo (two talking tomatoes from bedtime stories I used to tell my kids), "Mix Tape" (a series of frames illustrating lines from some of my favorite novelty songs), and an eight-page story following Mugg (my interlocutor in the *Perspective!* books) as he goes to yard sales. The last story was the only one where I was truly winging it (my plan had originally been for three stories, but the Singar and Mingo one ran shorter than I'd estimated and the mix tape premise didn't seem worth filling the rest of my pages with), and it's the one I had the most fun doing. I used the same method as I had with "The Harold Project"—starting with a simple premise and pulling random picture references from a sack every page to direct the story.

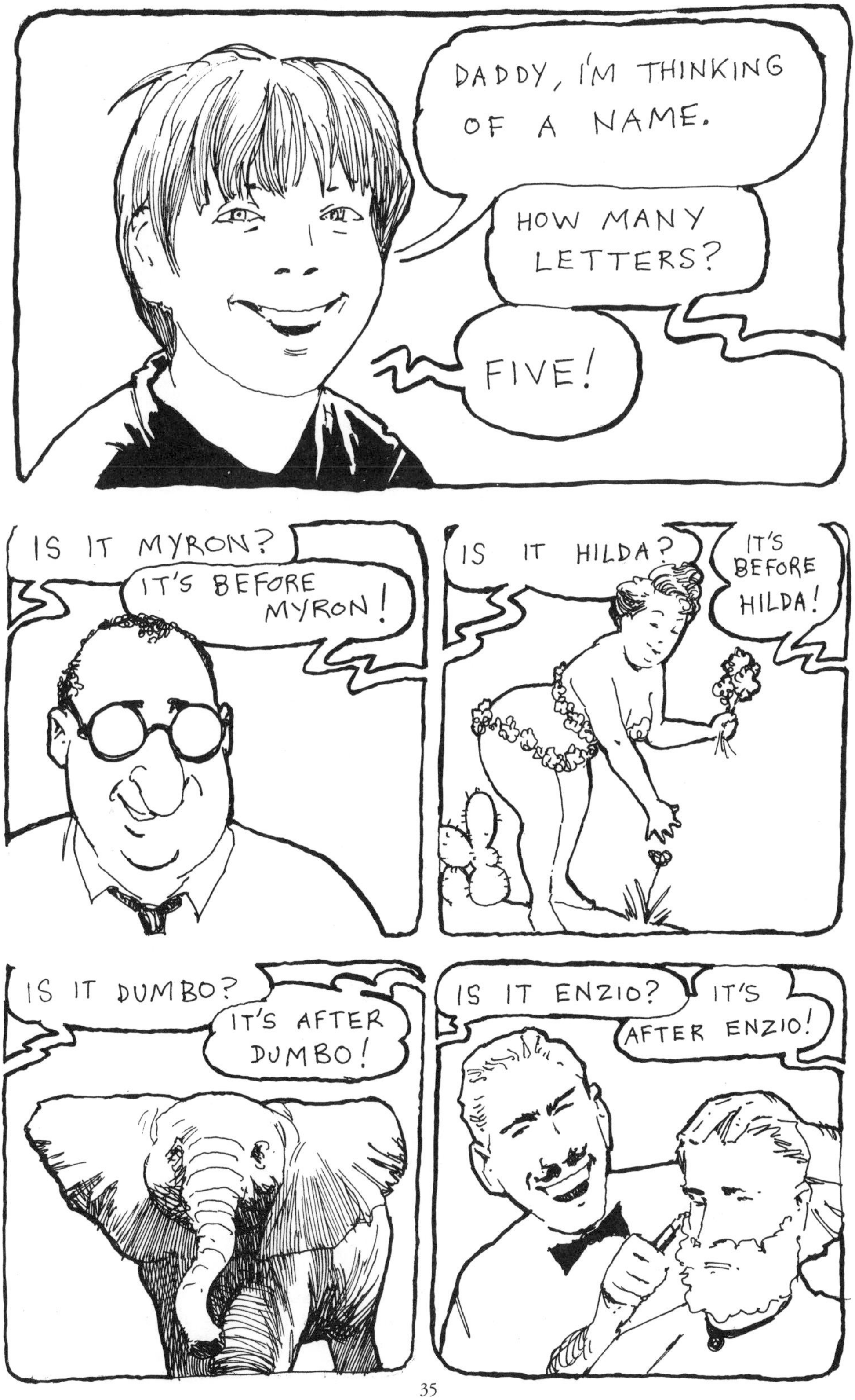
DADDY, I'M THINKING OF A NAME.
HOW MANY LETTERS?
FIVE!
IS IT MYRON?
IT'S BEFORE MYRON!
IS IT HILDA?
IT'S BEFORE HILDA!
IS IT DUMBO?
IT'S AFTER DUMBO!
IS IT ENZIO?
IT'S AFTER ENZIO!

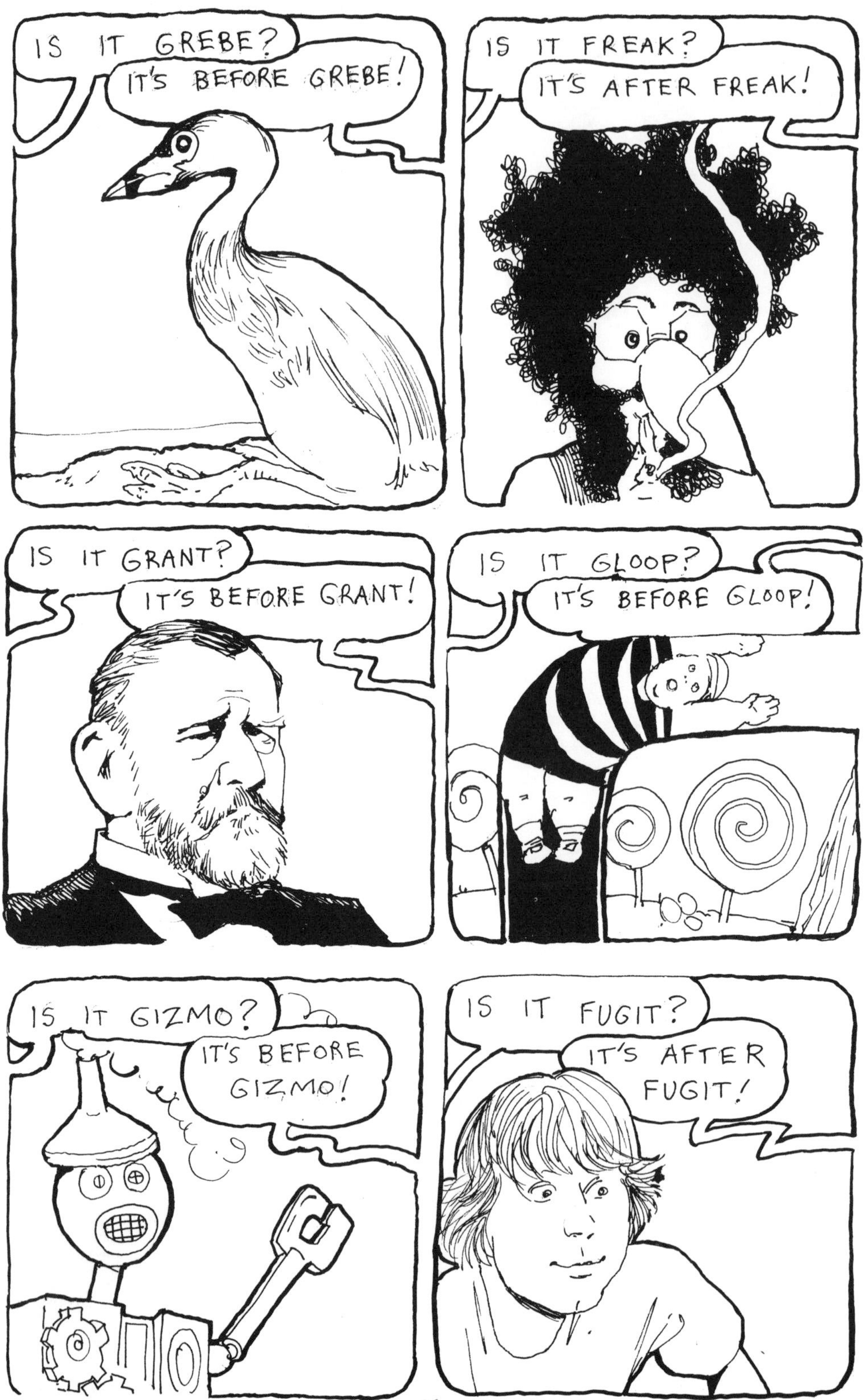

IS IT GREBE?
IT'S BEFORE GREBE!
IS IT FREAK?
IT'S AFTER FREAK!
IS IT GRANT?
IT'S BEFORE GRANT!
IS IT GLOOP?
IT'S BEFORE GLOOP!
IS IT GIZMO?
IT'S BEFORE GIZMO!
IS IT FUGIT?
IT'S AFTER FUGIT!

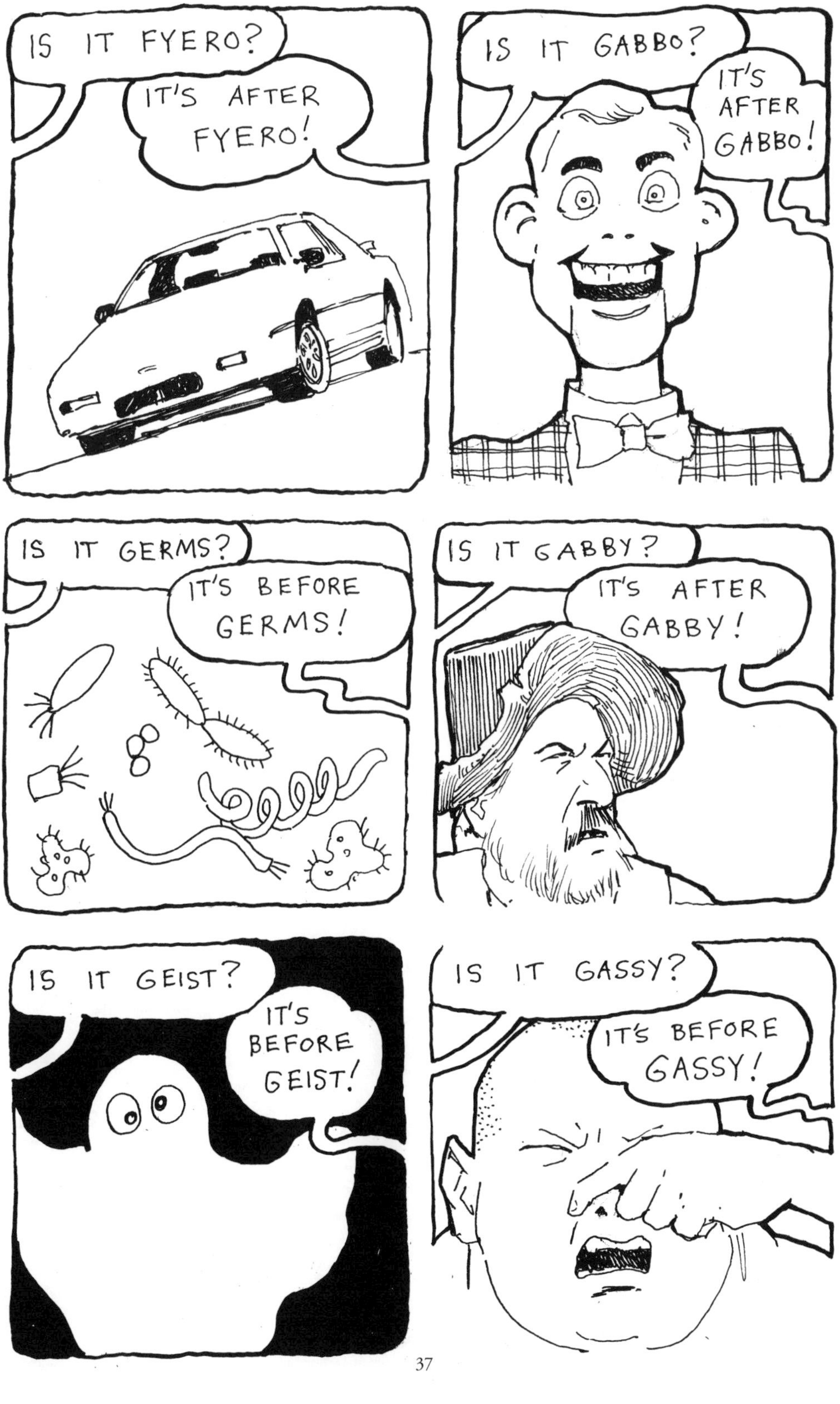
IS IT FYERO?
IT'S AFTER FYERO!
IS IT GABBO?
IT'S AFTER GABBO!
IS IT GERMS?
IT'S BEFORE GERMS!
IS IT GABBY?
IT'S AFTER GABBY!
IS IT GEIST?
IT'S BEFORE GEIST!
IS IT GASSY?
IT'S BEFORE GASSY!

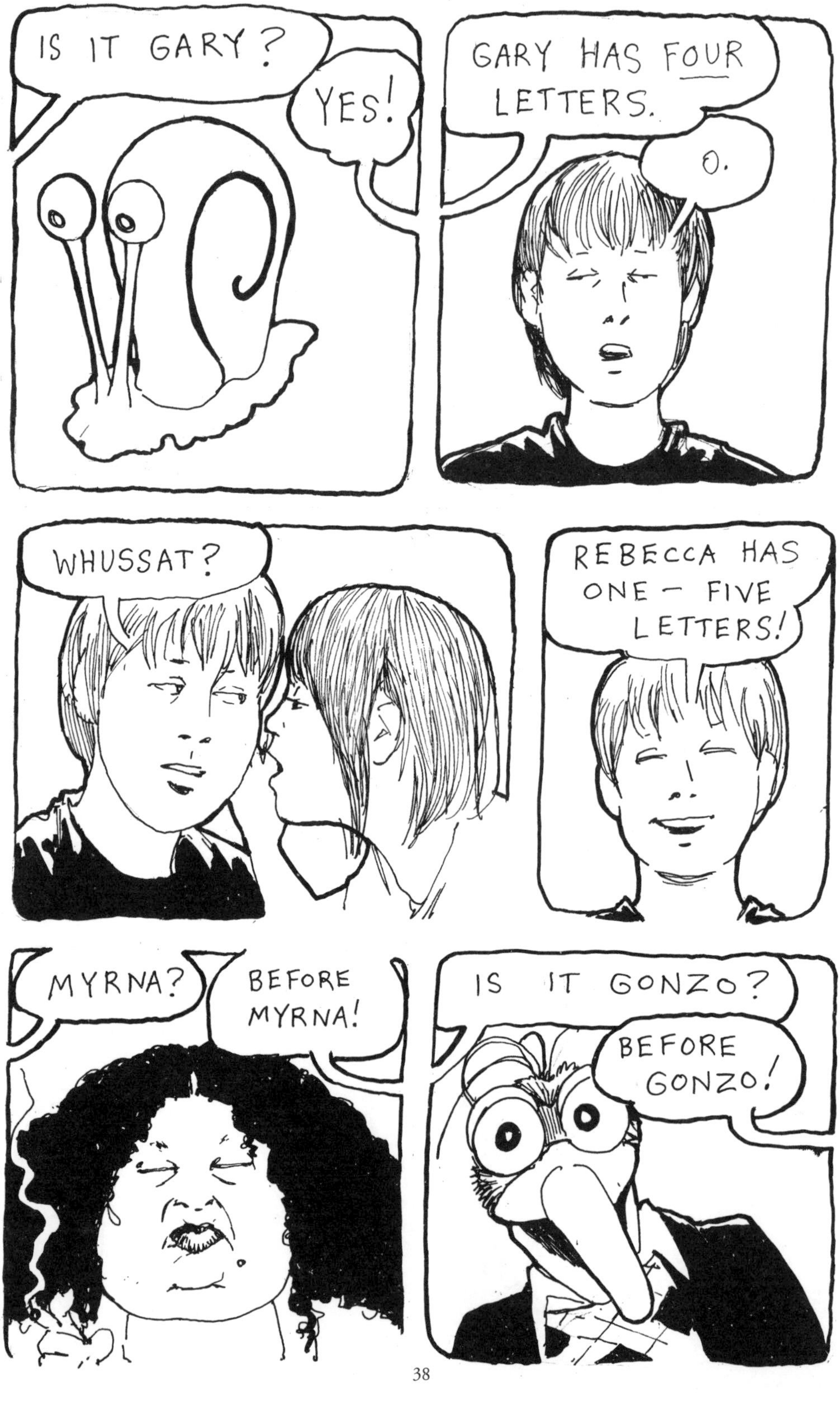
IS IT GARY?
YES!
GARY HAS FOUR LETTERS.
O.
WHUSSAT?
REBECCA HAS ONE - FIVE LETTERS!
MYRNA?
BEFORE MYRNA!
IS IT GONZO?
BEFORE GONZO!

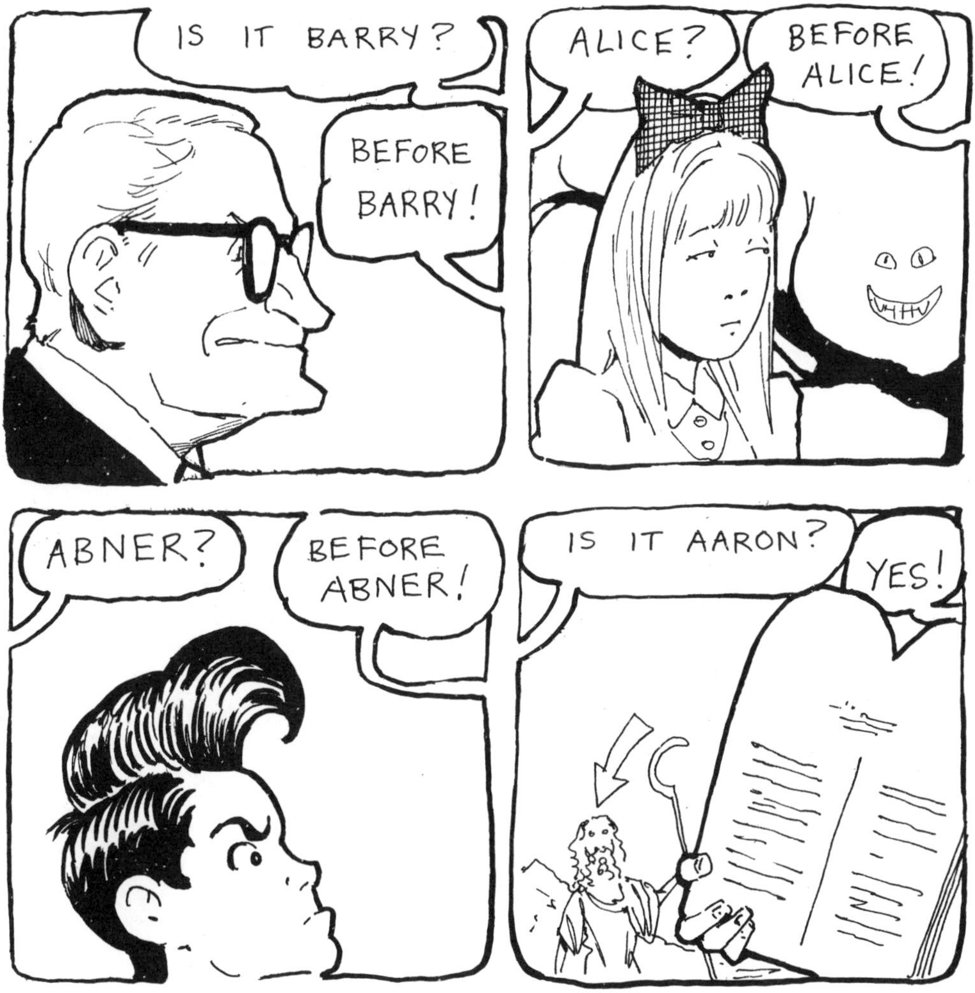
IS IT BARRY?
BEFORE BARRY!
ALICE?
BEFORE ALICE!
ABNER?
BEFORE ABNER!
IS IT AARON?
YES!

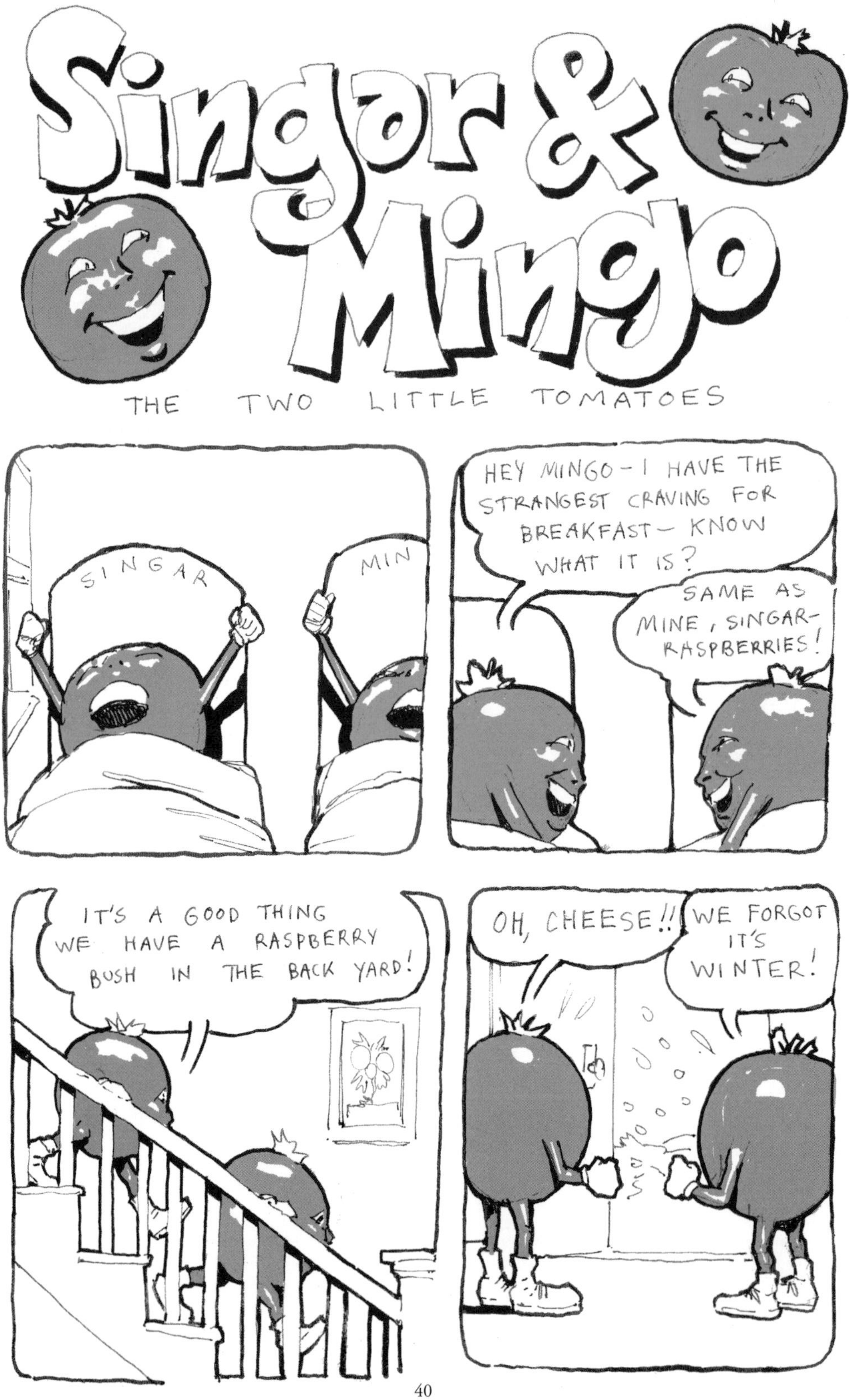
Singar & Mingo
THE TWO LITTLE TOMATOES
SINGAR
MIN
HEY MINGO - I HAVE THE STRANGEST CRAVING FOR BREAKFAST - KNOW WHAT IT IS?
SAME AS MINE, SINGAR- RASPBERRIES!
IT'S A GOOD THING WE HAVE A RASPBERRY BUSH IN THE BACK YARD!
OH, CHEESE!!
WE FORGOT IT'S WINTER!

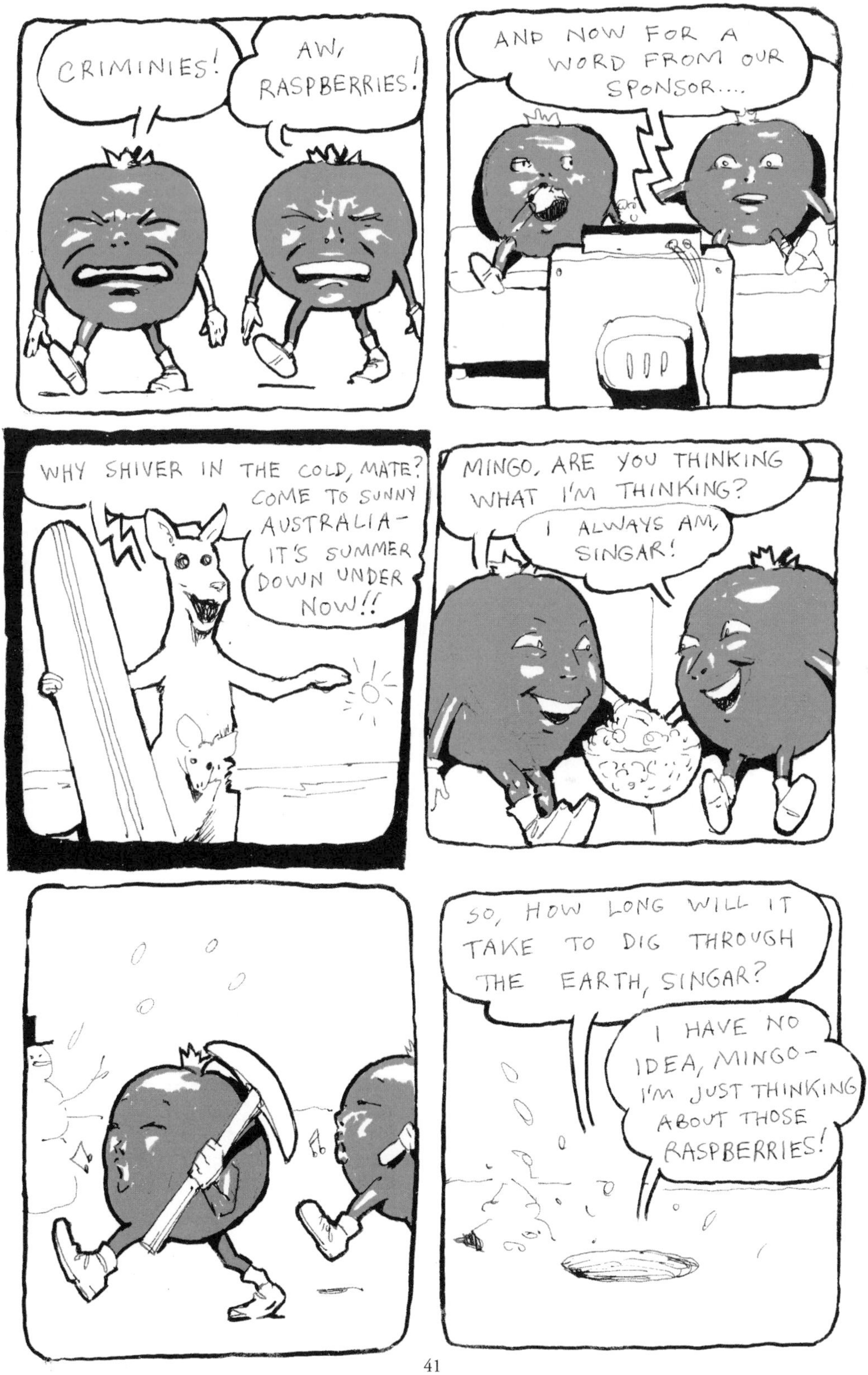
CRIMINIES!
AW, RASPBERRIES!
AND NOW FOR A WORD FROM OUR SPONSOR....
WHY SHIVER IN THE COLD, MATE? COME TO SUNNY AUSTRALIA- IT'S SUMMER DOWN UNDER NOW!!
MINGO, ARE YOU THINKING WHAT I'M THINKING?
I ALWAYS AM, SINGAR!
SO, HOW LONG WILL IT TAKE TO DIG THROUGH THE EARTH, SINGAR?
I HAVE NO IDEA, MINGO- I'M JUST THINKING ABOUT THOSE RASPBERRIES!

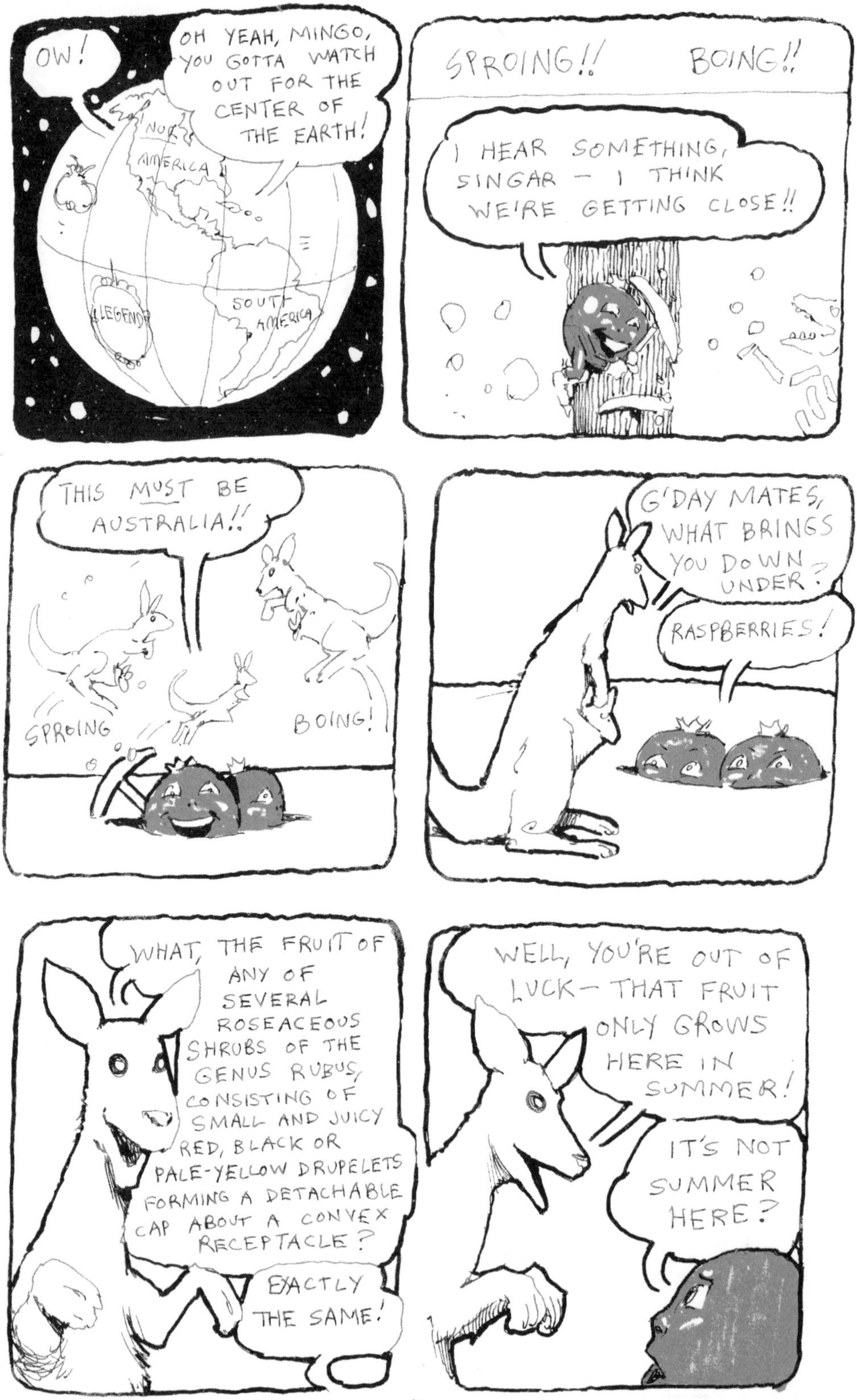
OW!
OH YEAH, MINGO, YOU GOTTA WATCH OUT FOR THE CENTER OF THE EARTH!
NORTH AMERICA
LEGEND
SOUTH AMERICA
SPROING!! BOING!!
I HEAR SOMETHING, SINGAR — I THINK WE'RE GETTING CLOSE!!
THIS MUST BE AUSTRALIA!!
SPROING
BOING!
G'DAY MATES, WHAT BRINGS YOU DOWN UNDER?
RASPBERRIES!
WHAT, THE FRUIT OF ANY OF SEVERAL ROSEACEOUS SHRUBS OF THE GENUS RUBUS, CONSISTING OF SMALL AND JUICY RED, BLACK OR PALE-YELLOW DRUPELETS FORMING A DETACHABLE CAP ABOUT A CONVEX RECEPTACLE?
EXACTLY THE SAME!
WELL, YOU'RE OUT OF LUCK — THAT FRUIT ONLY GROWS HERE IN SUMMER!
IT'S NOT SUMMER HERE?

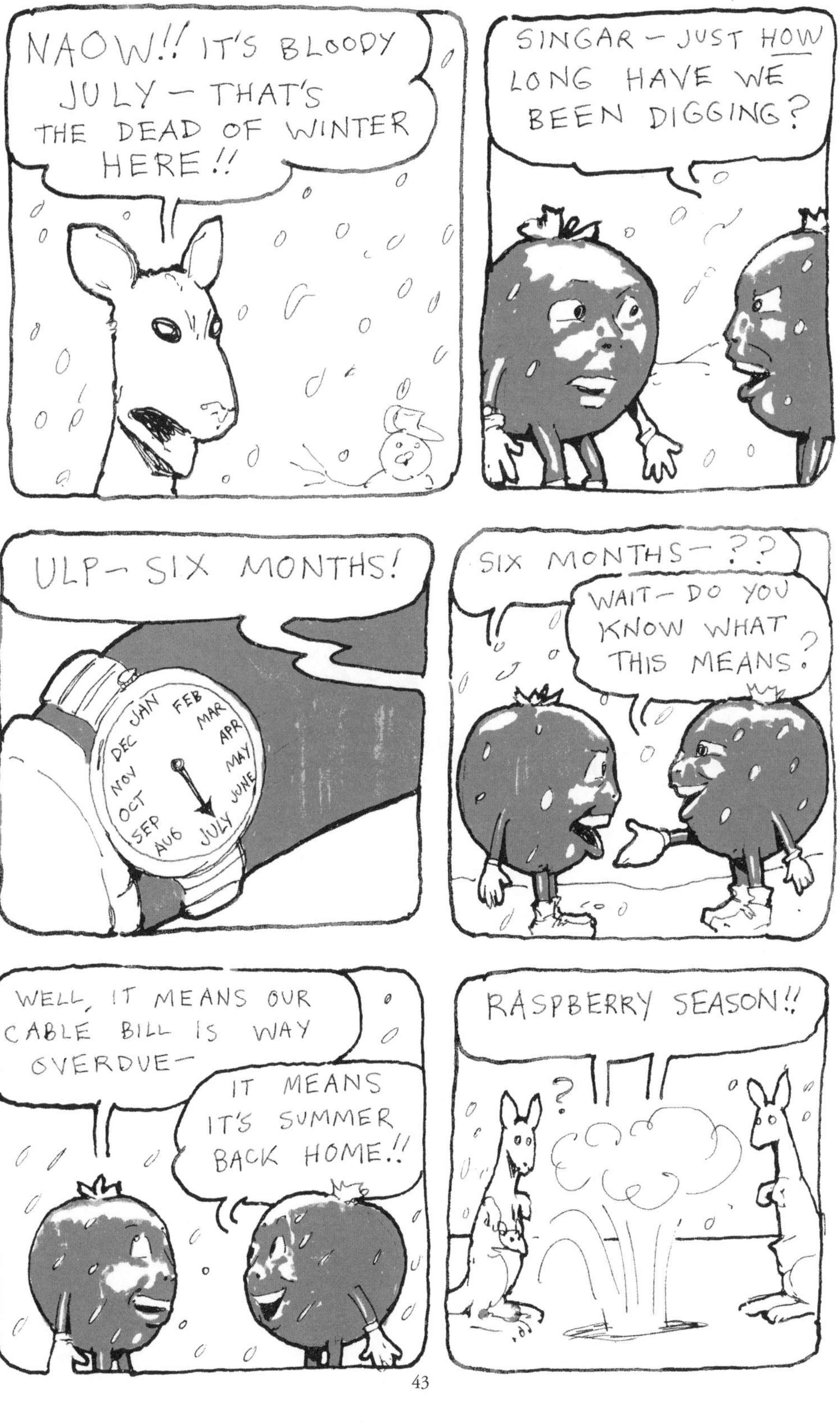
NAOW!! IT'S BLOODY JULY — THAT'S THE DEAD OF WINTER HERE!!
SINGAR — JUST HOW LONG HAVE WE BEEN DIGGING?
ULP — SIX MONTHS!
JAN FEB MAR APR MAY JUNE JULY AUG SEP OCT NOV DEC
SIX MONTHS — ??
WAIT — DO YOU KNOW WHAT THIS MEANS?
WELL, IT MEANS OUR CABLE BILL IS WAY OVERDUE —
IT MEANS IT'S SUMMER BACK HOME!!
RASPBERRY SEASON!!
?

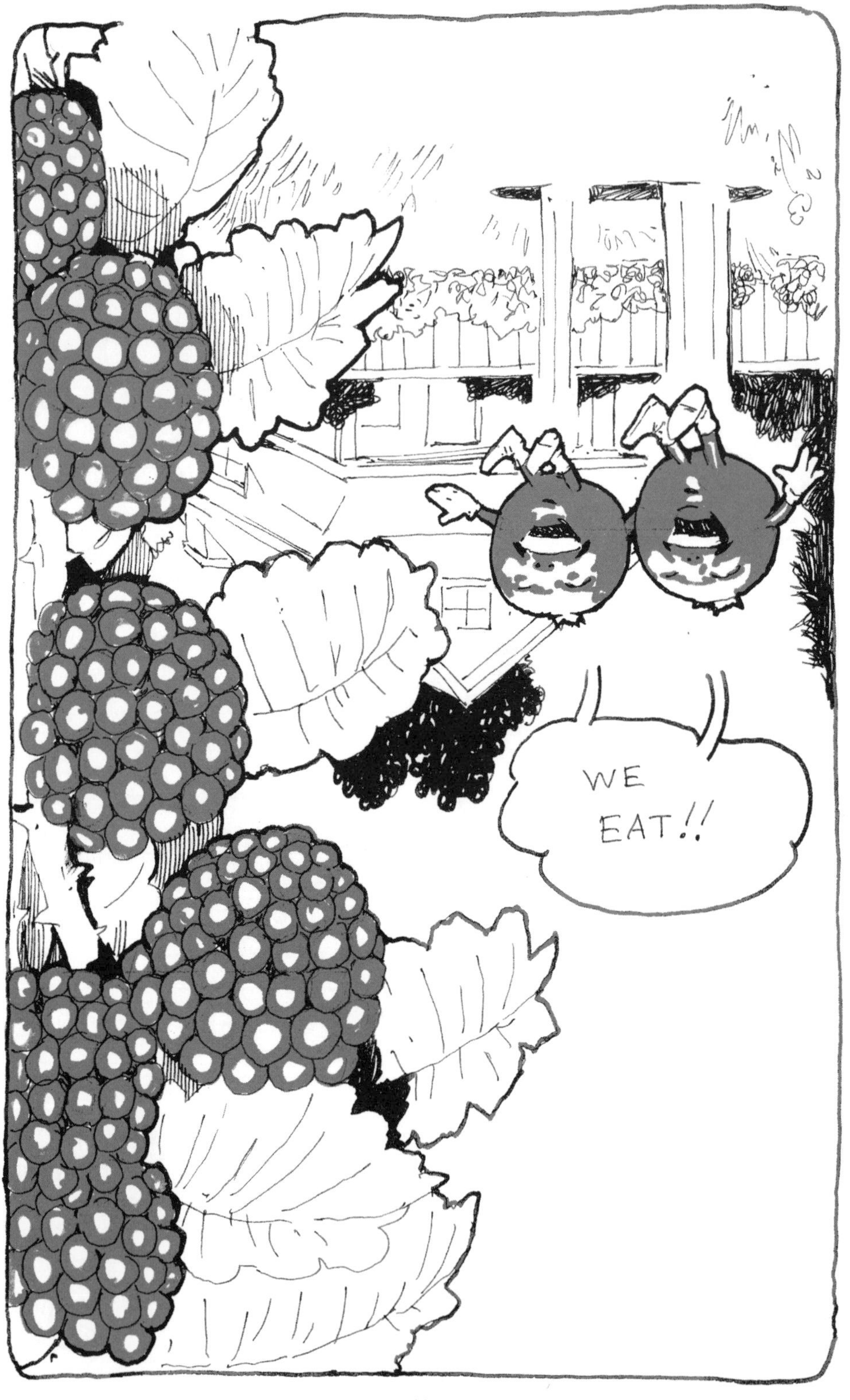
WE EAT!!

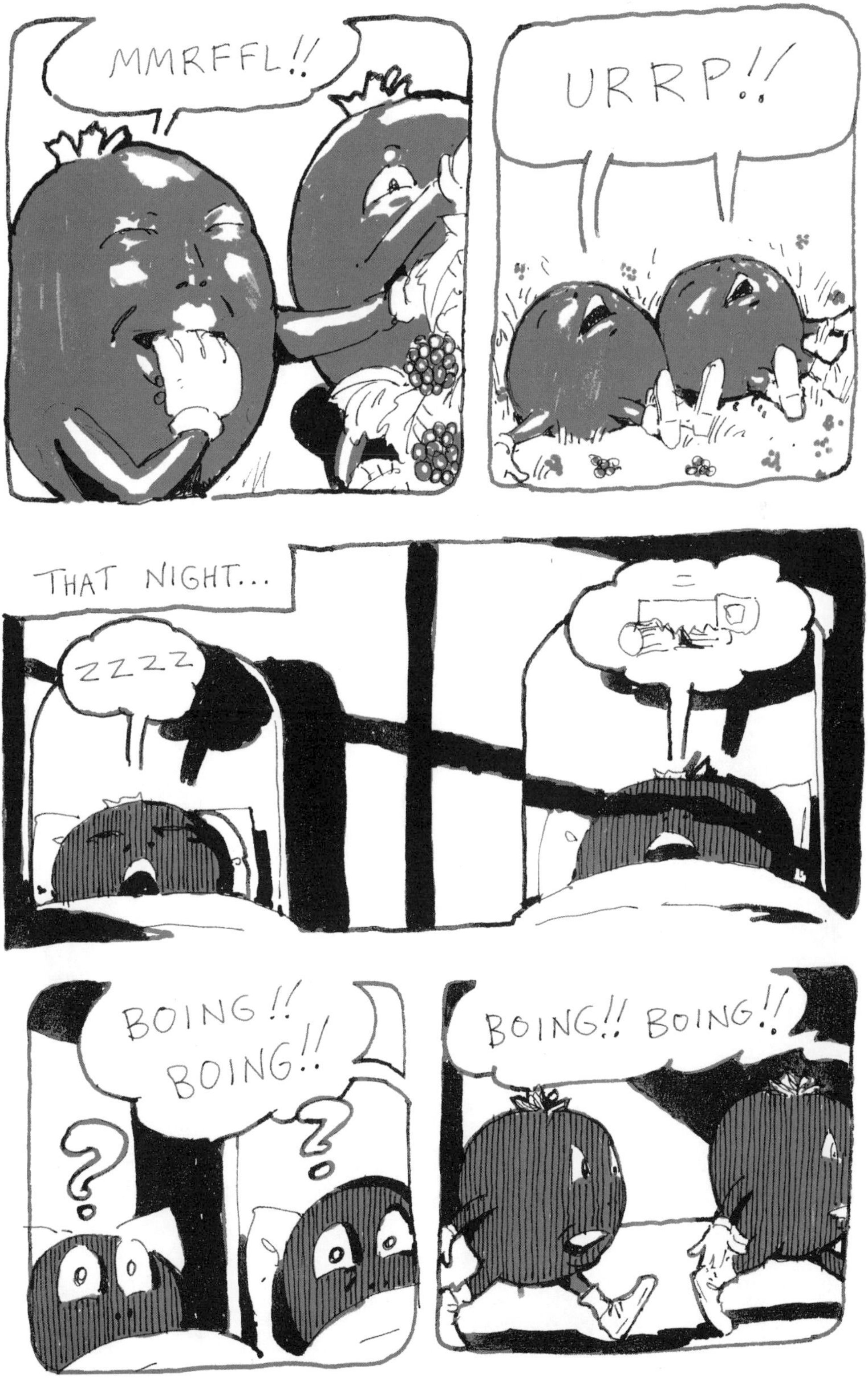
MMRFFL!!
URRP!!
THAT NIGHT...
ZZZZ
BOING!! BOING!!
BOING!! BOING!!

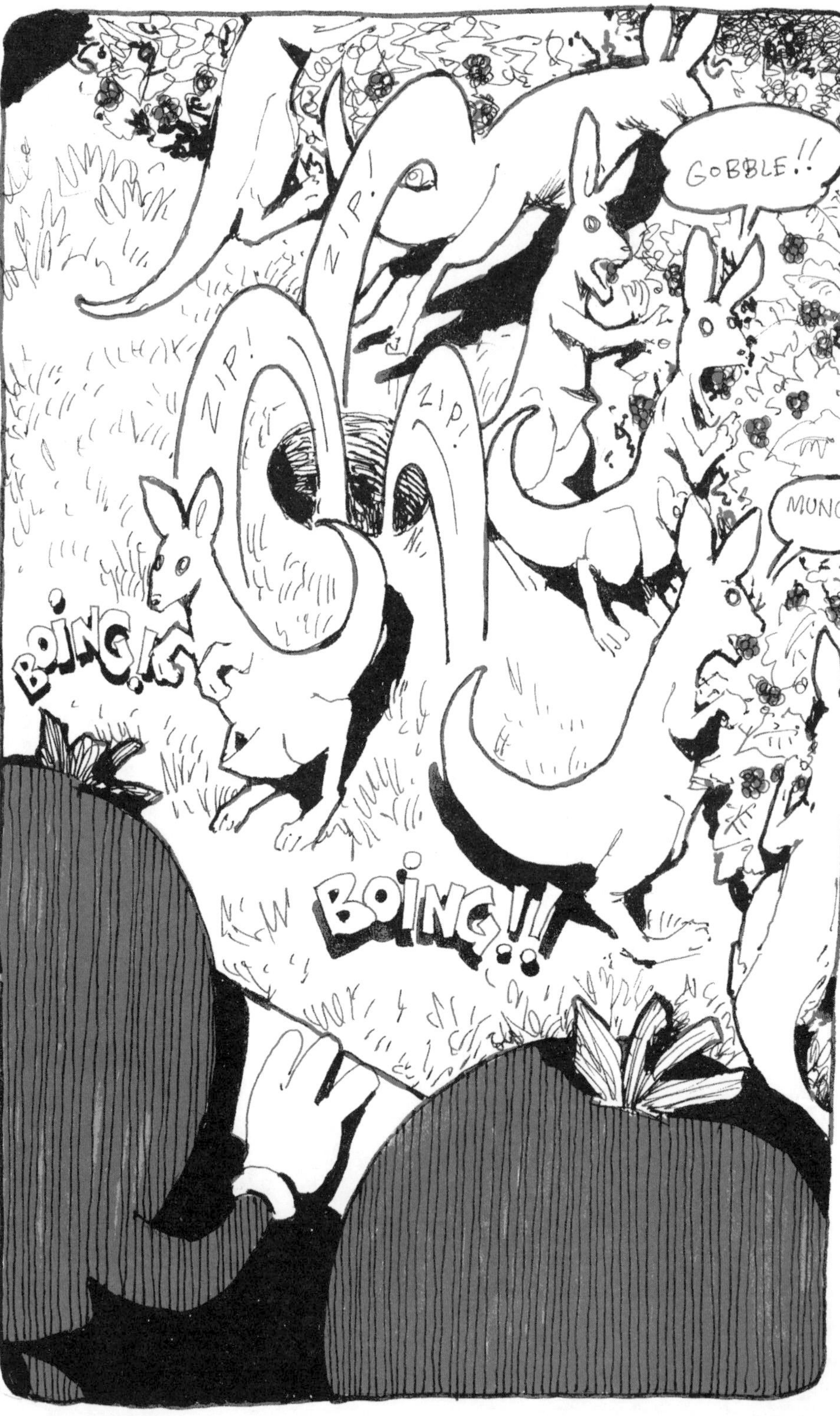
ZIP!
ZIP!
ZIP!
GOBBLE!!
MUNCH
BOING!!
BOING!!

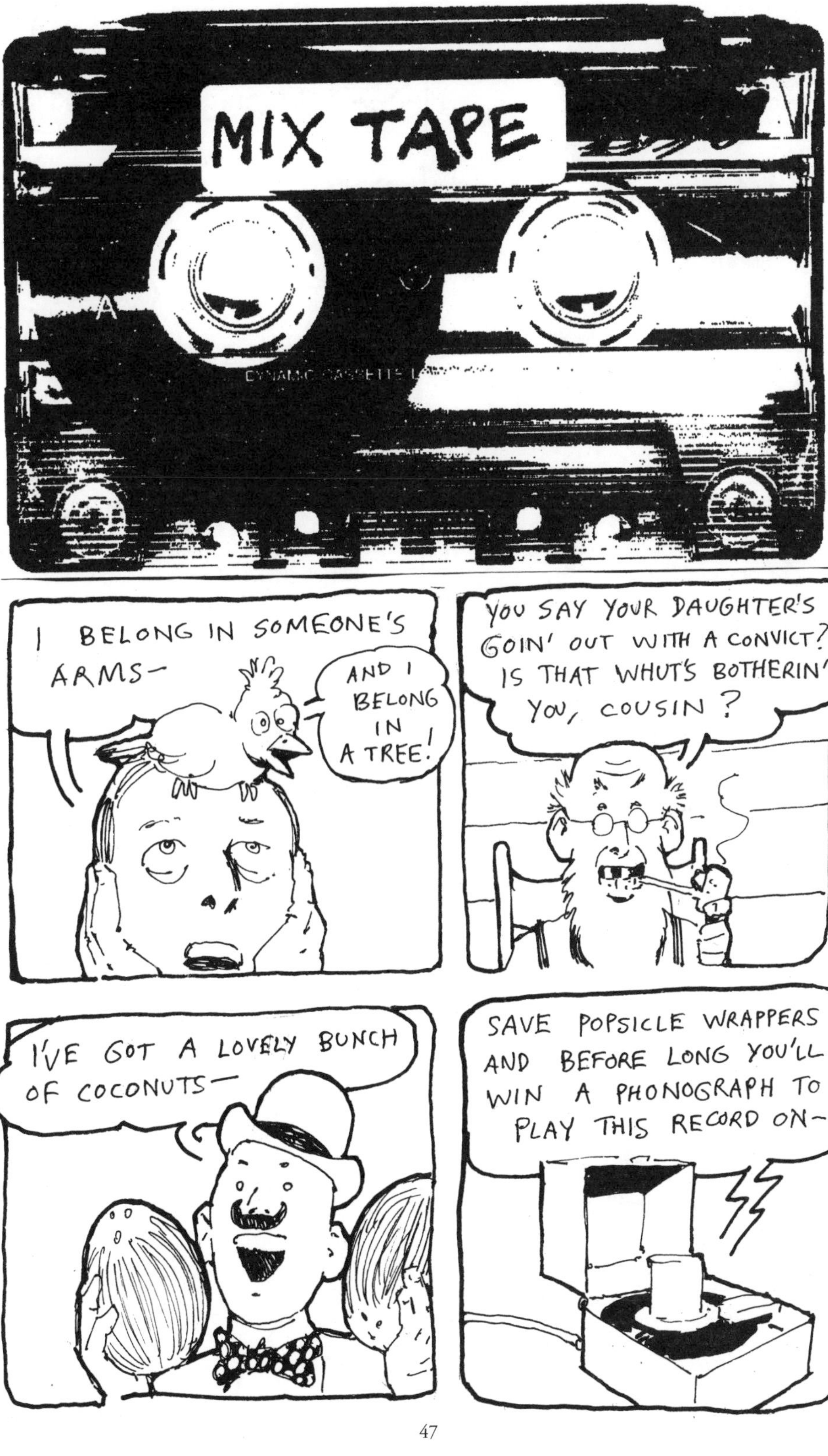
MIX TAPE
I BELONG IN SOMEONE'S ARMS—
AND I BELONG IN A TREE!
YOU SAY YOUR DAUGHTER'S GOIN' OUT WITH A CONVICT? IS THAT WHUT'S BOTHERIN' YOU, COUSIN?
I'VE GOT A LOVELY BUNCH OF COCONUTS—
SAVE POPSICLE WRAPPERS AND BEFORE LONG YOU'LL WIN A PHONOGRAPH TO PLAY THIS RECORD ON—

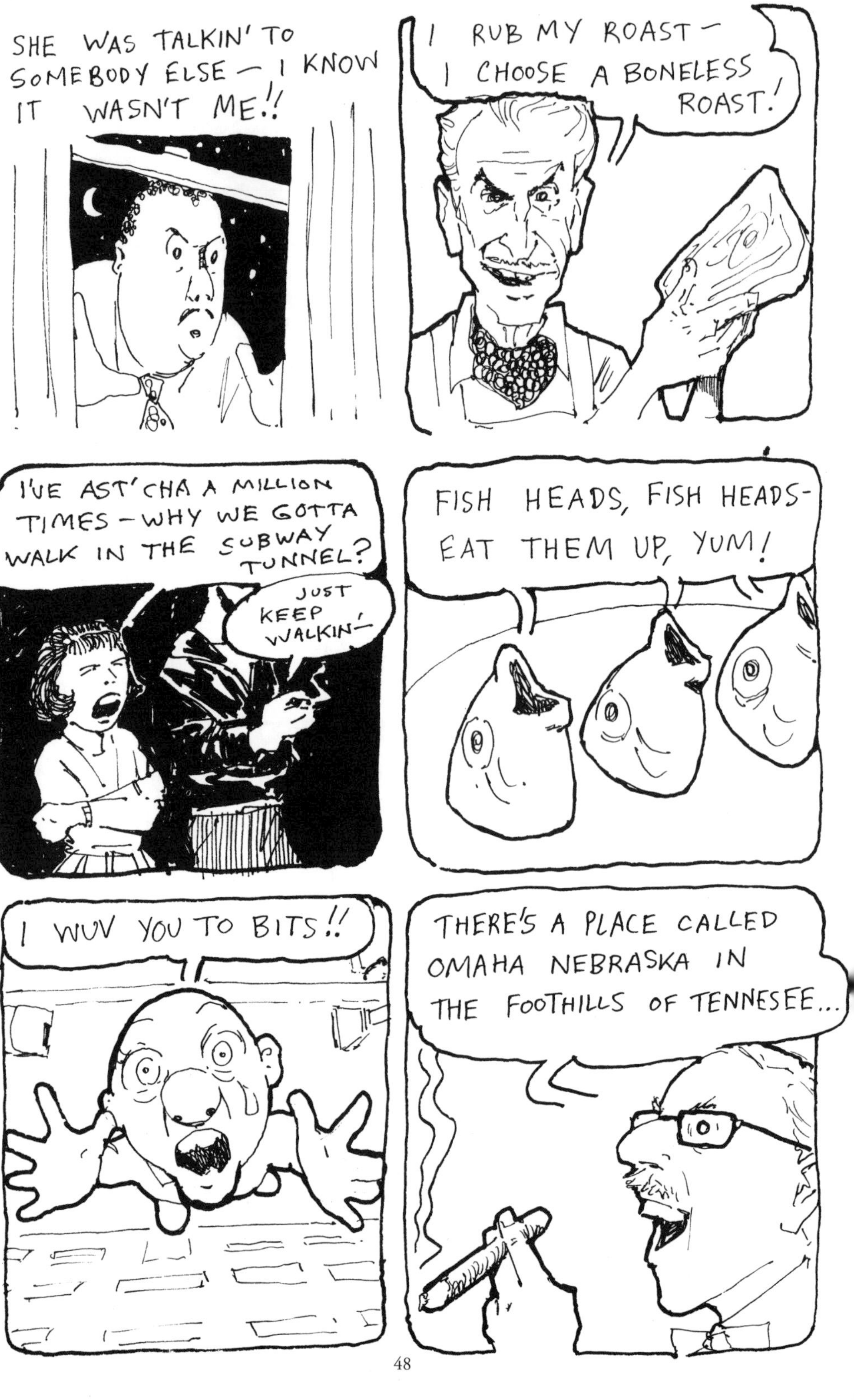
SHE WAS TALKIN' TO SOMEBODY ELSE — I KNOW IT WASN'T ME!!
I RUB MY ROAST — I CHOOSE A BONELESS ROAST!
I'VE AST'CHA A MILLION TIMES — WHY WE GOTTA WALK IN THE SUBWAY TUNNEL?
JUST KEEP WALKIN'!
FISH HEADS, FISH HEADS — EAT THEM UP, YUM!
I WUV YOU TO BITS!!
THERE'S A PLACE CALLED OMAHA NEBRASKA IN THE FOOTHILLS OF TENNESEE...

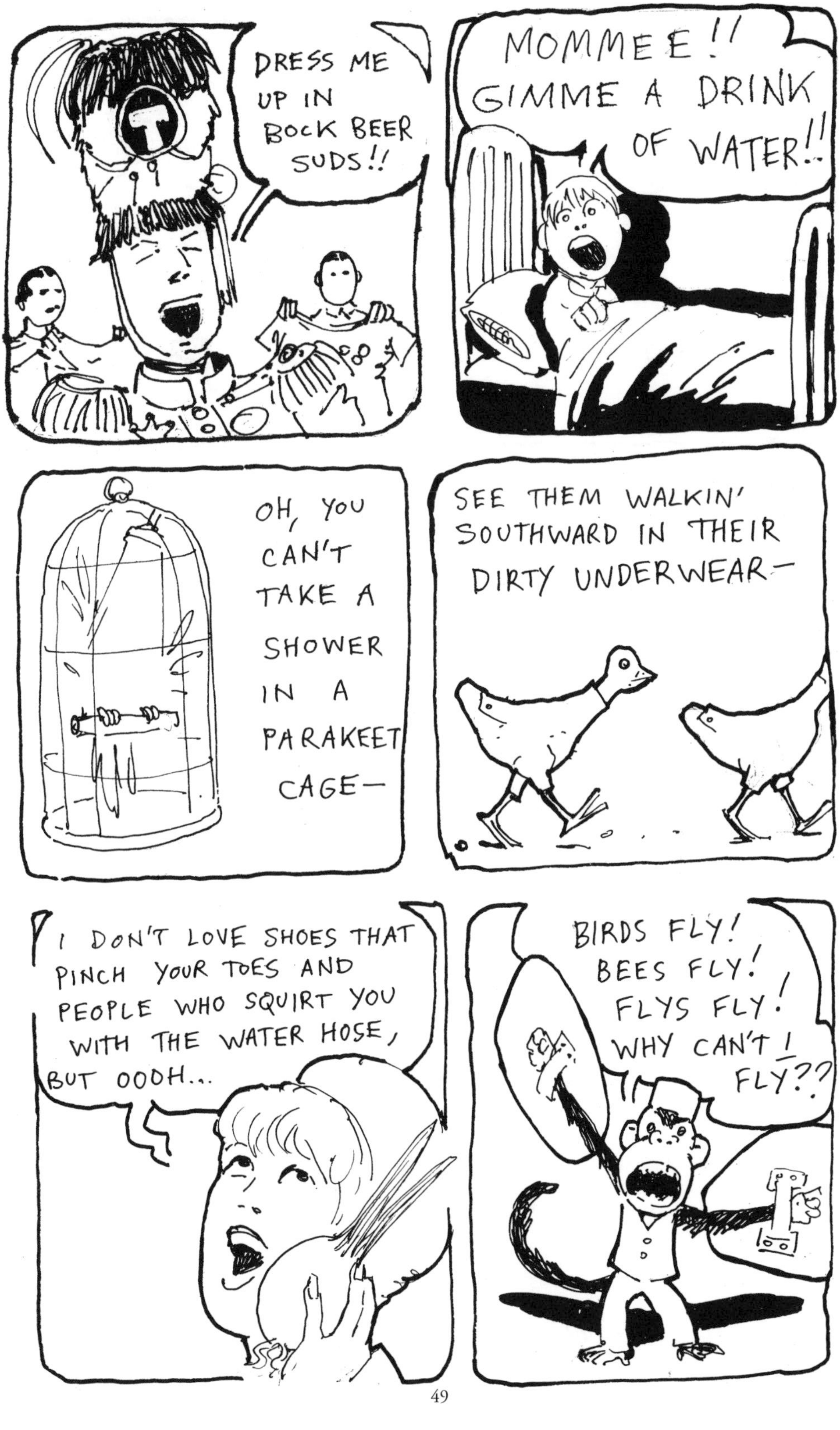
DRESS ME UP IN BOCK BEER SUDS!!
MOMMEE!! GIMME A DRINK OF WATER!!
OH, YOU CAN'T TAKE A SHOWER IN A PARAKEET CAGE—
SEE THEM WALKIN' SOUTHWARD IN THEIR DIRTY UNDERWEAR—
I DON'T LOVE SHOES THAT PINCH YOUR TOES AND PEOPLE WHO SQUIRT YOU WITH THE WATER HOSE, BUT OOOH...
BIRDS FLY! BEES FLY! FLYS FLY! WHY CAN'T I FLY??

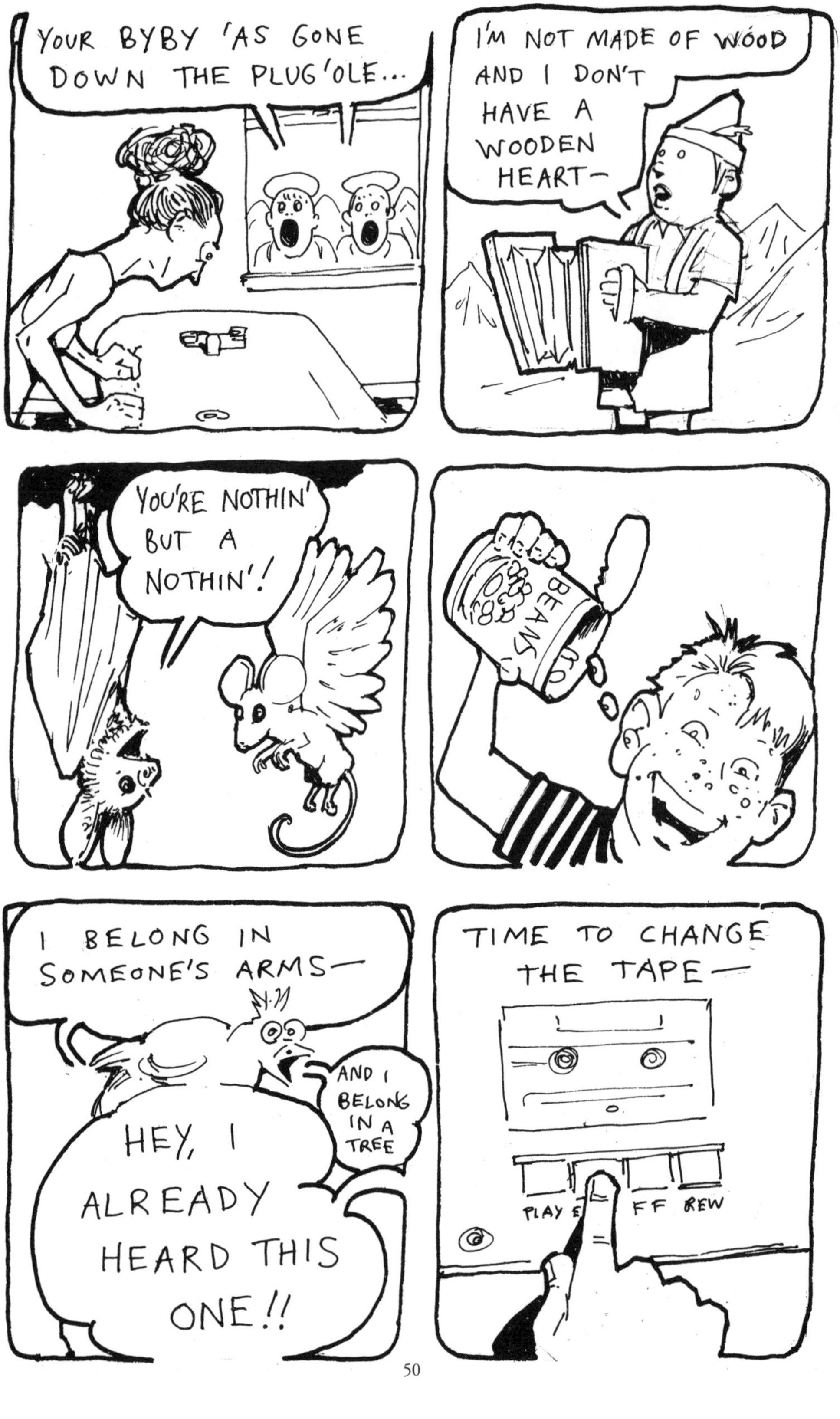
YOUR BYBY 'AS GONE DOWN THE PLUG'OLE...
I'M NOT MADE OF WOOD AND I DON'T HAVE A WOODEN HEART—
YOU'RE NOTHIN' BUT A NOTHIN'!
BEANS
I BELONG IN SOMEONE'S ARMS—
AND I BELONG IN A TREE
HEY, I ALREADY HEARD THIS ONE!!
TIME TO CHANGE THE TAPE—
PLAY
FF
REW

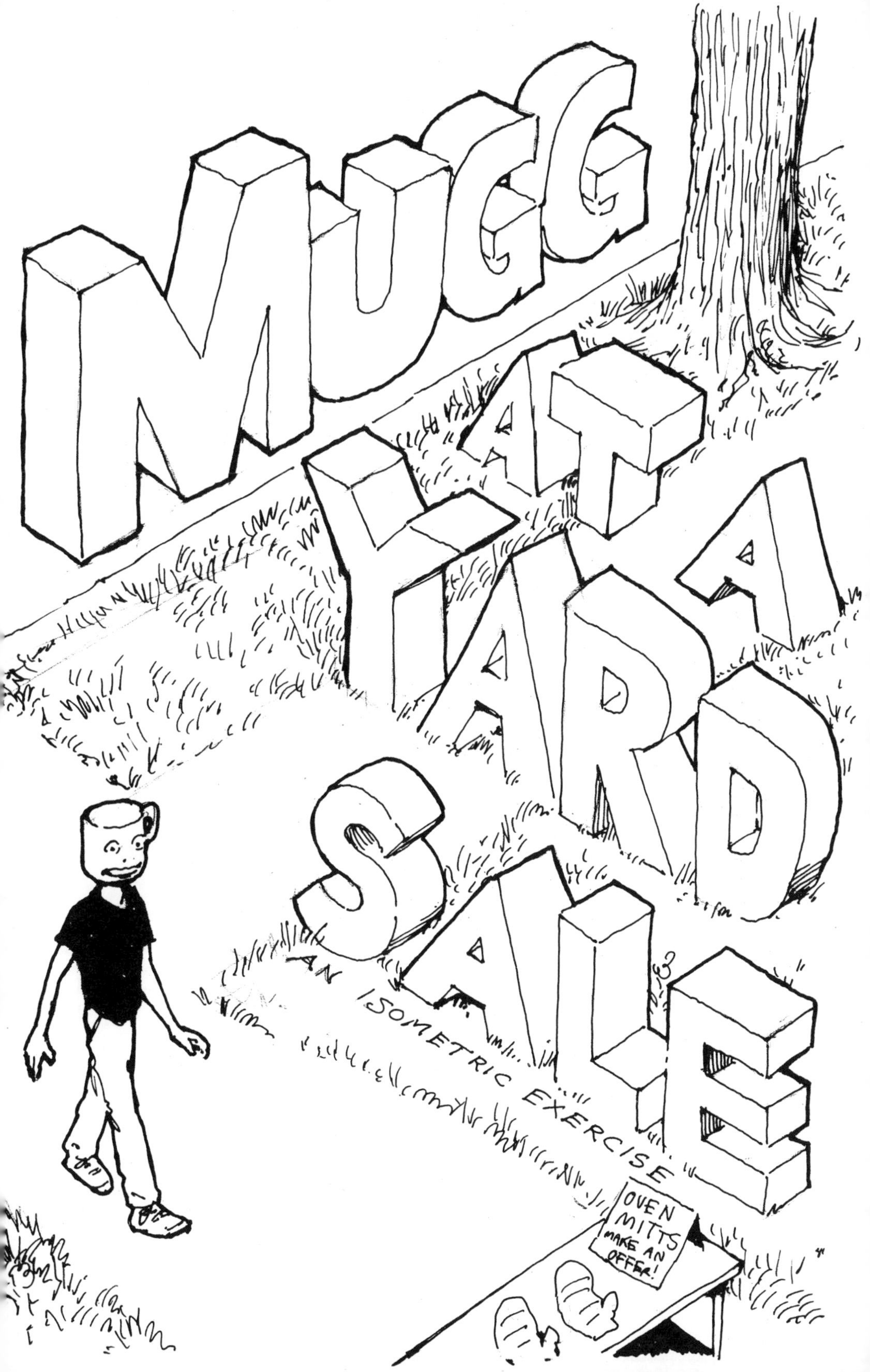
MUGG
AT
A
YARD
SALE
AN ISOMETRIC EXERCISE
OVEN MITTS
MAKE AN OFFER!

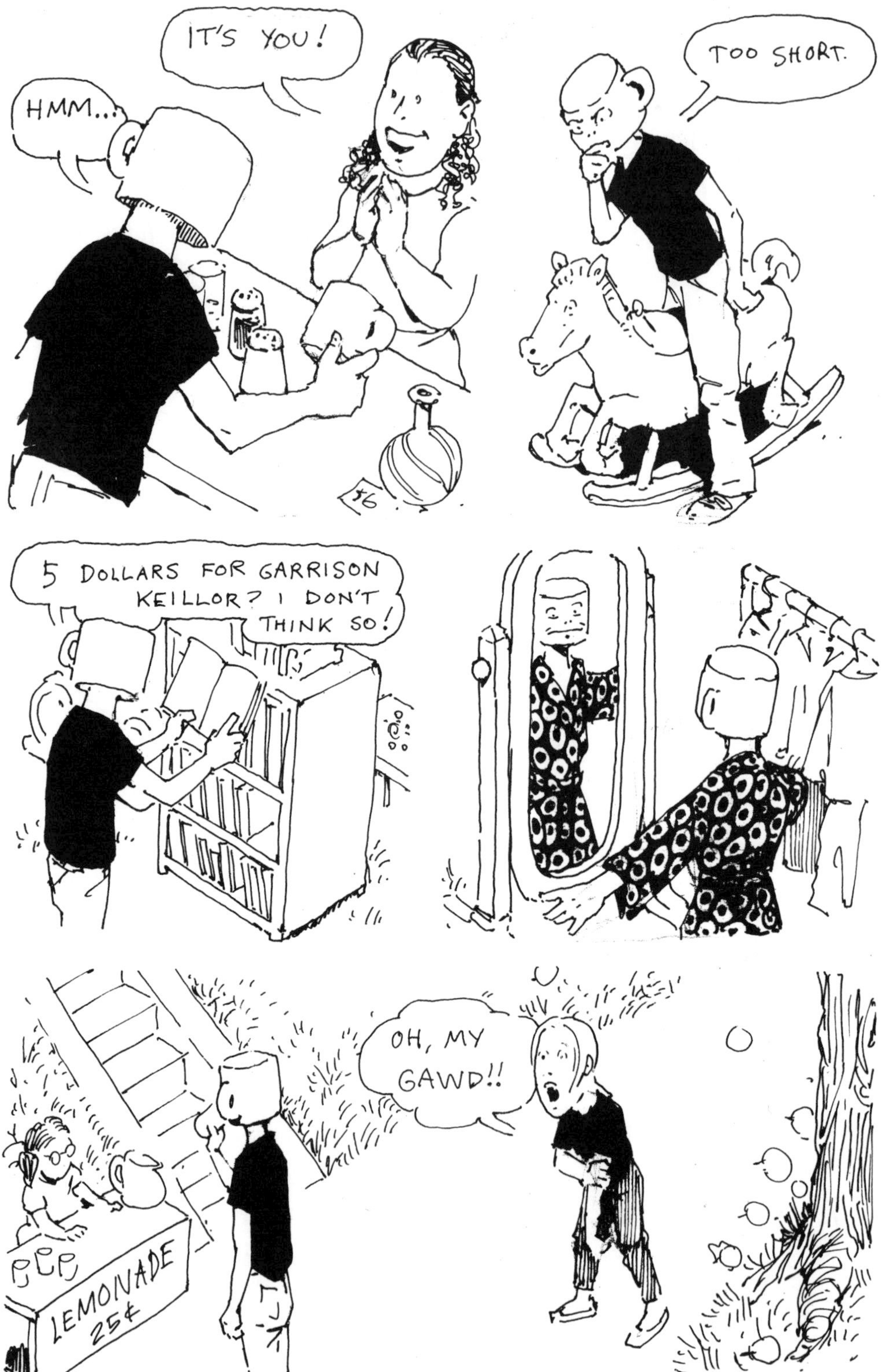
HMM...
IT'S YOU!
$6
TOO SHORT.
5 DOLLARS FOR GARRISON KEILLOR? I DON'T THINK SO!
LEMONADE 25¢
OH, MY GAWD!!

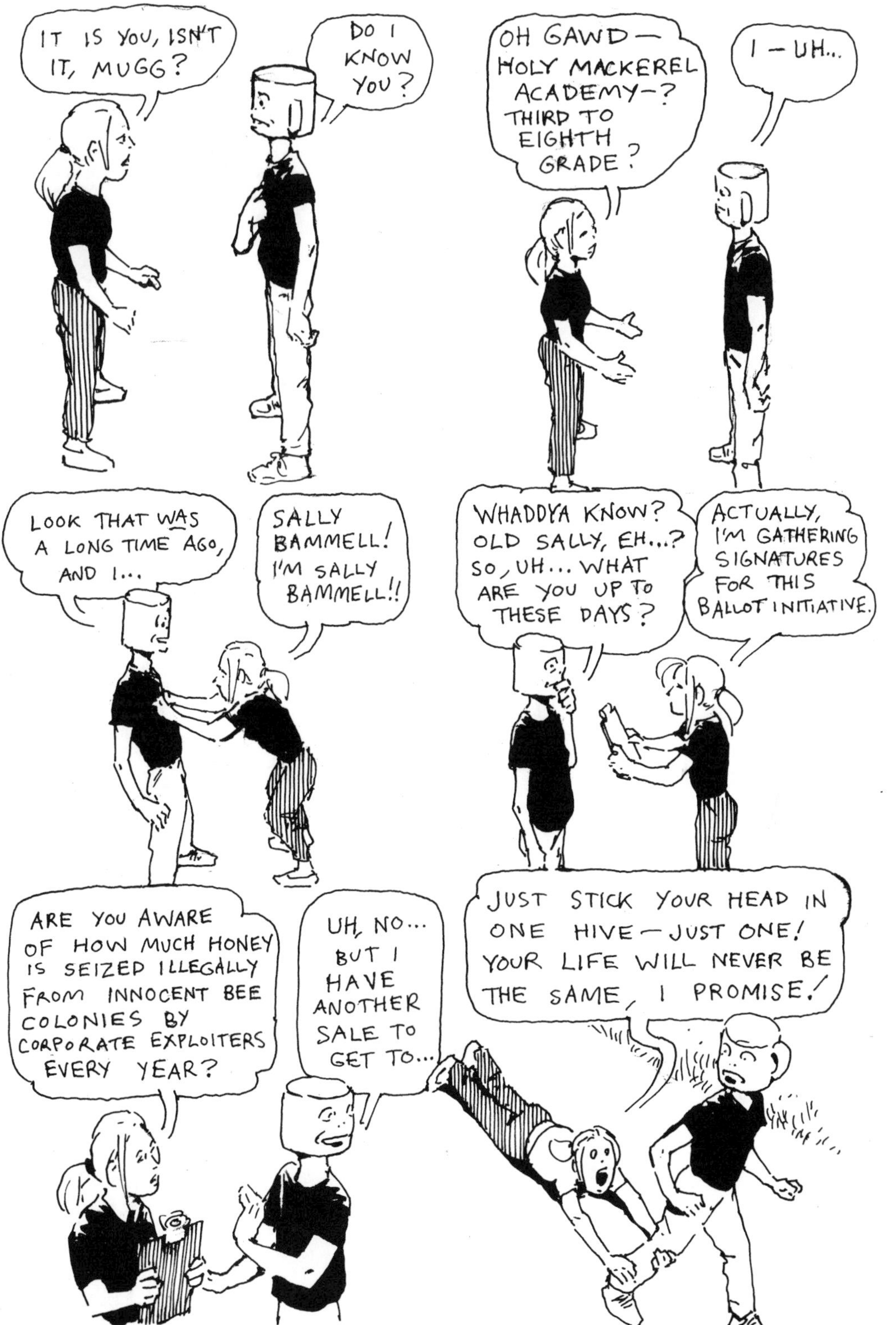
IT IS YOU, ISN'T IT, MUGG?
DO I KNOW YOU?
OH GAWD— HOLY MACKEREL ACADEMY—? THIRD TO EIGHTH GRADE?
I—UH...
LOOK THAT WAS A LONG TIME AGO, AND I...
SALLY BAMMELL! I'M SALLY BAMMELL!!
WHADDYA KNOW? OLD SALLY, EH...? SO, UH... WHAT ARE YOU UP TO THESE DAYS?
ACTUALLY, I'M GATHERING SIGNATURES FOR THIS BALLOT INITIATIVE.
ARE YOU AWARE OF HOW MUCH HONEY IS SEIZED ILLEGALLY FROM INNOCENT BEE COLONIES BY CORPORATE EXPLOITERS EVERY YEAR?
UH, NO... BUT I HAVE ANOTHER SALE TO GET TO...
JUST STICK YOUR HEAD IN ONE HIVE—JUST ONE! YOUR LIFE WILL NEVER BE THE SAME, I PROMISE!

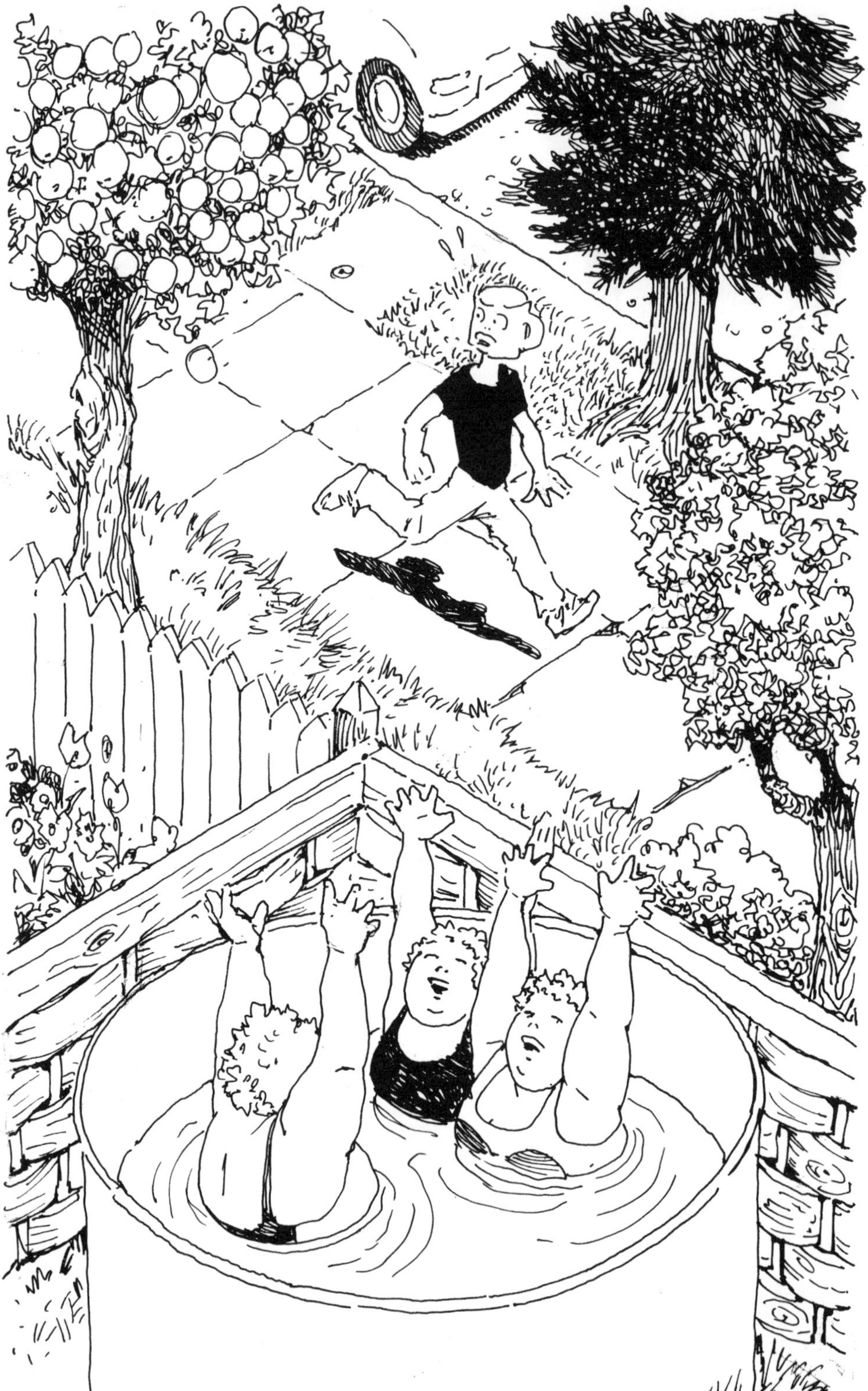

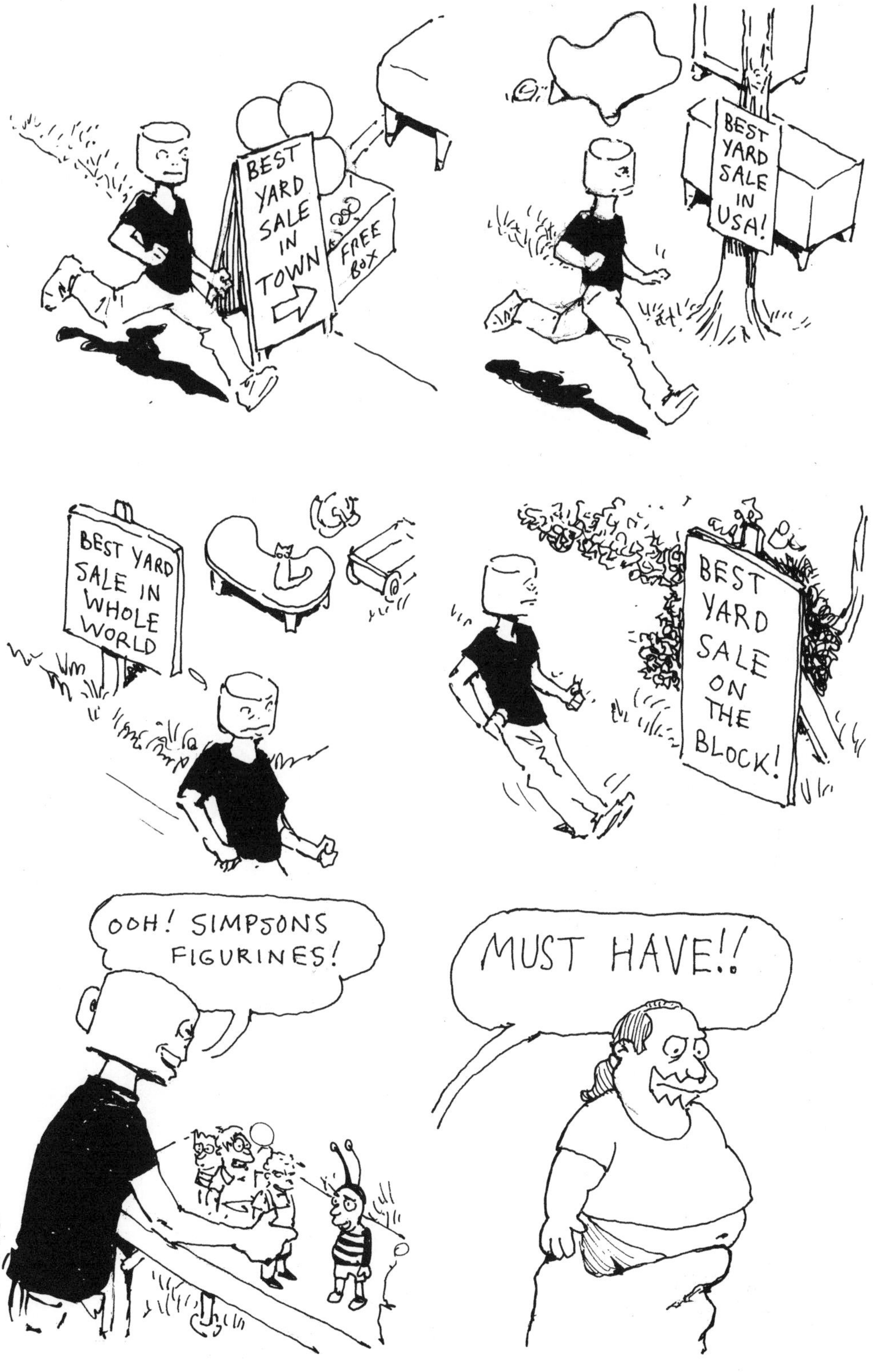
BEST YARD SALE IN TOWN
FREE BOX
BEST YARD SALE IN USA!
BEST YARD SALE IN WHOLE WORLD
BEST YARD SALE ON THE BLOCK!
OOH! SIMPSONS FIGURINES!
MUST HAVE!!

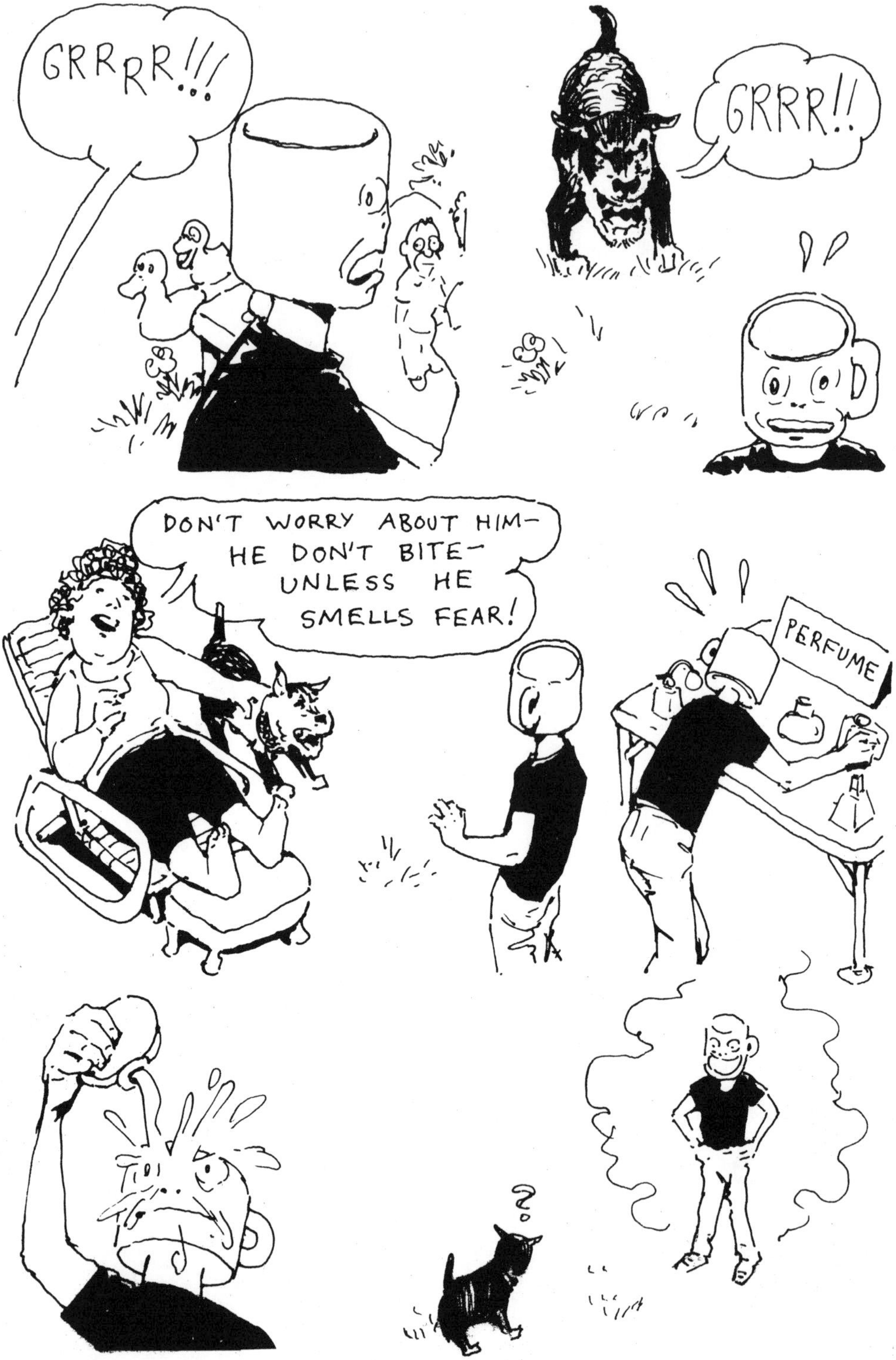
GRRRR!!!
GRRR!!
DON'T WORRY ABOUT HIM- HE DON'T BITE- UNLESS HE SMELLS FEAR!
PERFUME

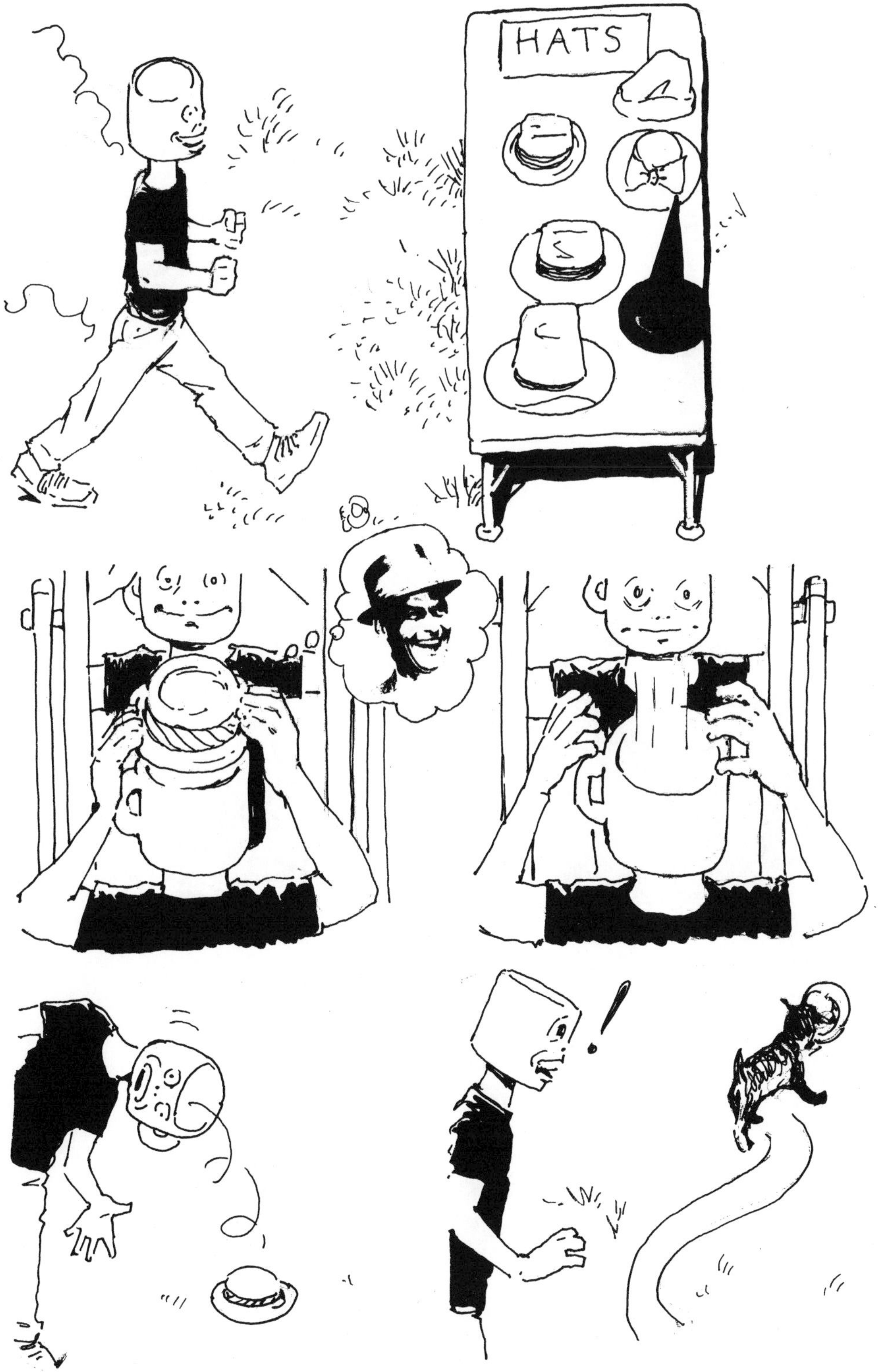
HATS

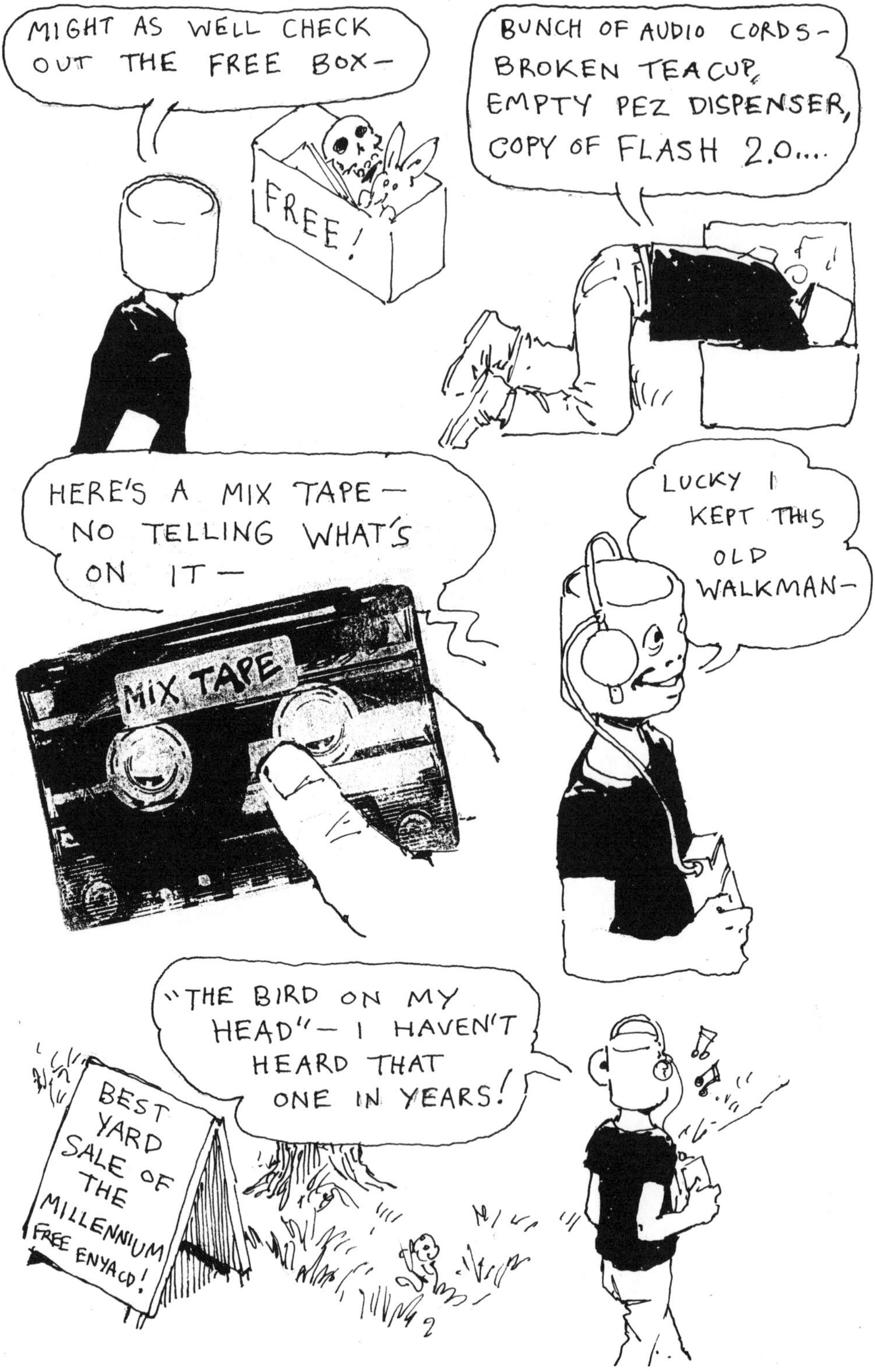
MIGHT AS WELL CHECK OUT THE FREE BOX—
FREE!
BUNCH OF AUDIO CORDS— BROKEN TEACUP, EMPTY PEZ DISPENSER, COPY OF FLASH 2.0....
HERE'S A MIX TAPE— NO TELLING WHAT'S ON IT—
MIX TAPE
LUCKY I KEPT THIS OLD WALKMAN—
"THE BIRD ON MY HEAD"— I HAVEN'T HEARD THAT ONE IN YEARS!
BEST YARD SALE OF THE MILLENNIUM
FREE ENYA CD!

JESUSLAND

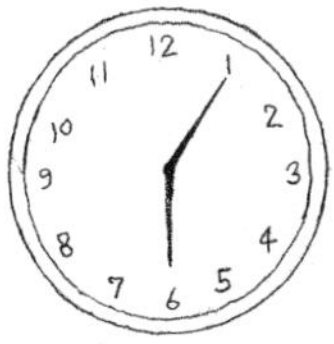

NOTES ON "JESUSLAND"

This story was drawn in the immediate aftermath of the 2004 presidential election, when Democrats were in shock and awe at how thoroughly John Kerry had been routed by the Republicans working off of Karl Rove's playbook. Particularly shocking to me was how Protestant Evangelicals and the Catholic Church, which had always been historic enemies, now had teamed up to defeat a Catholic candidate. This fantasy about a battle to establish a state religion was my way of getting those two groups at each other's throats again. Also it gave me a chance to draw President Bush as a rabbit.

The short, wordless comic at the end came about because I ran out of story on "Jesusland." This tends to happen when I have a very definite story in mind—I get anxious that I'm not going to be able to get it all on paper, and therefore rush to tell it all before I run out of time—only to find I've come to the end early and have to somehow fill pages, either by vamping or by starting something entirely new. That's what I did this time.

Religion seems to have been in the air at the time. Cartoonist Chad Essley was present at this session, and he drew a story about the time two Mormon missionaries came to his door and he took advantage of their visit to formally resign from the church.

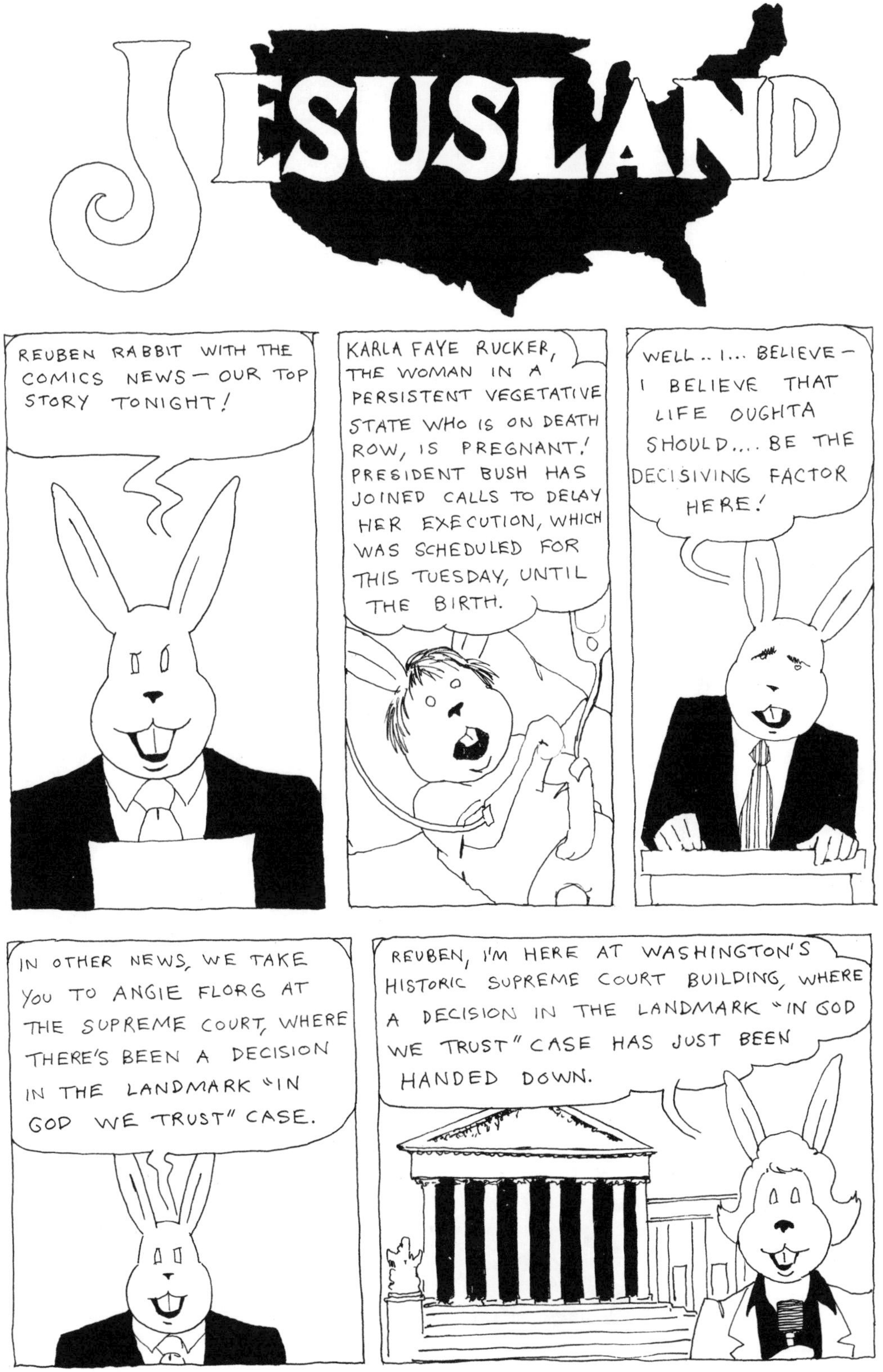
JESUSLAND
REUBEN RABBIT WITH THE COMICS NEWS— OUR TOP STORY TONIGHT!
KARLA FAYE RUCKER, THE WOMAN IN A PERSISTENT VEGETATIVE STATE WHO IS ON DEATH ROW, IS PREGNANT! PRESIDENT BUSH HAS JOINED CALLS TO DELAY HER EXECUTION, WHICH WAS SCHEDULED FOR THIS TUESDAY, UNTIL THE BIRTH.
WELL.. I... BELIEVE— I BELIEVE THAT LIFE OUGHTA SHOULD.... BE THE DECISIVING FACTOR HERE!
IN OTHER NEWS, WE TAKE YOU TO ANGIE FLORG AT THE SUPREME COURT, WHERE THERE'S BEEN A DECISION IN THE LANDMARK "IN GOD WE TRUST" CASE.
REUBEN, I'M HERE AT WASHINGTON'S HISTORIC SUPREME COURT BUILDING, WHERE A DECISION IN THE LANDMARK "IN GOD WE TRUST" CASE HAS JUST BEEN HANDED DOWN.

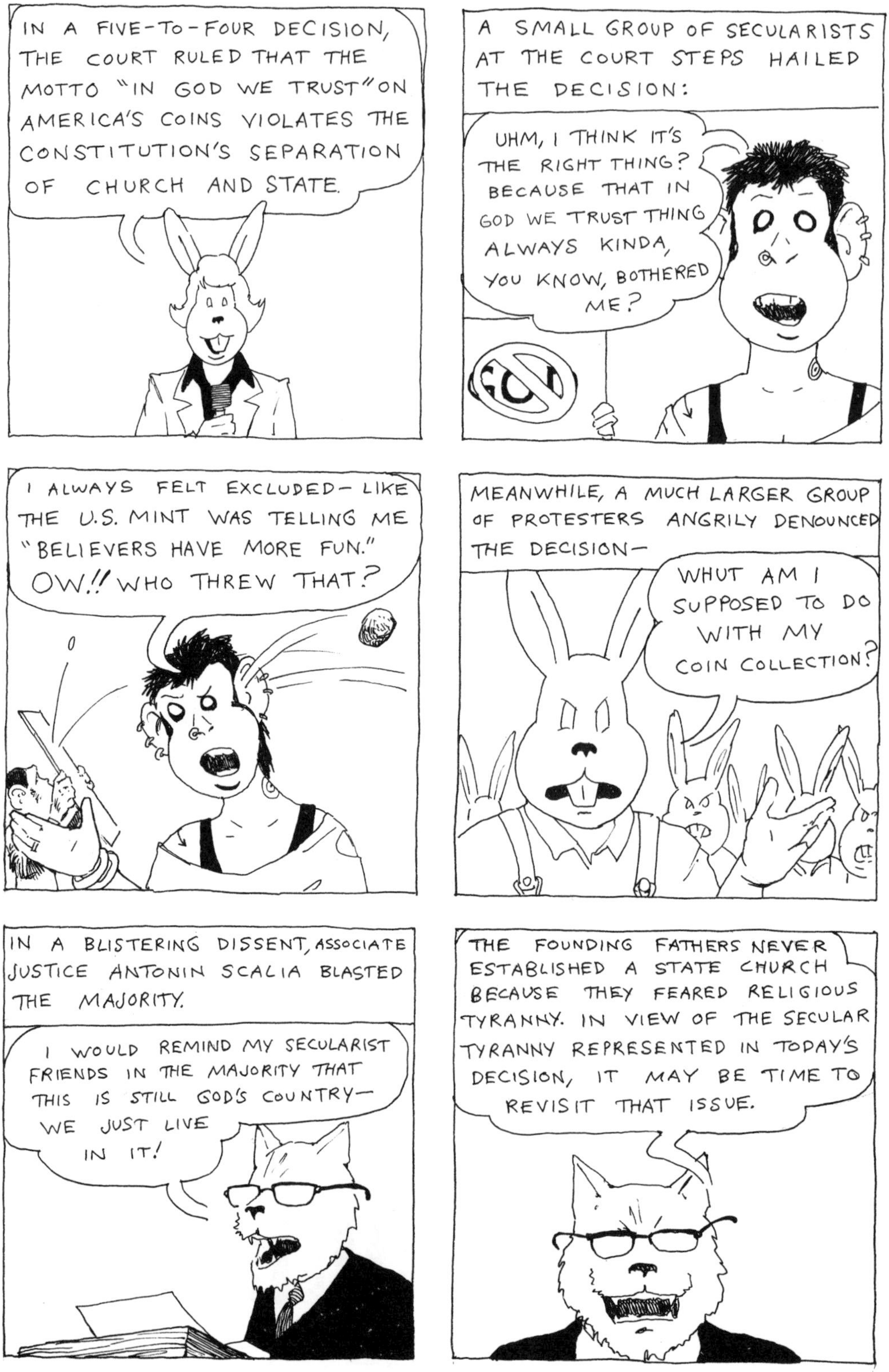
IN A FIVE-TO-FOUR DECISION, THE COURT RULED THAT THE MOTTO "IN GOD WE TRUST" ON AMERICA'S COINS VIOLATES THE CONSTITUTION'S SEPARATION OF CHURCH AND STATE.
A SMALL GROUP OF SECULARISTS AT THE COURT STEPS HAILED THE DECISION:
UHM, I THINK IT'S THE RIGHT THING? BECAUSE THAT IN GOD WE TRUST THING ALWAYS KINDA, YOU KNOW, BOTHERED ME?
I ALWAYS FELT EXCLUDED—LIKE THE U.S. MINT WAS TELLING ME "BELIEVERS HAVE MORE FUN." OW!! WHO THREW THAT?
MEANWHILE, A MUCH LARGER GROUP OF PROTESTERS ANGRILY DENOUNCED THE DECISION—
WHUT AM I SUPPOSED TO DO WITH MY COIN COLLECTION?
IN A BLISTERING DISSENT, ASSOCIATE JUSTICE ANTONIN SCALIA BLASTED THE MAJORITY.
I WOULD REMIND MY SECULARIST FRIENDS IN THE MAJORITY THAT THIS IS STILL GOD'S COUNTRY—WE JUST LIVE IN IT!
THE FOUNDING FATHERS NEVER ESTABLISHED A STATE CHURCH BECAUSE THEY FEARED RELIGIOUS TYRANNY. IN VIEW OF THE SECULAR TYRANNY REPRESENTED IN TODAY'S DECISION, IT MAY BE TIME TO REVISIT THAT ISSUE.

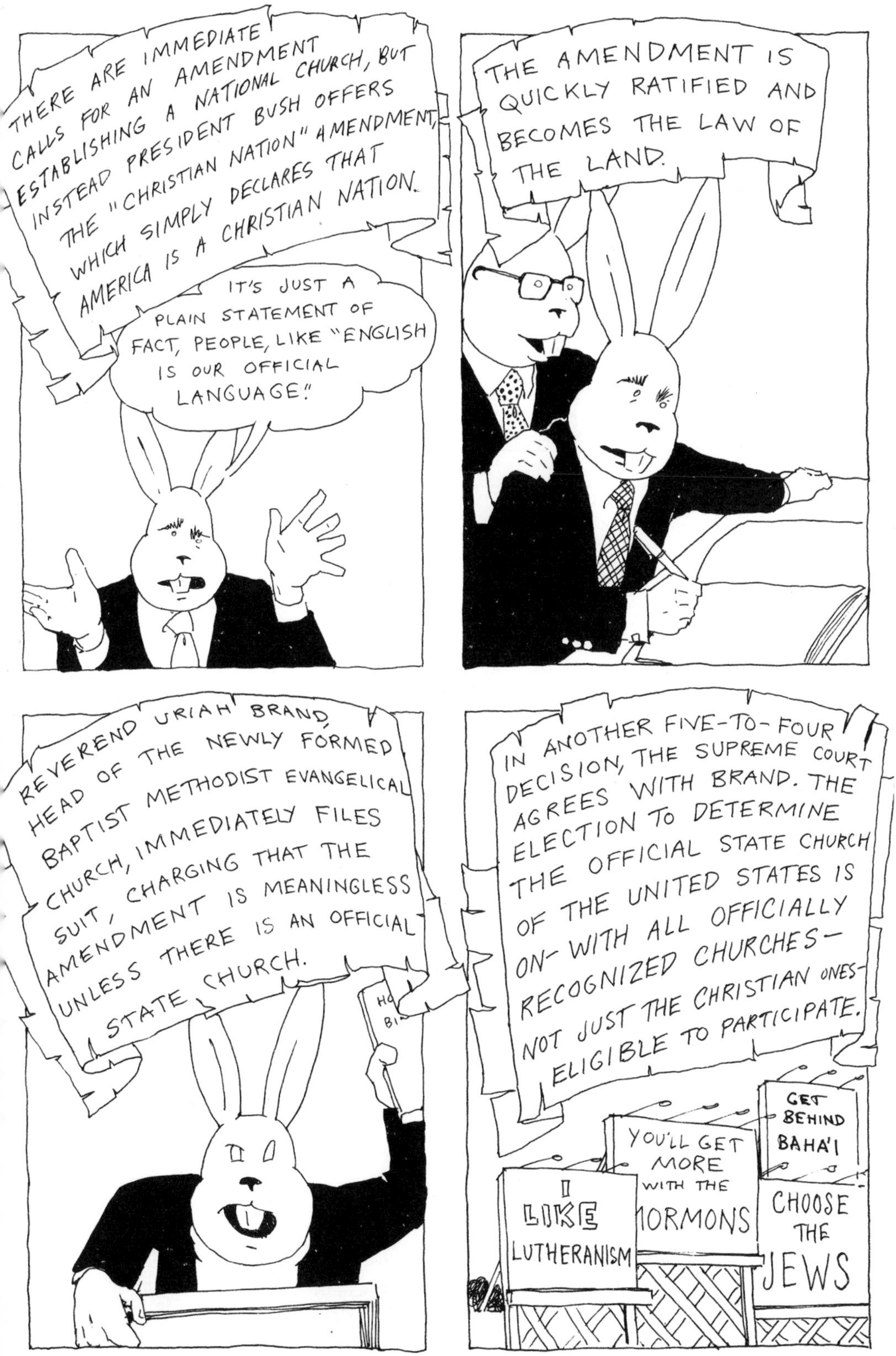
THERE ARE IMMEDIATE CALLS FOR AN AMENDMENT ESTABLISHING A NATIONAL CHURCH, BUT INSTEAD PRESIDENT BUSH OFFERS THE "CHRISTIAN NATION" AMENDMENT, WHICH SIMPLY DECLARES THAT AMERICA IS A CHRISTIAN NATION.
IT'S JUST A PLAIN STATEMENT OF FACT, PEOPLE, LIKE "ENGLISH IS OUR OFFICIAL LANGUAGE!"
THE AMENDMENT IS QUICKLY RATIFIED AND BECOMES THE LAW OF THE LAND.
REVEREND URIAH BRAND, HEAD OF THE NEWLY FORMED BAPTIST METHODIST EVANGELICAL CHURCH, IMMEDIATELY FILES SUIT, CHARGING THAT THE AMENDMENT IS MEANINGLESS UNLESS THERE IS AN OFFICIAL STATE CHURCH.
IN ANOTHER FIVE-TO-FOUR DECISION, THE SUPREME COURT AGREES WITH BRAND. THE ELECTION TO DETERMINE THE OFFICIAL STATE CHURCH OF THE UNITED STATES IS ON- WITH ALL OFFICIALLY RECOGNIZED CHURCHES- NOT JUST THE CHRISTIAN ONES- ELIGIBLE TO PARTICIPATE.
GET BEHIND BAHA'I
YOU'LL GET MORE WITH THE MORMONS
I LIKE LUTHERANISM
CHOOSE THE JEWS

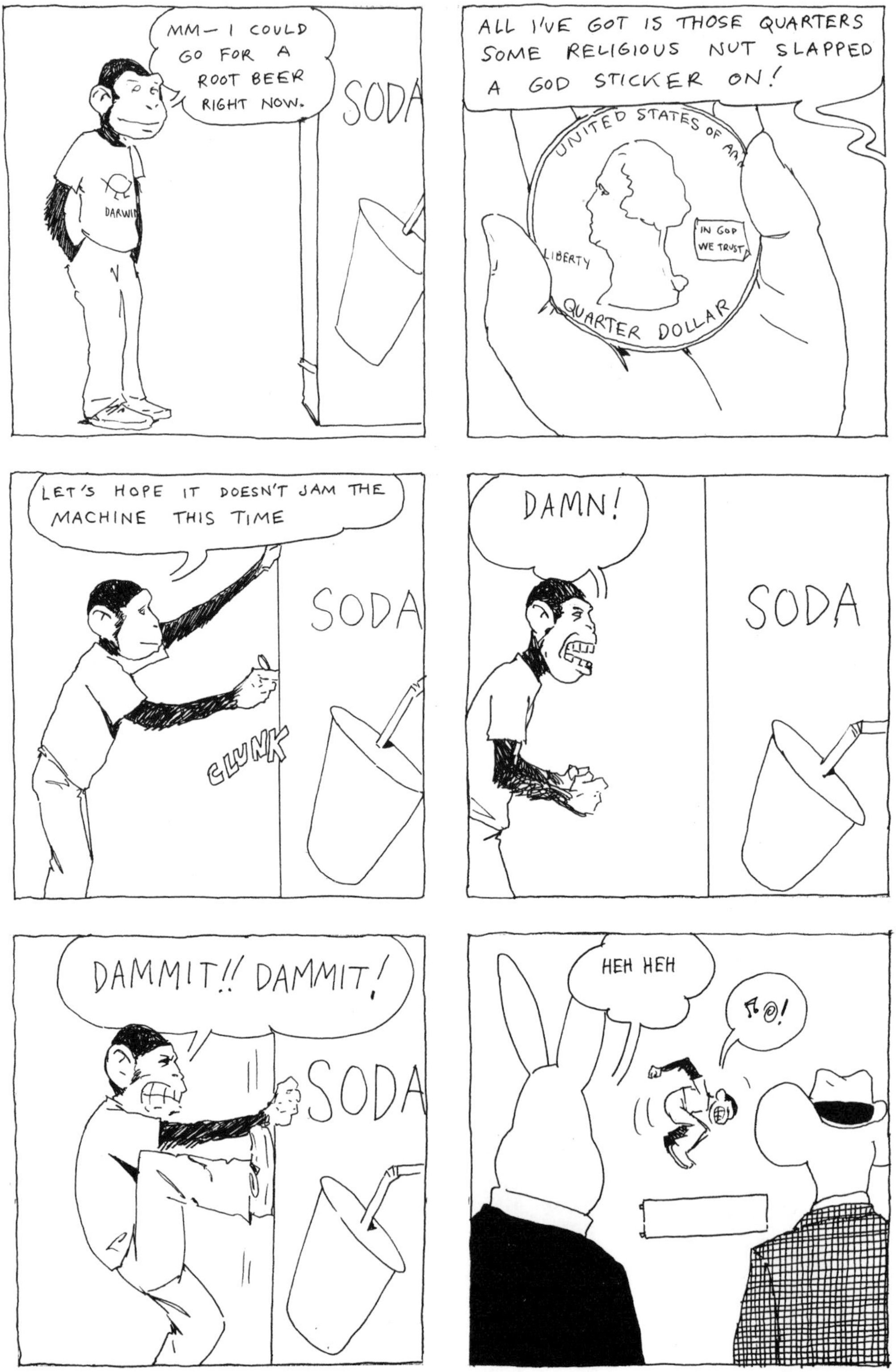
MM— I COULD GO FOR A ROOT BEER RIGHT NOW.
DARWIN
SODA
ALL I'VE GOT IS THOSE QUARTERS SOME RELIGIOUS NUT SLAPPED A GOD STICKER ON!
UNITED STATES OF AM
LIBERTY
IN GOD WE TRUST
QUARTER DOLLAR
LET'S HOPE IT DOESN'T JAM THE MACHINE THIS TIME
SODA
CLUNK
DAMN!
SODA
DAMMIT!! DAMMIT!
SODA
HEH HEH

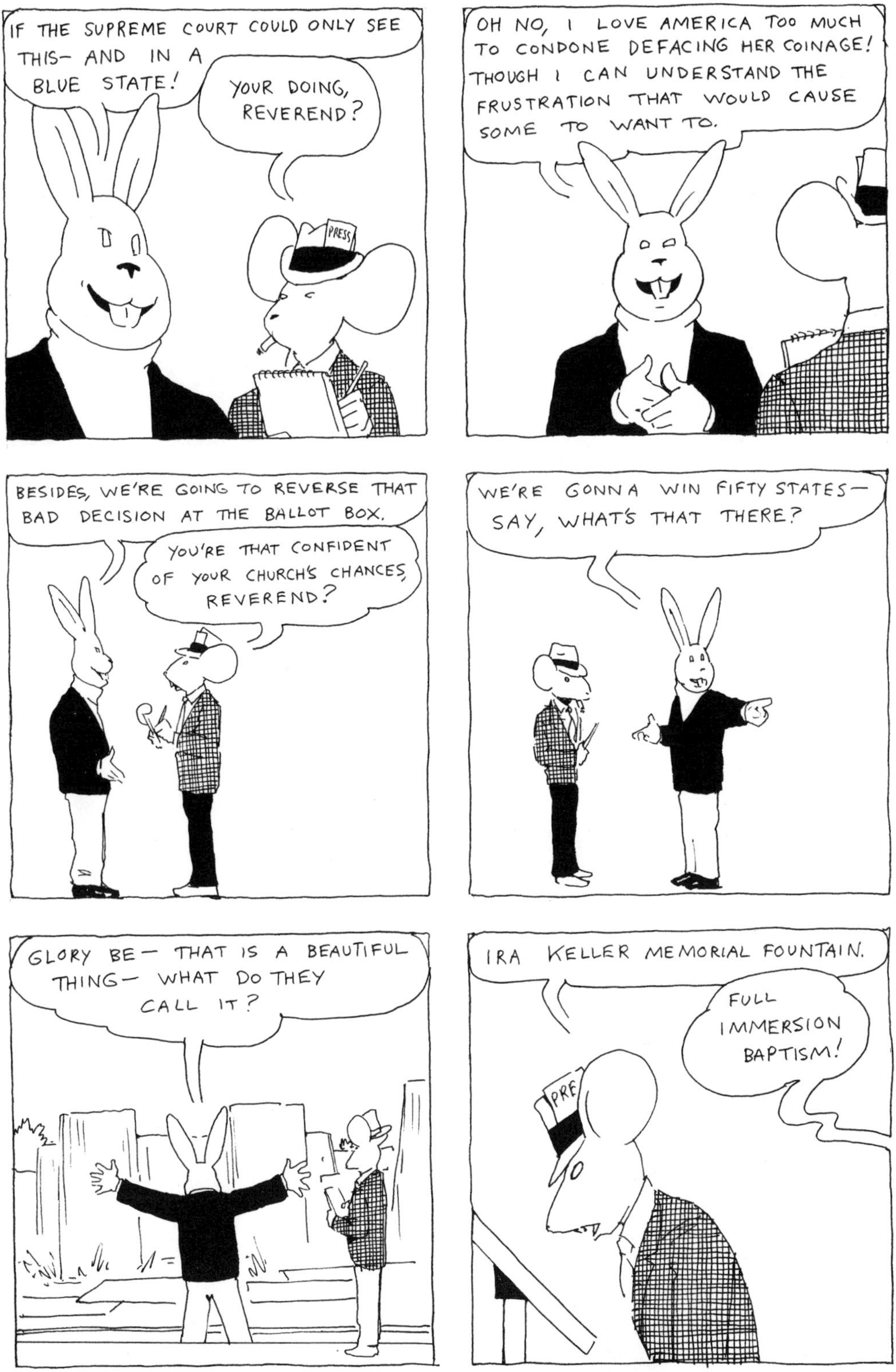
IF THE SUPREME COURT COULD ONLY SEE THIS— AND IN A BLUE STATE!
YOUR DOING, REVEREND?
PRESS
OH NO, I LOVE AMERICA TOO MUCH TO CONDONE DEFACING HER COINAGE! THOUGH I CAN UNDERSTAND THE FRUSTRATION THAT WOULD CAUSE SOME TO WANT TO.
BESIDES, WE'RE GOING TO REVERSE THAT BAD DECISION AT THE BALLOT BOX.
YOU'RE THAT CONFIDENT OF YOUR CHURCH'S CHANCES, REVEREND?
WE'RE GONNA WIN FIFTY STATES— SAY, WHAT'S THAT THERE?
GLORY BE— THAT IS A BEAUTIFUL THING— WHAT DO THEY CALL IT?
IRA KELLER MEMORIAL FOUNTAIN.
FULL IMMERSION BAPTISM!

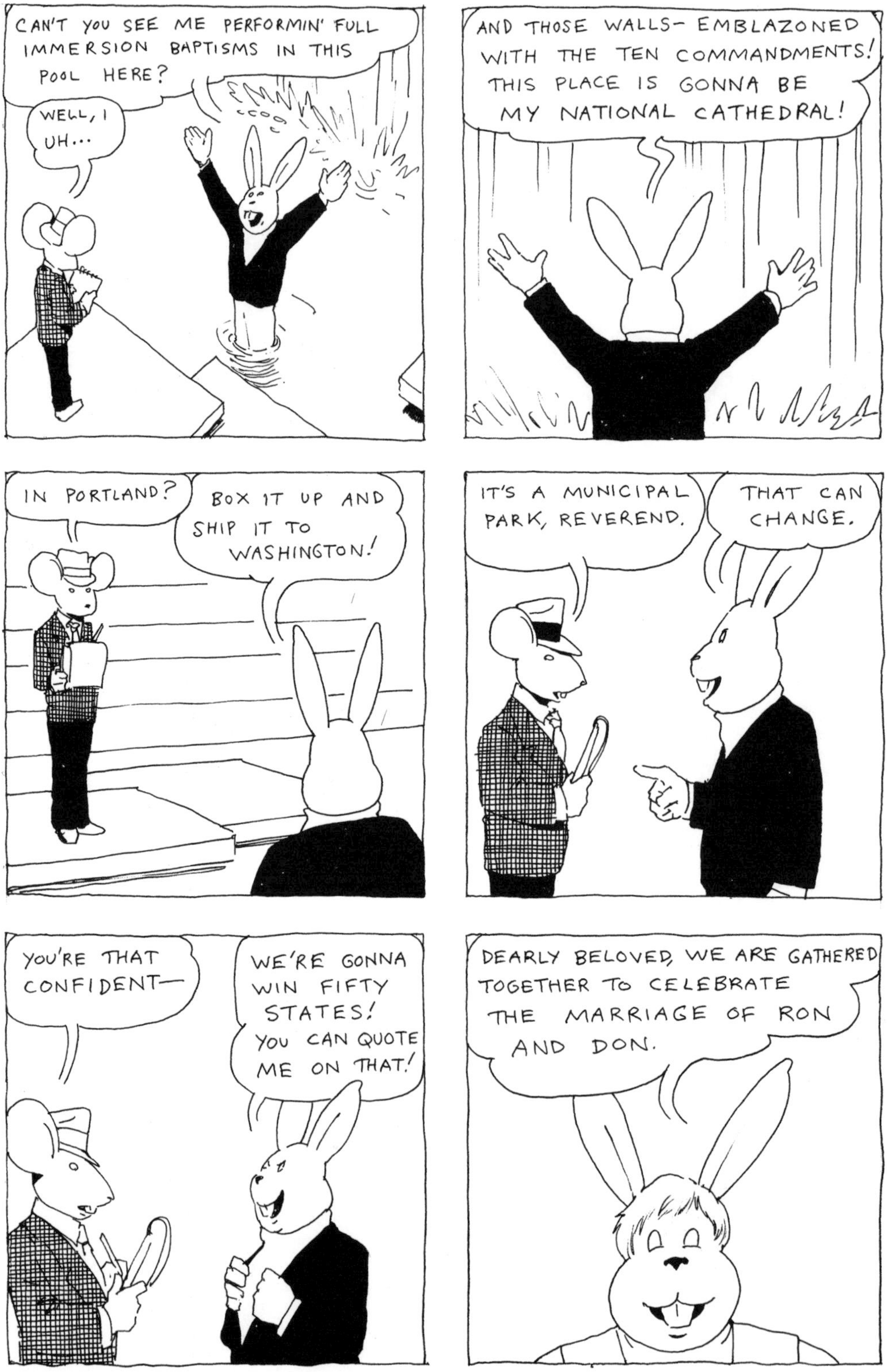
CAN'T YOU SEE ME PERFORMIN' FULL IMMERSION BAPTISMS IN THIS POOL HERE?
WELL, I UH...
AND THOSE WALLS— EMBLAZONED WITH THE TEN COMMANDMENTS! THIS PLACE IS GONNA BE MY NATIONAL CATHEDRAL!
IN PORTLAND?
BOX IT UP AND SHIP IT TO WASHINGTON!
IT'S A MUNICIPAL PARK, REVEREND.
THAT CAN CHANGE.
YOU'RE THAT CONFIDENT—
WE'RE GONNA WIN FIFTY STATES! YOU CAN QUOTE ME ON THAT!
DEARLY BELOVED, WE ARE GATHERED TOGETHER TO CELEBRATE THE MARRIAGE OF RON AND DON.

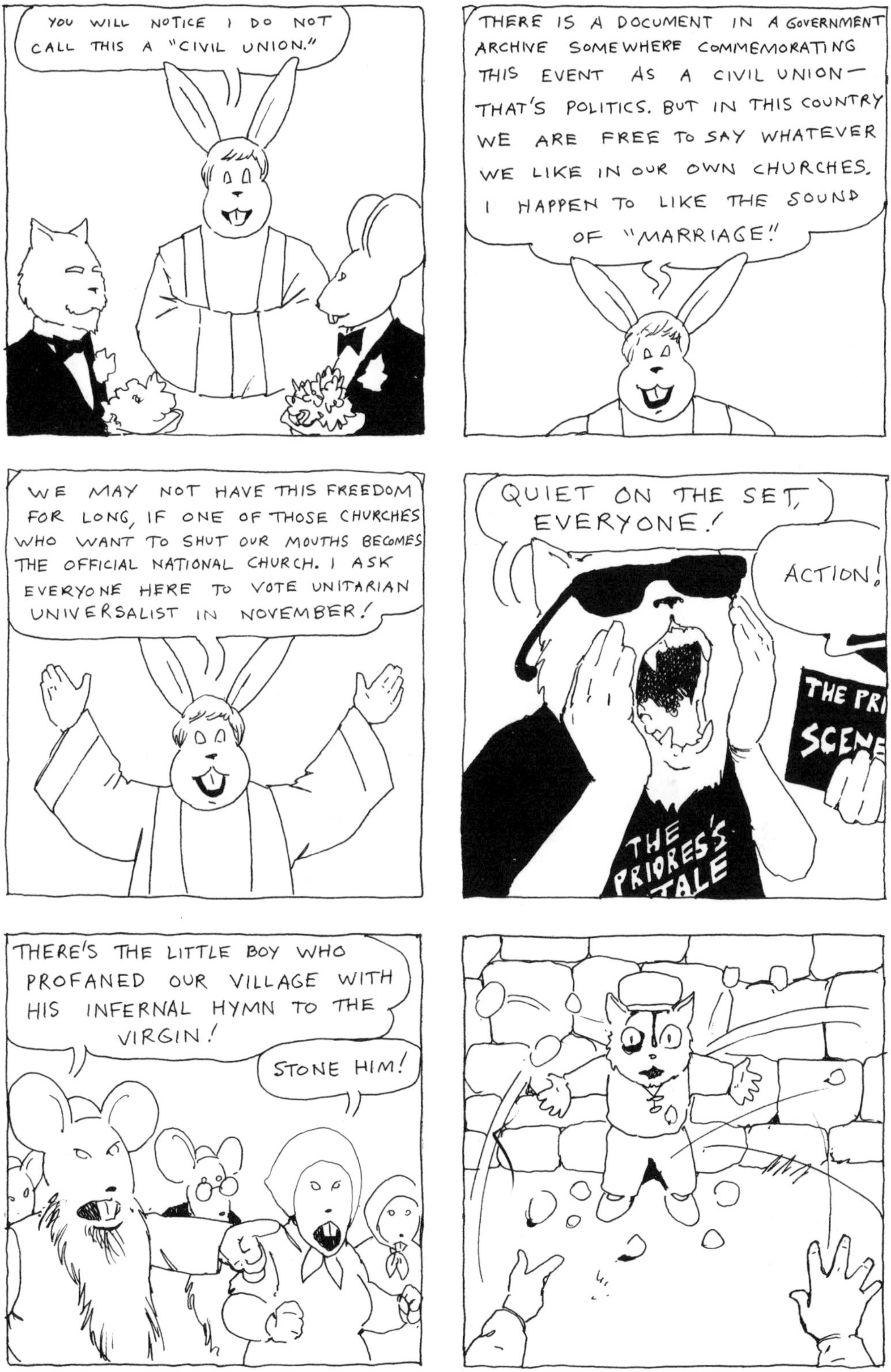
YOU WILL NOTICE I DO NOT CALL THIS A "CIVIL UNION."
THERE IS A DOCUMENT IN A GOVERNMENT ARCHIVE SOMEWHERE COMMEMORATING THIS EVENT AS A CIVIL UNION— THAT'S POLITICS. BUT IN THIS COUNTRY WE ARE FREE TO SAY WHATEVER WE LIKE IN OUR OWN CHURCHES. I HAPPEN TO LIKE THE SOUND OF "MARRIAGE!"
WE MAY NOT HAVE THIS FREEDOM FOR LONG, IF ONE OF THOSE CHURCHES WHO WANT TO SHUT OUR MOUTHS BECOMES THE OFFICIAL NATIONAL CHURCH. I ASK EVERYONE HERE TO VOTE UNITARIAN UNIVERSALIST IN NOVEMBER!
QUIET ON THE SET, EVERYONE!
ACTION!
THE PRIORESS'S TALE
THERE'S THE LITTLE BOY WHO PROFANED OUR VILLAGE WITH HIS INFERNAL HYMN TO THE VIRGIN!
STONE HIM!

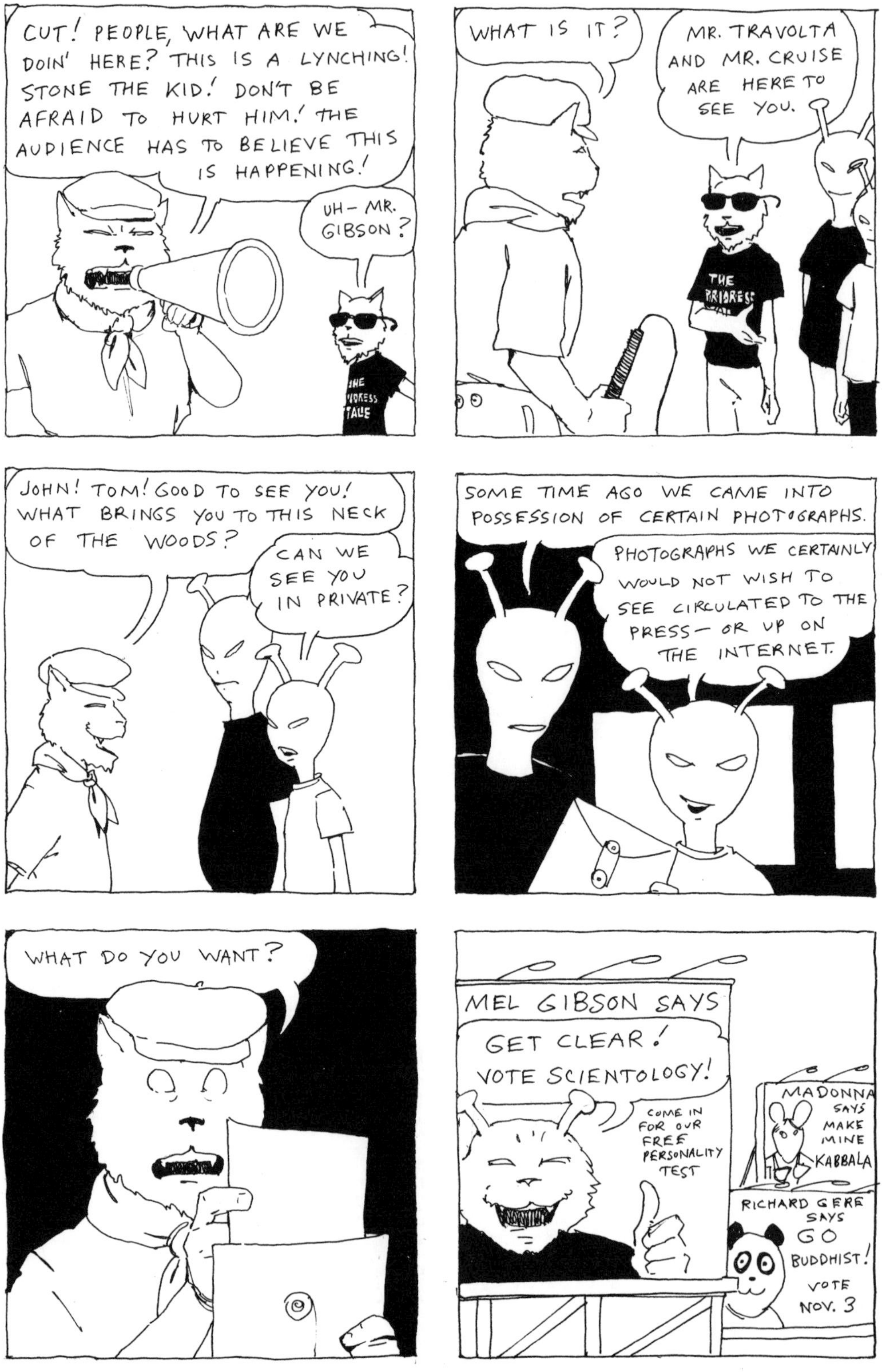
CUT! PEOPLE, WHAT ARE WE DOIN' HERE? THIS IS A LYNCHING! STONE THE KID! DON'T BE AFRAID TO HURT HIM! THE AUDIENCE HAS TO BELIEVE THIS IS HAPPENING!
UH— MR. GIBSON?
WHAT IS IT?
MR. TRAVOLTA AND MR. CRUISE ARE HERE TO SEE YOU.
JOHN! TOM! GOOD TO SEE YOU! WHAT BRINGS YOU TO THIS NECK OF THE WOODS?
CAN WE SEE YOU IN PRIVATE?
SOME TIME AGO WE CAME INTO POSSESSION OF CERTAIN PHOTOGRAPHS.
PHOTOGRAPHS WE CERTAINLY WOULD NOT WISH TO SEE CIRCULATED TO THE PRESS— OR UP ON THE INTERNET.
WHAT DO YOU WANT?
MEL GIBSON SAYS
GET CLEAR! VOTE SCIENTOLOGY!
COME IN FOR OUR FREE PERSONALITY TEST
MADONNA SAYS MAKE MINE KABBALA
RICHARD GERE SAYS GO BUDDHIST!
VOTE NOV. 3

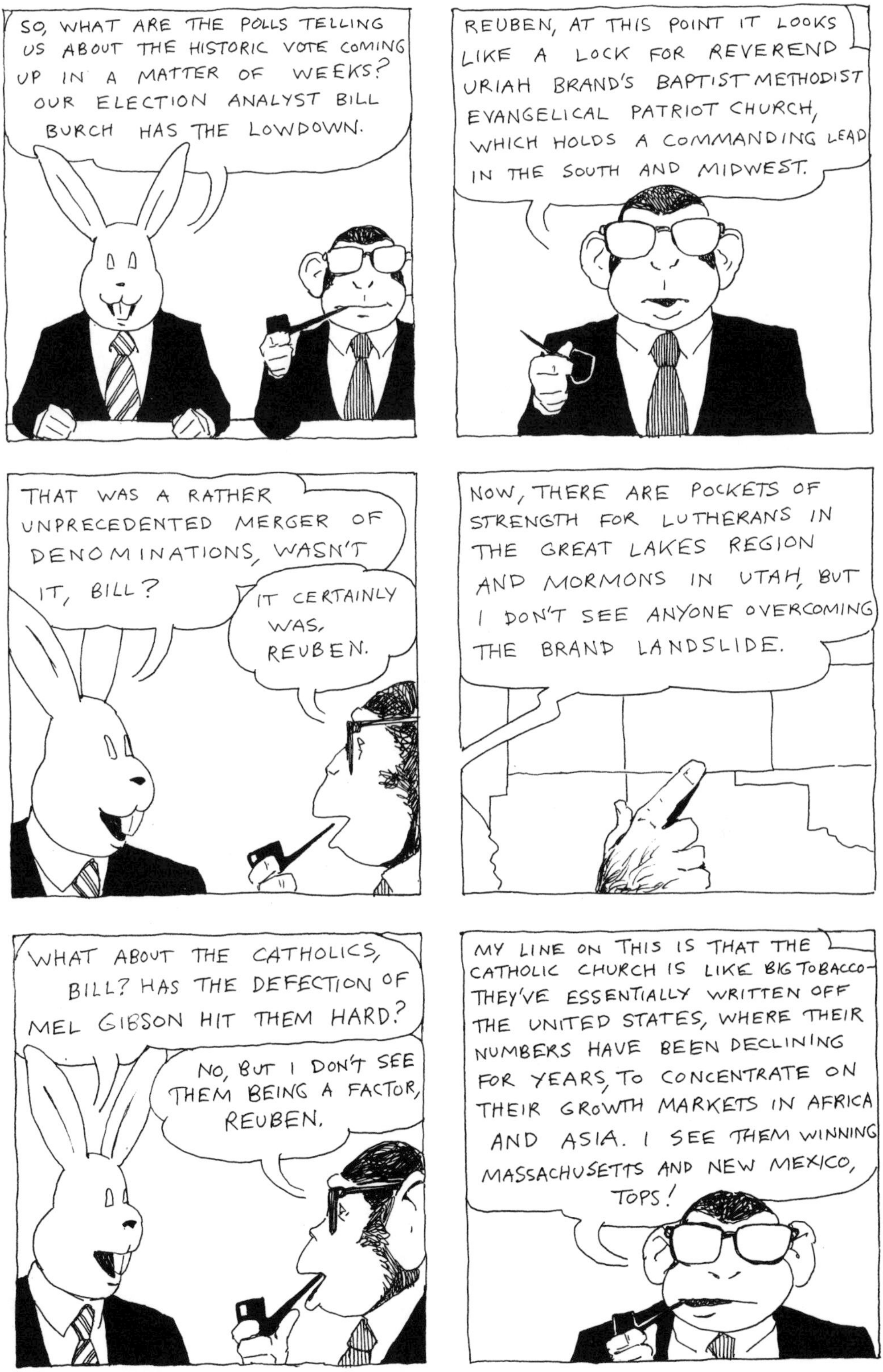
SO, WHAT ARE THE POLLS TELLING US ABOUT THE HISTORIC VOTE COMING UP IN A MATTER OF WEEKS? OUR ELECTION ANALYST BILL BURCH HAS THE LOWDOWN.
REUBEN, AT THIS POINT IT LOOKS LIKE A LOCK FOR REVEREND URIAH BRAND'S BAPTIST METHODIST EVANGELICAL PATRIOT CHURCH, WHICH HOLDS A COMMANDING LEAD IN THE SOUTH AND MIDWEST.
THAT WAS A RATHER UNPRECEDENTED MERGER OF DENOMINATIONS, WASN'T IT, BILL?
IT CERTAINLY WAS, REUBEN.
NOW, THERE ARE POCKETS OF STRENGTH FOR LUTHERANS IN THE GREAT LAKES REGION AND MORMONS IN UTAH, BUT I DON'T SEE ANYONE OVERCOMING THE BRAND LANDSLIDE.
WHAT ABOUT THE CATHOLICS, BILL? HAS THE DEFECTION OF MEL GIBSON HIT THEM HARD?
NO, BUT I DON'T SEE THEM BEING A FACTOR, REUBEN.
MY LINE ON THIS IS THAT THE CATHOLIC CHURCH IS LIKE BIG TOBACCO- THEY'VE ESSENTIALLY WRITTEN OFF THE UNITED STATES, WHERE THEIR NUMBERS HAVE BEEN DECLINING FOR YEARS, TO CONCENTRATE ON THEIR GROWTH MARKETS IN AFRICA AND ASIA. I SEE THEM WINNING MASSACHUSETTS AND NEW MEXICO, TOPS!

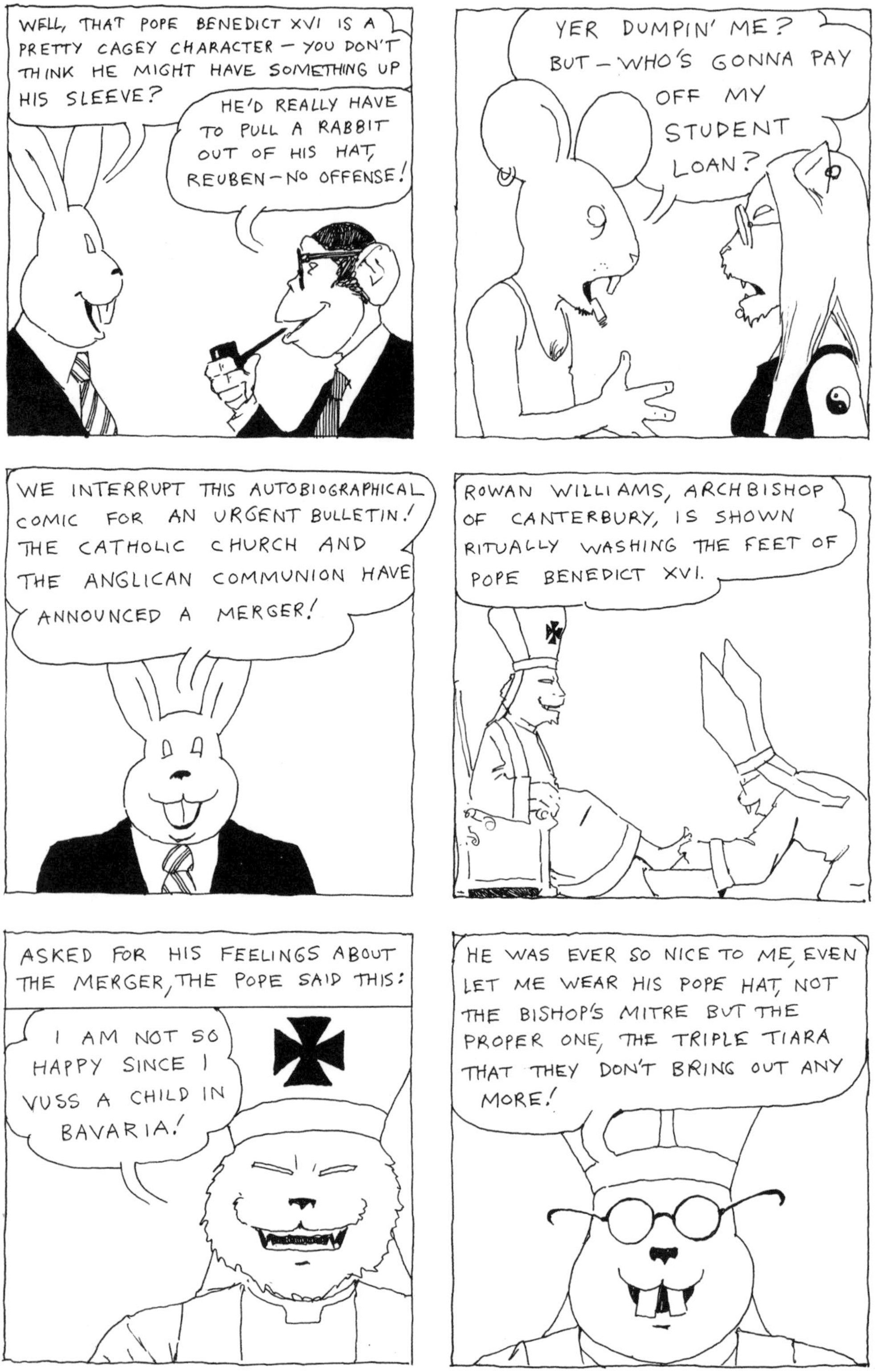

WELL, THAT POPE BENEDICT XVI IS A PRETTY CAGEY CHARACTER — YOU DON'T THINK HE MIGHT HAVE SOMETHING UP HIS SLEEVE?
HE'D REALLY HAVE TO PULL A RABBIT OUT OF HIS HAT, REUBEN—NO OFFENSE!
YER DUMPIN' ME? BUT—WHO'S GONNA PAY OFF MY STUDENT LOAN?
WE INTERRUPT THIS AUTOBIOGRAPHICAL COMIC FOR AN URGENT BULLETIN! THE CATHOLIC CHURCH AND THE ANGLICAN COMMUNION HAVE ANNOUNCED A MERGER!
ROWAN WILLIAMS, ARCHBISHOP OF CANTERBURY, IS SHOWN RITUALLY WASHING THE FEET OF POPE BENEDICT XVI.
ASKED FOR HIS FEELINGS ABOUT THE MERGER, THE POPE SAID THIS:
I AM NOT SO HAPPY SINCE I VUSS A CHILD IN BAVARIA!
HE WAS EVER SO NICE TO ME, EVEN LET ME WEAR HIS POPE HAT, NOT THE BISHOP'S MITRE BUT THE PROPER ONE, THE TRIPLE TIARA THAT THEY DON'T BRING OUT ANY MORE!

WERE NEGOTIATIONS DIFFICULT?

NO— THE HOLY FATHER AGREED TO ALL OF OUR MAJOR POINTS. HENRY VIII IS BEING GRANTED A RETROACTIVE DIVORCE AND THE CHURCH HAS PROMISED EXPEDITED ANNULMENTS FOR ALL OUR PRIESTS WHO WISH TO REMAIN IN THE MINISTRY!

AND BENEDICT SAYS I CAN USE THE VATICAN WHENEVER HE'S OUT OF THE COUNTRY! AFTER ALL—

...WE'RE ALL BROTHERS IN CHRIST!

THE NEWS IS GREETED WITH JUBILATION IN BRITAIN...

OW IT'S LONG OVERDUE, INNIT? WE NEVER REALLY WANTED OUR OWN CHURCH! IT WAS ALL THEM TOFFS LIKE HENRY VIII AND THAT LOT!

I REMEMBER— DURIN' THE WAR, WHENEVER WE'D 'EAR A JERRY BOMB COMIN' WE'D ALWAYS BE SURE TO STAND NEAR THE CATHOLIC—

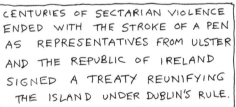

CENTURIES OF SECTARIAN VIOLENCE ENDED WITH THE STROKE OF A PEN AS REPRESENTATIVES FROM ULSTER AND THE REPUBLIC OF IRELAND SIGNED A TREATY REUNIFYING THE ISLAND UNDER DUBLIN'S RULE.

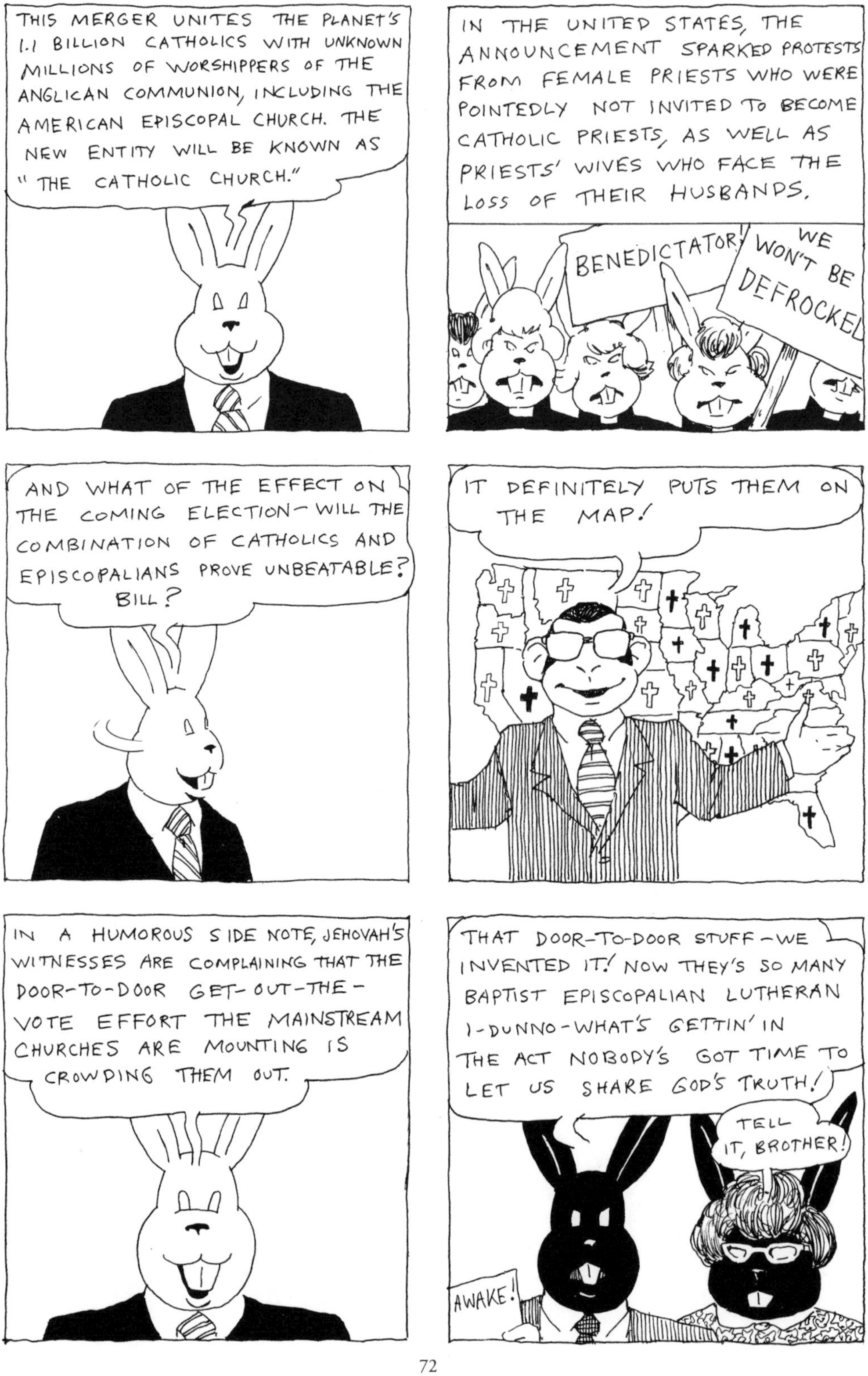
THIS MERGER UNITES THE PLANET'S 1.1 BILLION CATHOLICS WITH UNKNOWN MILLIONS OF WORSHIPPERS OF THE ANGLICAN COMMUNION, INCLUDING THE AMERICAN EPISCOPAL CHURCH. THE NEW ENTITY WILL BE KNOWN AS "THE CATHOLIC CHURCH."
IN THE UNITED STATES, THE ANNOUNCEMENT SPARKED PROTESTS FROM FEMALE PRIESTS WHO WERE POINTEDLY NOT INVITED TO BECOME CATHOLIC PRIESTS, AS WELL AS PRIESTS' WIVES WHO FACE THE LOSS OF THEIR HUSBANDS.
BENEDICTATOR!
WE WON'T BE DEFROCKED
AND WHAT OF THE EFFECT ON THE COMING ELECTION— WILL THE COMBINATION OF CATHOLICS AND EPISCOPALIANS PROVE UNBEATABLE? BILL?
IT DEFINITELY PUTS THEM ON THE MAP!
IN A HUMOROUS SIDE NOTE, JEHOVAH'S WITNESSES ARE COMPLAINING THAT THE DOOR-TO-DOOR GET-OUT-THE-VOTE EFFORT THE MAINSTREAM CHURCHES ARE MOUNTING IS CROWDING THEM OUT.
THAT DOOR-TO-DOOR STUFF—WE INVENTED IT! NOW THEY'S SO MANY BAPTIST EPISCOPALIAN LUTHERAN I-DUNNO-WHAT'S GETTIN' IN THE ACT NOBODY'S GOT TIME TO LET US SHARE GOD'S TRUTH!
TELL IT, BROTHER!
AWAKE!

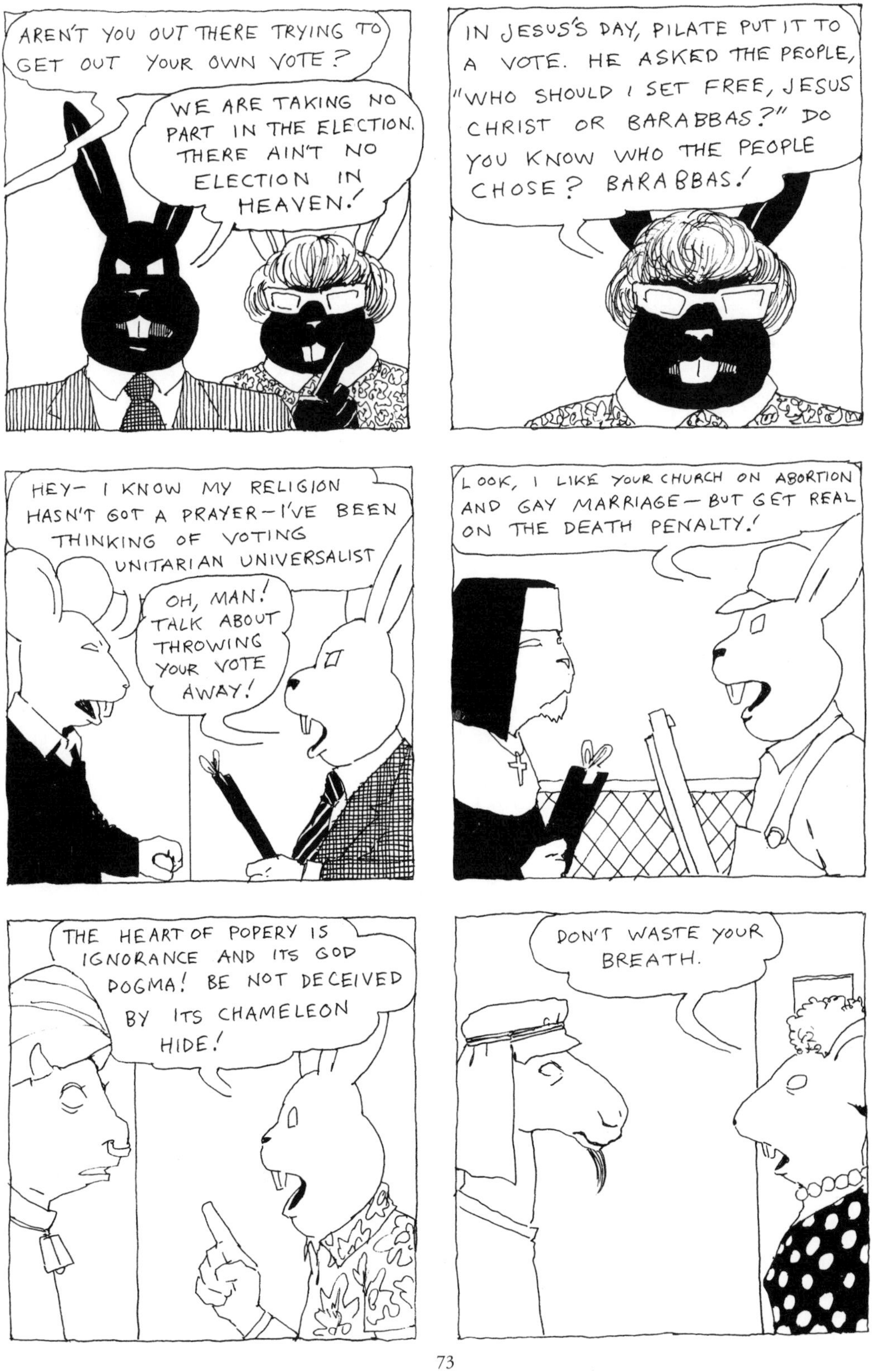
AREN'T YOU OUT THERE TRYING TO GET OUT YOUR OWN VOTE?
WE ARE TAKING NO PART IN THE ELECTION. THERE AIN'T NO ELECTION IN HEAVEN!
IN JESUS'S DAY, PILATE PUT IT TO A VOTE. HE ASKED THE PEOPLE, "WHO SHOULD I SET FREE, JESUS CHRIST OR BARABBAS?" DO YOU KNOW WHO THE PEOPLE CHOSE? BARABBAS!
HEY— I KNOW MY RELIGION HASN'T GOT A PRAYER—I'VE BEEN THINKING OF VOTING UNITARIAN UNIVERSALIST
OH, MAN! TALK ABOUT THROWING YOUR VOTE AWAY!
LOOK, I LIKE YOUR CHURCH ON ABORTION AND GAY MARRIAGE— BUT GET REAL ON THE DEATH PENALTY!
THE HEART OF POPERY IS IGNORANCE AND ITS GOD DOGMA! BE NOT DECEIVED BY ITS CHAMELEON HIDE!
DON'T WASTE YOUR BREATH.

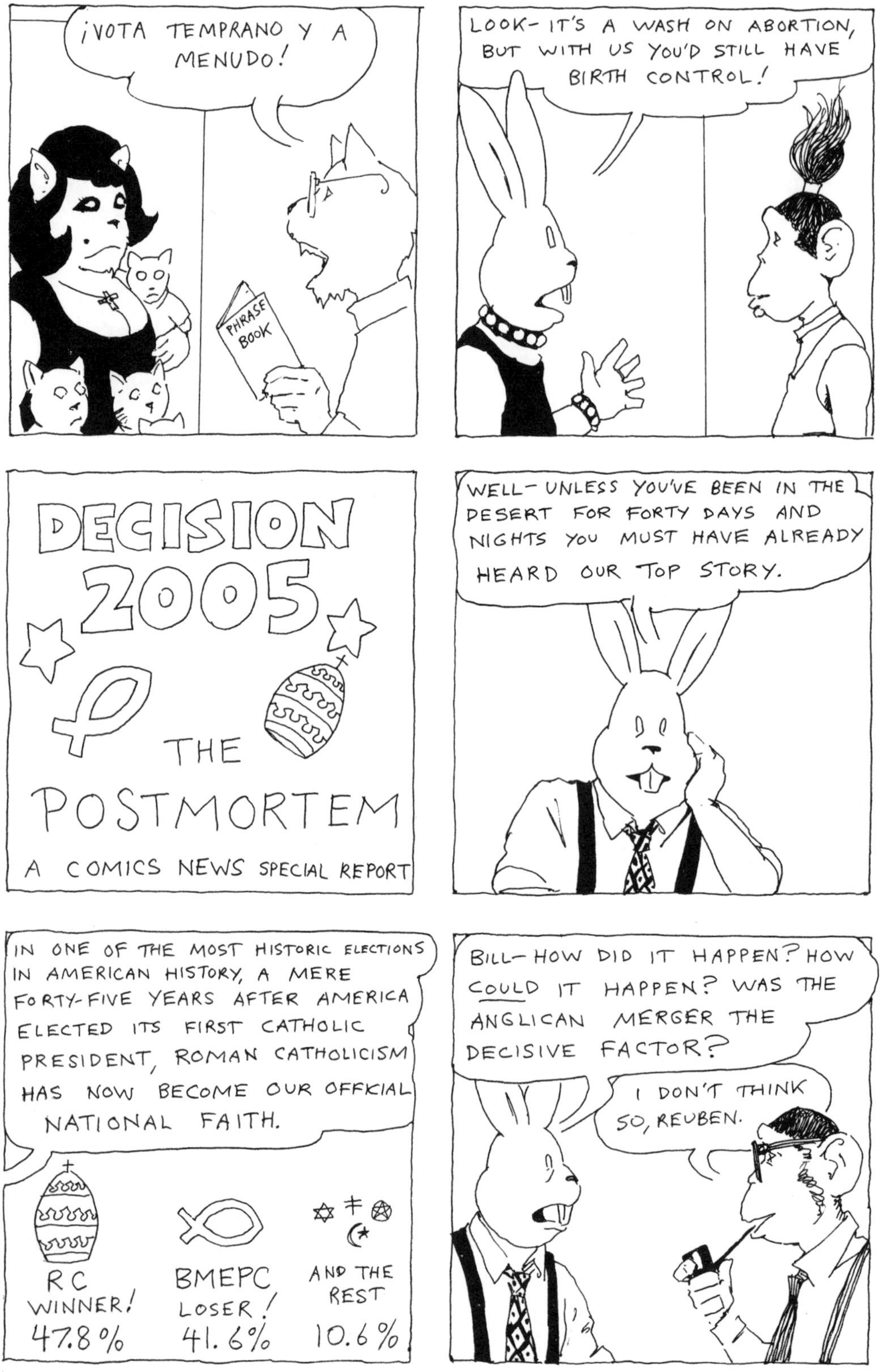
¡VOTA TEMPRANO Y A MENUDO!
PHRASE BOOK
LOOK— IT'S A WASH ON ABORTION, BUT WITH US YOU'D STILL HAVE BIRTH CONTROL!
DECISION 2005
THE POSTMORTEM
A COMICS NEWS SPECIAL REPORT
WELL— UNLESS YOU'VE BEEN IN THE DESERT FOR FORTY DAYS AND NIGHTS YOU MUST HAVE ALREADY HEARD OUR TOP STORY.
IN ONE OF THE MOST HISTORIC ELECTIONS IN AMERICAN HISTORY, A MERE FORTY-FIVE YEARS AFTER AMERICA ELECTED ITS FIRST CATHOLIC PRESIDENT, ROMAN CATHOLICISM HAS NOW BECOME OUR OFFICIAL NATIONAL FAITH.
RC WINNER! 47.8%
BMEPC LOSER! 41.6%
AND THE REST 10.6%
BILL— HOW DID IT HAPPEN? HOW COULD IT HAPPEN? WAS THE ANGLICAN MERGER THE DECISIVE FACTOR?
I DON'T THINK SO, REUBEN.

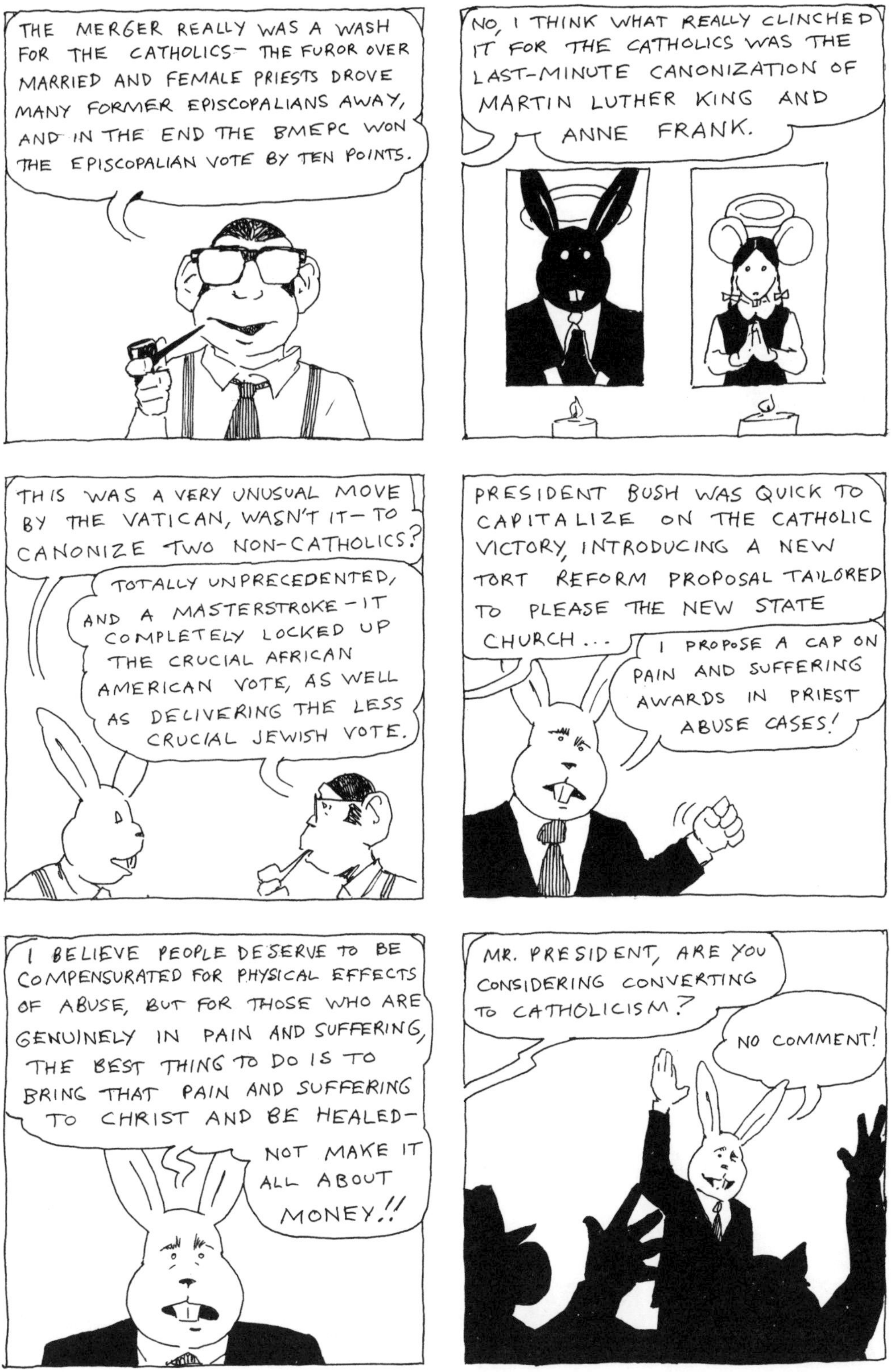
THE MERGER REALLY WAS A WASH FOR THE CATHOLICS— THE FUROR OVER MARRIED AND FEMALE PRIESTS DROVE MANY FORMER EPISCOPALIANS AWAY, AND IN THE END THE BMEPC WON THE EPISCOPALIAN VOTE BY TEN POINTS.
NO, I THINK WHAT REALLY CLINCHED IT FOR THE CATHOLICS WAS THE LAST-MINUTE CANONIZATION OF MARTIN LUTHER KING AND ANNE FRANK.
THIS WAS A VERY UNUSUAL MOVE BY THE VATICAN, WASN'T IT— TO CANONIZE TWO NON-CATHOLICS?
TOTALLY UNPRECEDENTED, AND A MASTERSTROKE—IT COMPLETELY LOCKED UP THE CRUCIAL AFRICAN AMERICAN VOTE, AS WELL AS DELIVERING THE LESS CRUCIAL JEWISH VOTE.
PRESIDENT BUSH WAS QUICK TO CAPITALIZE ON THE CATHOLIC VICTORY, INTRODUCING A NEW TORT REFORM PROPOSAL TAILORED TO PLEASE THE NEW STATE CHURCH...
I PROPOSE A CAP ON PAIN AND SUFFERING AWARDS IN PRIEST ABUSE CASES!
I BELIEVE PEOPLE DESERVE TO BE COMPENSURATED FOR PHYSICAL EFFECTS OF ABUSE, BUT FOR THOSE WHO ARE GENUINELY IN PAIN AND SUFFERING, THE BEST THING TO DO IS TO BRING THAT PAIN AND SUFFERING TO CHRIST AND BE HEALED—
NOT MAKE IT ALL ABOUT MONEY!!
MR. PRESIDENT, ARE YOU CONSIDERING CONVERTING TO CATHOLICISM?
NO COMMENT!

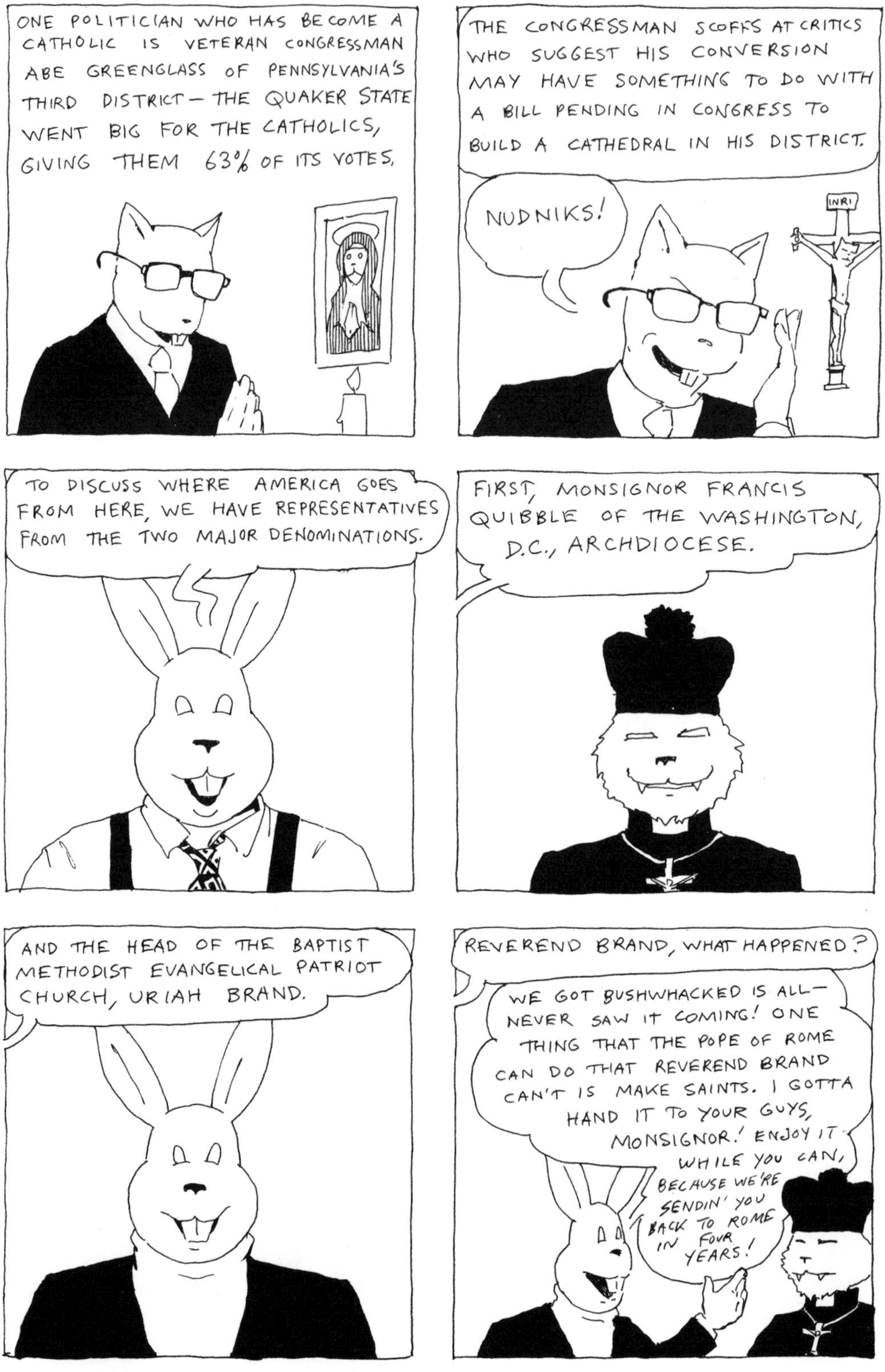
ONE POLITICIAN WHO HAS BECOME A CATHOLIC IS VETERAN CONGRESSMAN ABE GREENGLASS OF PENNSYLVANIA'S THIRD DISTRICT — THE QUAKER STATE WENT BIG FOR THE CATHOLICS, GIVING THEM 63% OF ITS VOTES.
THE CONGRESSMAN SCOFFS AT CRITICS WHO SUGGEST HIS CONVERSION MAY HAVE SOMETHING TO DO WITH A BILL PENDING IN CONGRESS TO BUILD A CATHEDRAL IN HIS DISTRICT.
NUDNIKS!
INRI
TO DISCUSS WHERE AMERICA GOES FROM HERE, WE HAVE REPRESENTATIVES FROM THE TWO MAJOR DENOMINATIONS.
FIRST, MONSIGNOR FRANCIS QUIBBLE OF THE WASHINGTON, D.C., ARCHDIOCESE.
AND THE HEAD OF THE BAPTIST METHODIST EVANGELICAL PATRIOT CHURCH, URIAH BRAND.
REVEREND BRAND, WHAT HAPPENED?
WE GOT BUSHWHACKED IS ALL— NEVER SAW IT COMING! ONE THING THAT THE POPE OF ROME CAN DO THAT REVEREND BRAND CAN'T IS MAKE SAINTS. I GOTTA HAND IT TO YOUR GUYS, MONSIGNOR! ENJOY IT WHILE YOU CAN,
BECAUSE WE'RE SENDIN' YOU BACK TO ROME IN FOUR YEARS!

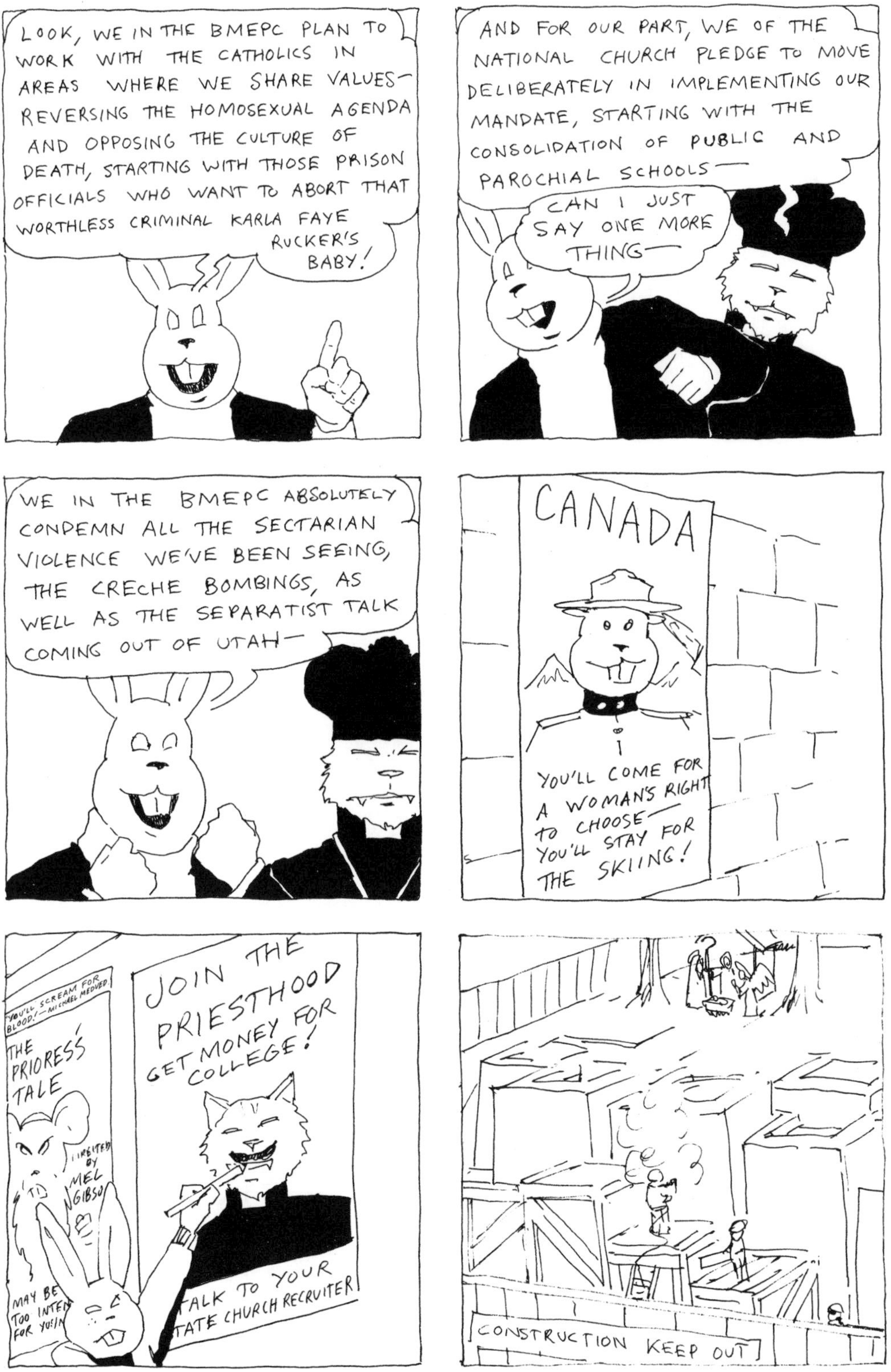
LOOK, WE IN THE BMEPC PLAN TO WORK WITH THE CATHOLICS IN AREAS WHERE WE SHARE VALUES— REVERSING THE HOMOSEXUAL AGENDA AND OPPOSING THE CULTURE OF DEATH, STARTING WITH THOSE PRISON OFFICIALS WHO WANT TO ABORT THAT WORTHLESS CRIMINAL KARLA FAYE RUCKER'S BABY!
AND FOR OUR PART, WE OF THE NATIONAL CHURCH PLEDGE TO MOVE DELIBERATELY IN IMPLEMENTING OUR MANDATE, STARTING WITH THE CONSOLIDATION OF PUBLIC AND PAROCHIAL SCHOOLS—
CAN I JUST SAY ONE MORE THING—
WE IN THE BMEPC ABSOLUTELY CONDEMN ALL THE SECTARIAN VIOLENCE WE'VE BEEN SEEING, THE CRECHE BOMBINGS, AS WELL AS THE SEPARATIST TALK COMING OUT OF UTAH—
CANADA
YOU'LL COME FOR A WOMAN'S RIGHT TO CHOOSE— YOU'LL STAY FOR THE SKIING!
"YOU'LL SCREAM FOR BLOOD!" —MICHAEL MEDVED
THE PRIORESS TALE
IRECTED BY MEL GIBSO
MAY BE TOO INTEN FOR YOU!
JOIN THE PRIESTHOOD
GET MONEY FOR COLLEGE!
TALK TO YOUR TATE CHURCH RECRUITER
CONSTRUCTION KEEP OUT

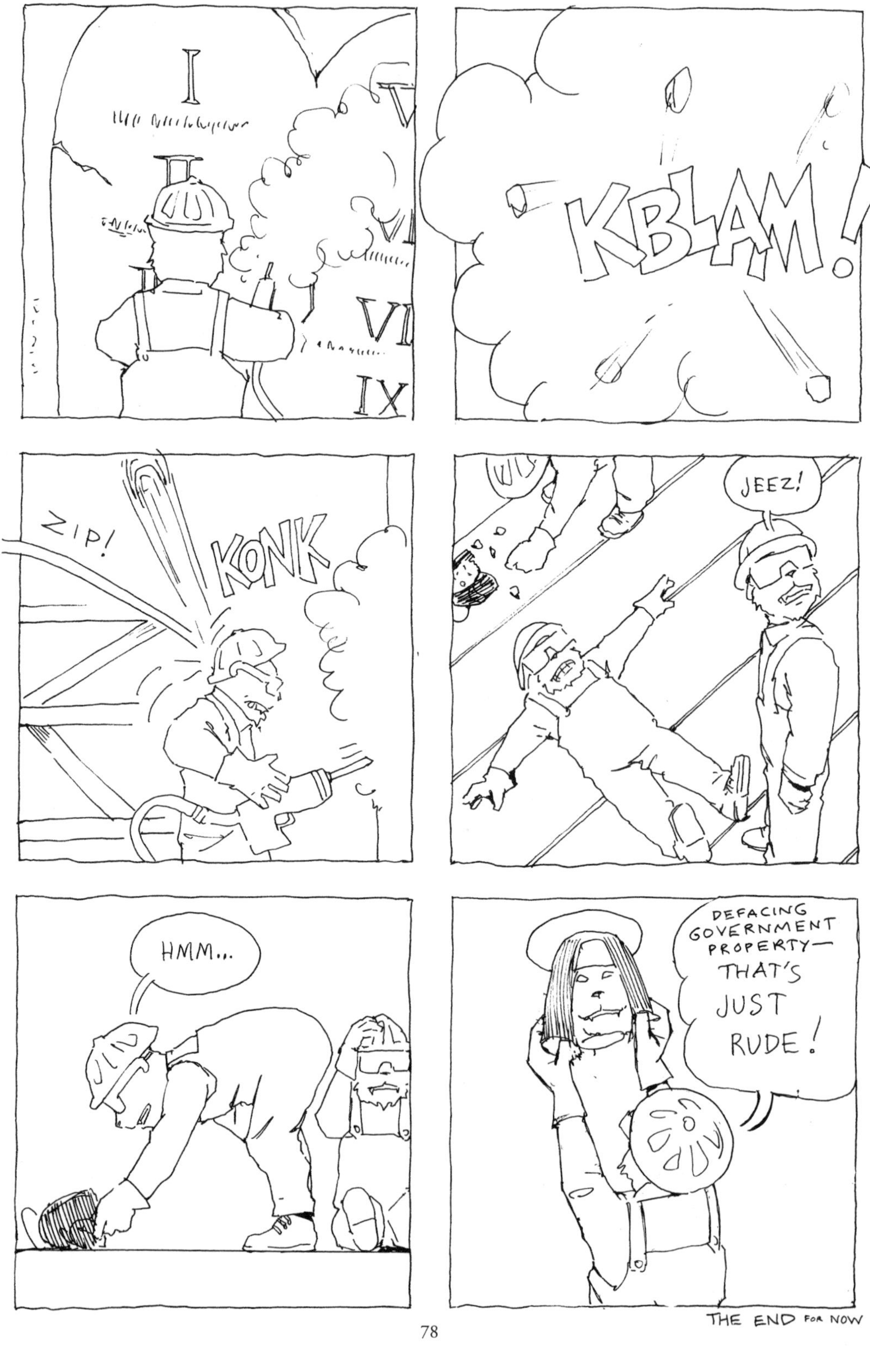
I
IX
KBLAM!
ZIP!
KONK
JEEZ!
HMM...
DEFACING GOVERNMENT PROPERTY— THAT'S JUST RUDE!

THE END FOR NOW

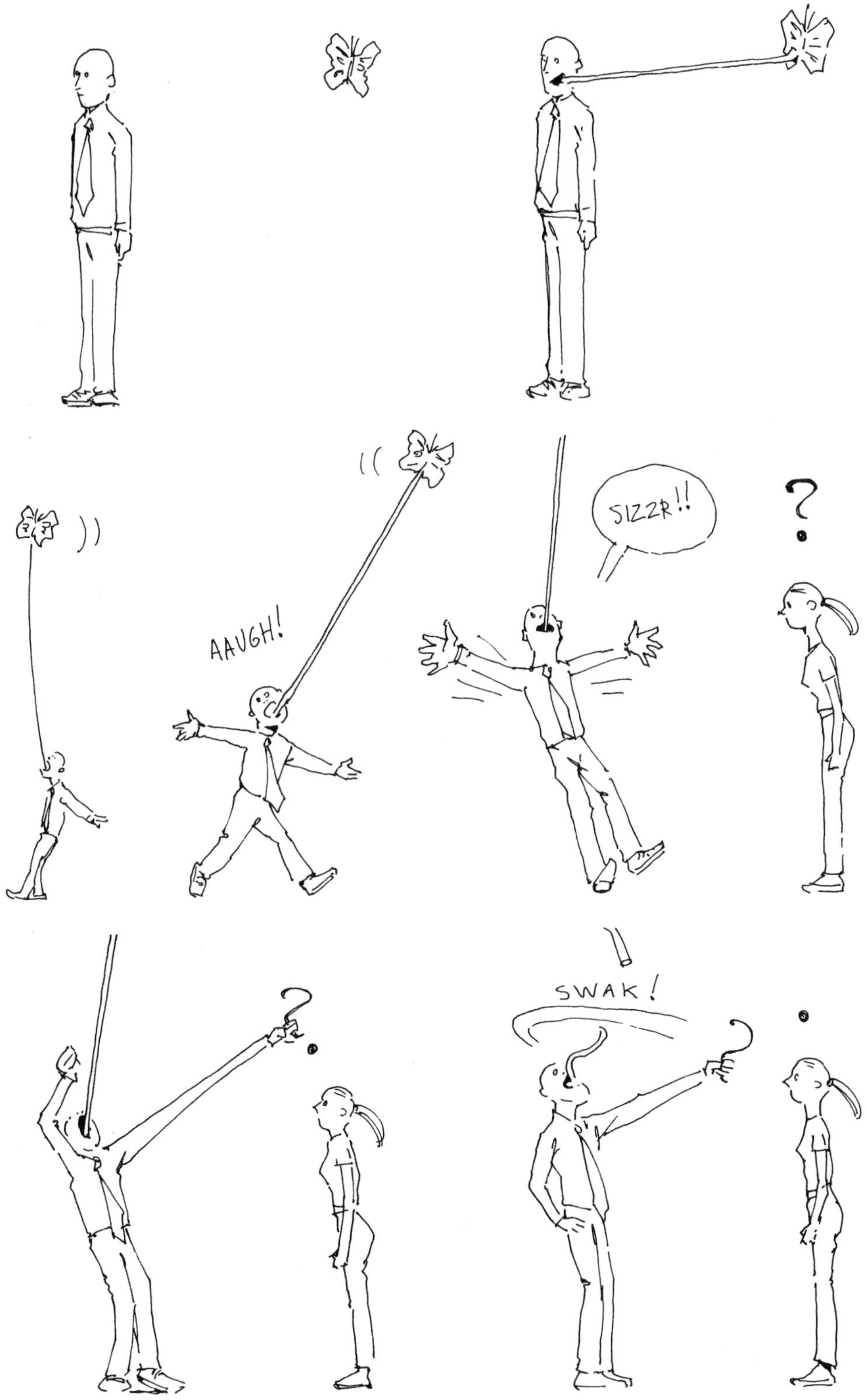
AAUGH!
SIZZR!!
SWAK!

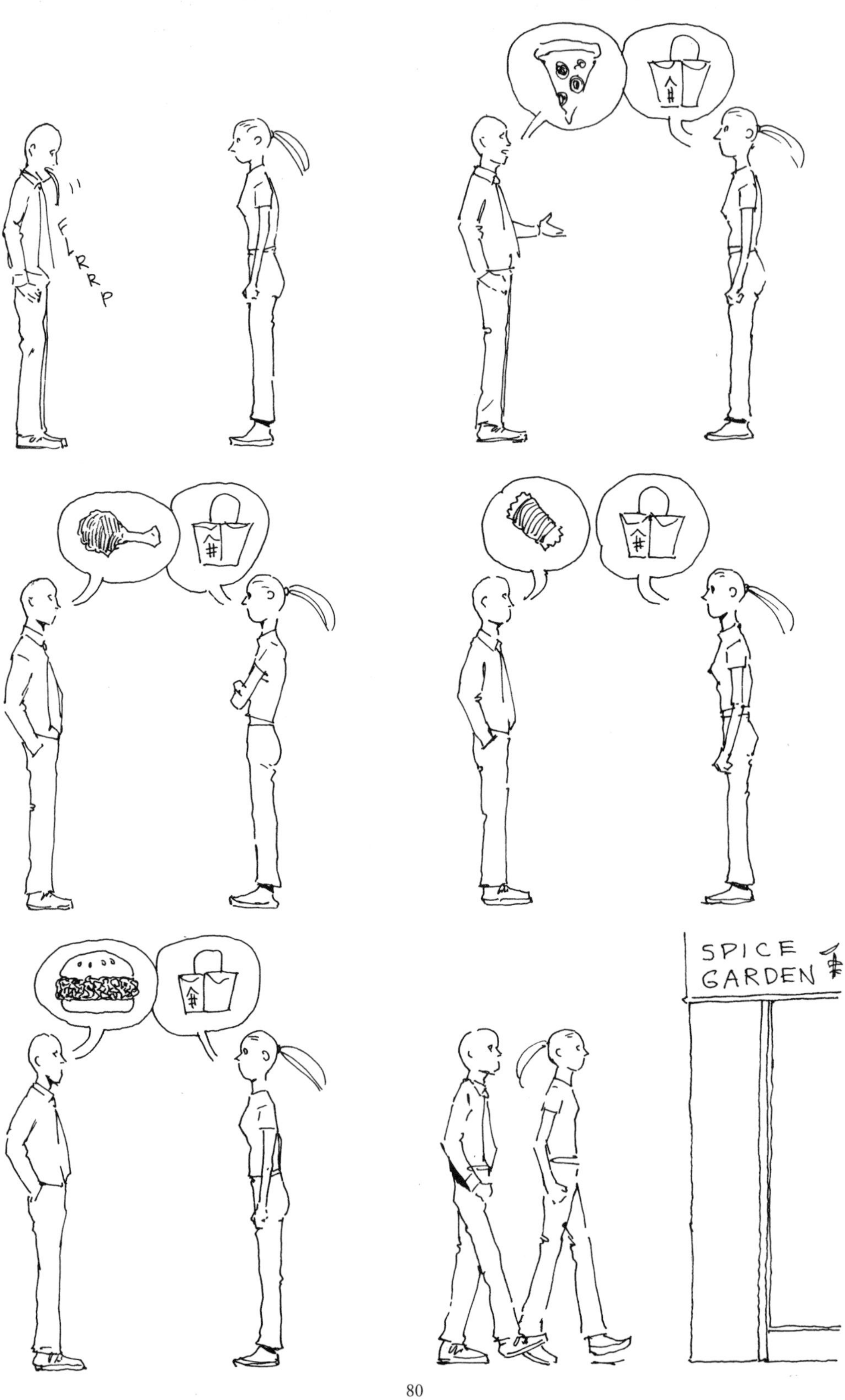
FLRRP
SPICE
GARDEN

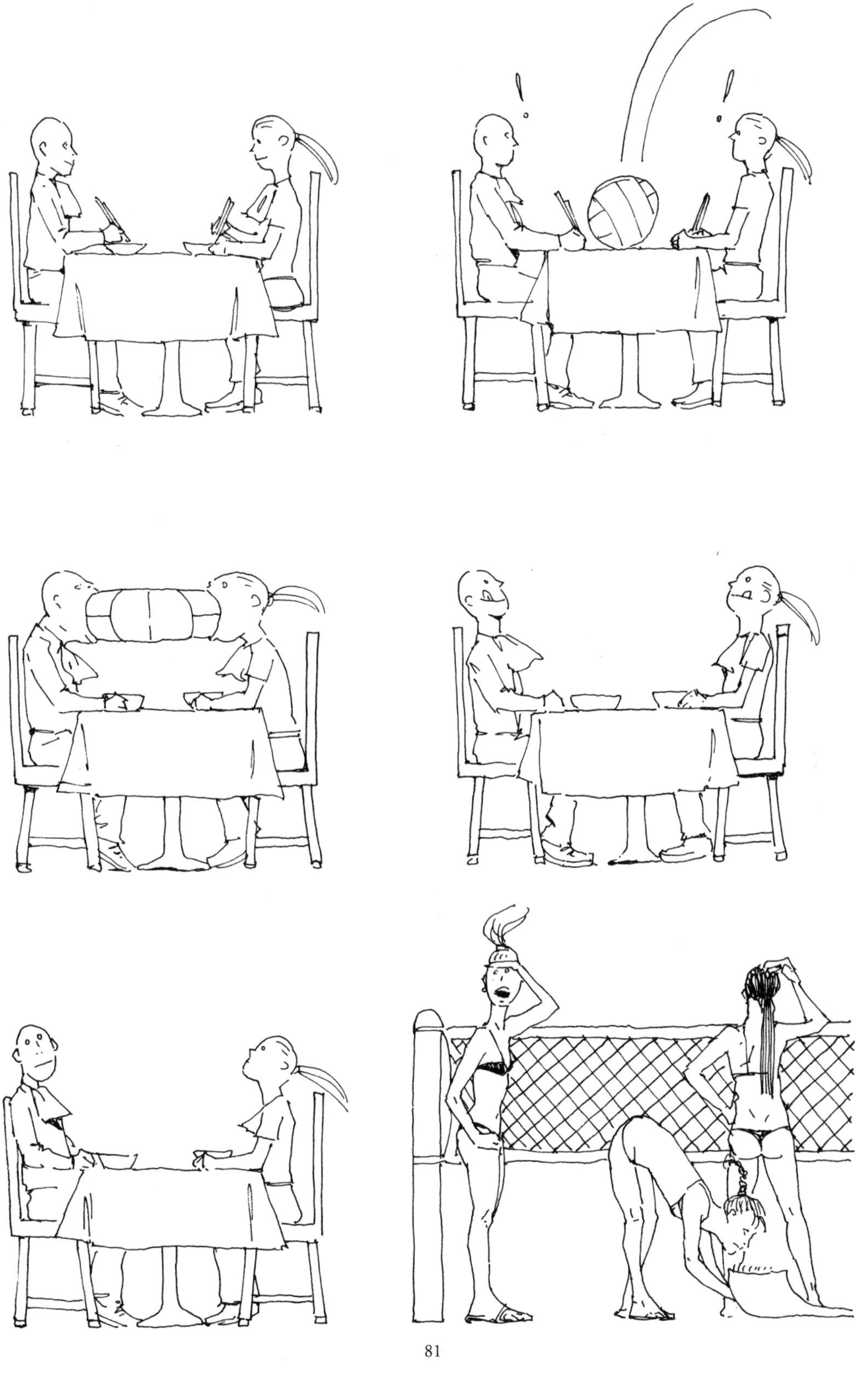
!
!

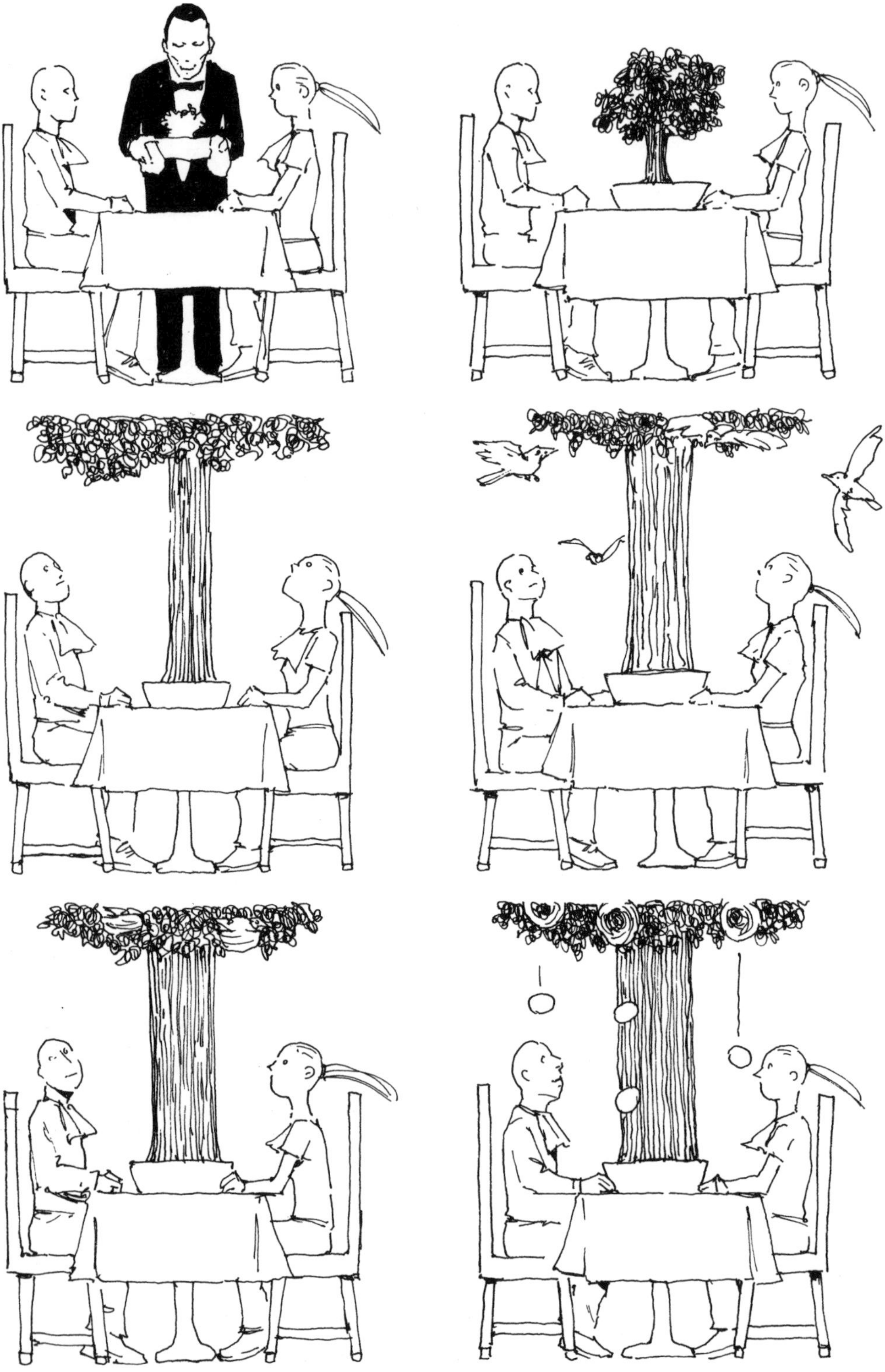

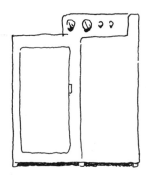

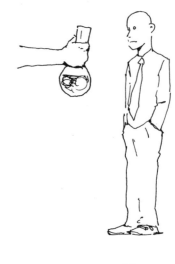
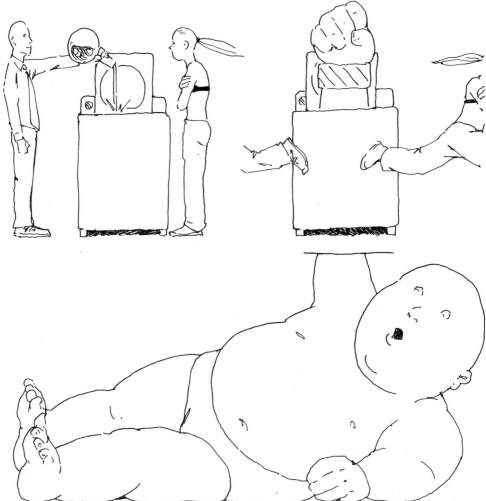

EVERYBODY GETS IT WRONG!

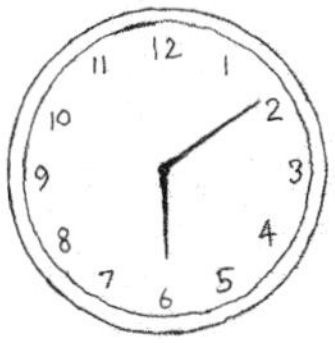
12
1
2
3
4
5
6
7
8
9
10
11

NOTES ON "EVERYBODY GETS IT WRONG!"

I got the original idea for this essay in comics form when I read an interview in a magazine with a cartoonist whose name I have forgotten. He was making some point about the difference between prose and comics, saying that there was "no equivalent" in comics for first-person narrative. I knew immediately that he was wrong, and that "subjective camera" or "point of view" was the exact equivalent of first-person prose, not just for comics but for film and television as well. It was an awkward insight for me, since my first graphic novel, *David Chelsea in Love*, had been an autobiographical comic almost devoid of point-of-view shots. I had mentioned this observation in interviews over the years, but eventually I realized that the most effective way to make my point was to draw a comic about it.

When this story was originally published by Top Shelf as half of the minicomic *24x2*, most reviewers dismissed my argument, and as far as I can tell it led to no great increase in autobiographical comics told in first person by other cartoonists— unlike in video games, where the first-person shooter mode has become the norm, but I don't suppose I can take credit for that. It did lead me to use first-person viewpoints more in my own work, notably in two stories which will appear in my second collection of 24-hour comics: "Sleepless"—a dream narrative seen from the eyes of a central character who is never seen (except once in a mirror)—and "The Girl with the Keyhole Eyes," an autobiographical comic in which I appear only in mirrors or as a hand holding a beer glass. I later reworked the story in color for *Dark Horse Presents*.

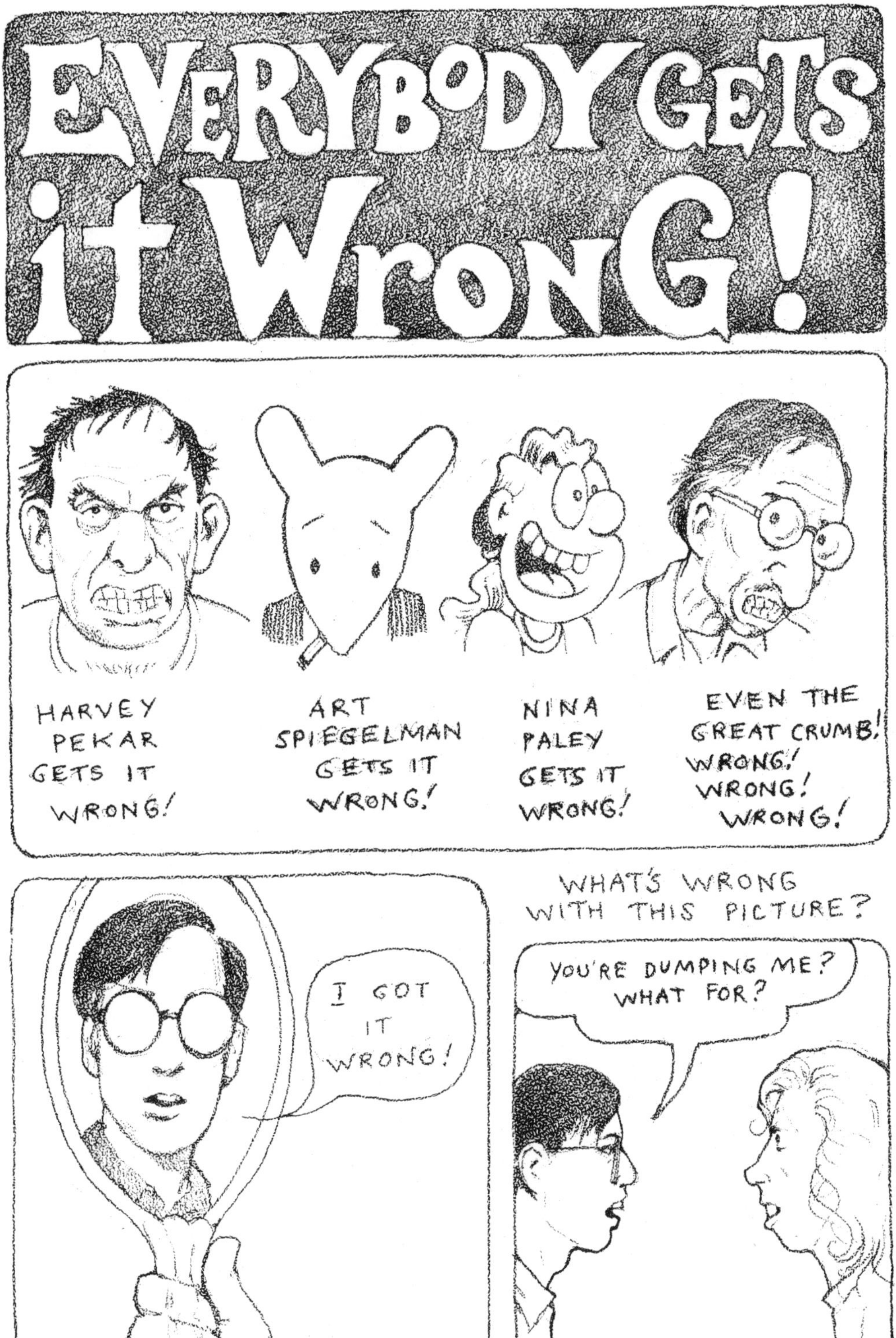
EVERYBODY GETS it WRONG!
HARVEY PEKAR GETS IT WRONG!
ART SPIEGELMAN GETS IT WRONG!
NINA PALEY GETS IT WRONG!
EVEN THE GREAT CRUMB! WRONG! WRONG! WRONG!
I GOT IT WRONG!
WHAT'S WRONG WITH THIS PICTURE?
YOU'RE DUMPING ME? WHAT FOR?

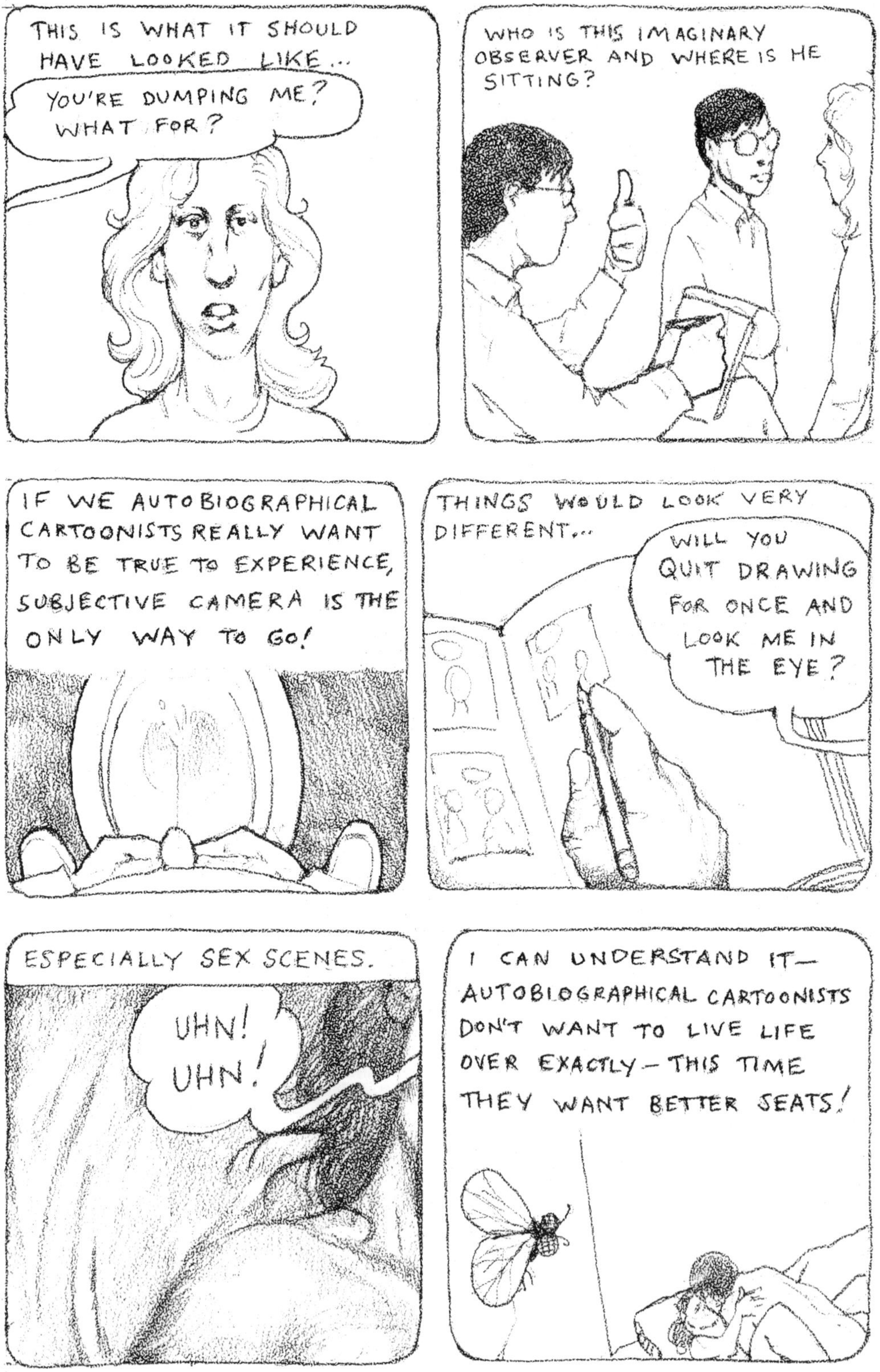
THIS IS WHAT IT SHOULD HAVE LOOKED LIKE...
YOU'RE DUMPING ME? WHAT FOR?
WHO IS THIS IMAGINARY OBSERVER AND WHERE IS HE SITTING?
IF WE AUTOBIOGRAPHICAL CARTOONISTS REALLY WANT TO BE TRUE TO EXPERIENCE, SUBJECTIVE CAMERA IS THE ONLY WAY TO GO!
THINGS WOULD LOOK VERY DIFFERENT...
WILL YOU QUIT DRAWING FOR ONCE AND LOOK ME IN THE EYE?
ESPECIALLY SEX SCENES.
UHN! UHN!
I CAN UNDERSTAND IT— AUTOBIOGRAPHICAL CARTOONISTS DON'T WANT TO LIVE LIFE OVER EXACTLY — THIS TIME THEY WANT BETTER SEATS!

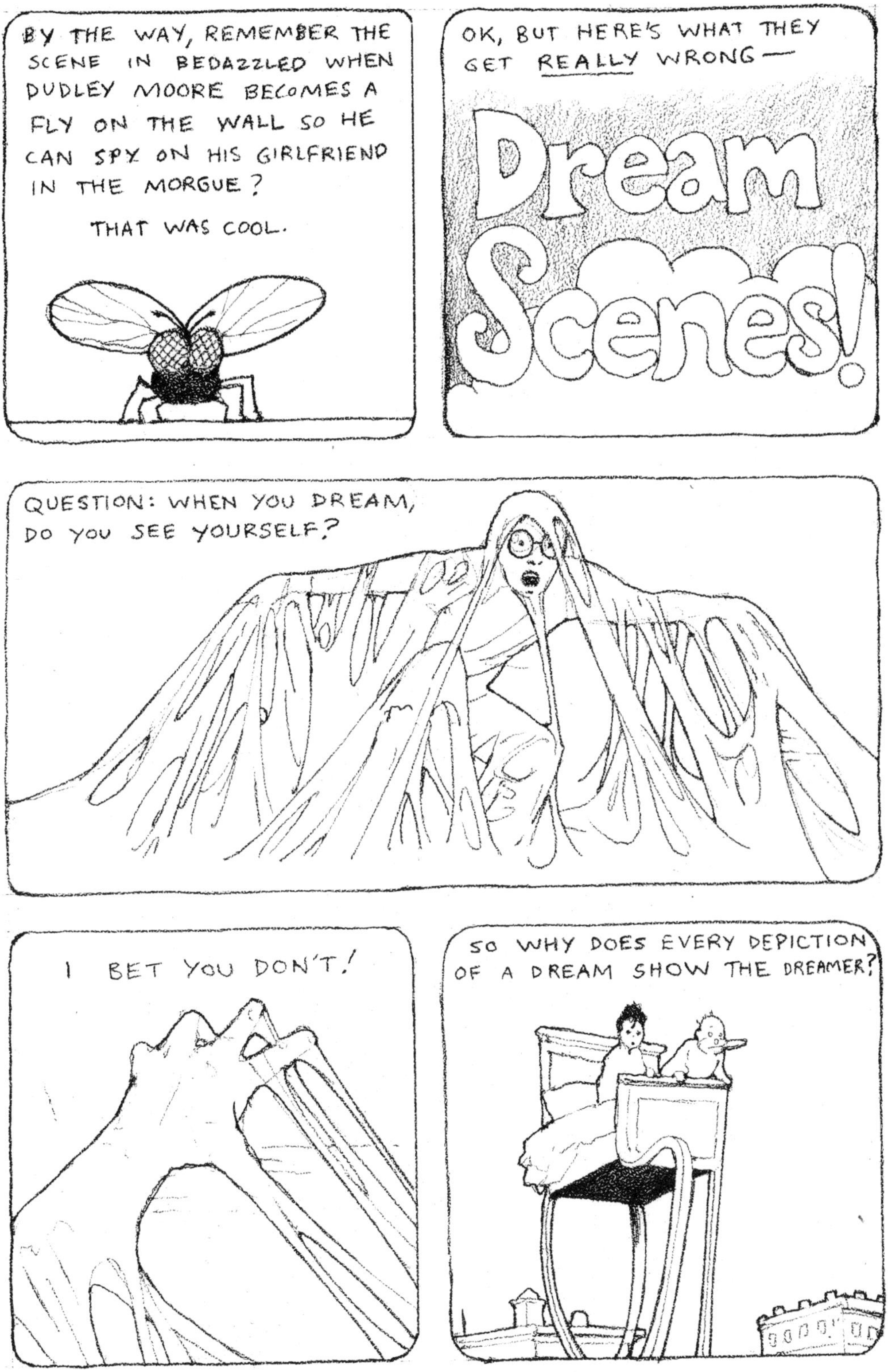
BY THE WAY, REMEMBER THE SCENE IN BEDAZZLED WHEN DUDLEY MOORE BECOMES A FLY ON THE WALL SO HE CAN SPY ON HIS GIRLFRIEND IN THE MORGUE?
THAT WAS COOL.
OK, BUT HERE'S WHAT THEY GET REALLY WRONG—
Dream Scenes!
QUESTION: WHEN YOU DREAM, DO YOU SEE YOURSELF?
I BET YOU DON'T!
SO WHY DOES EVERY DEPICTION OF A DREAM SHOW THE DREAMER?

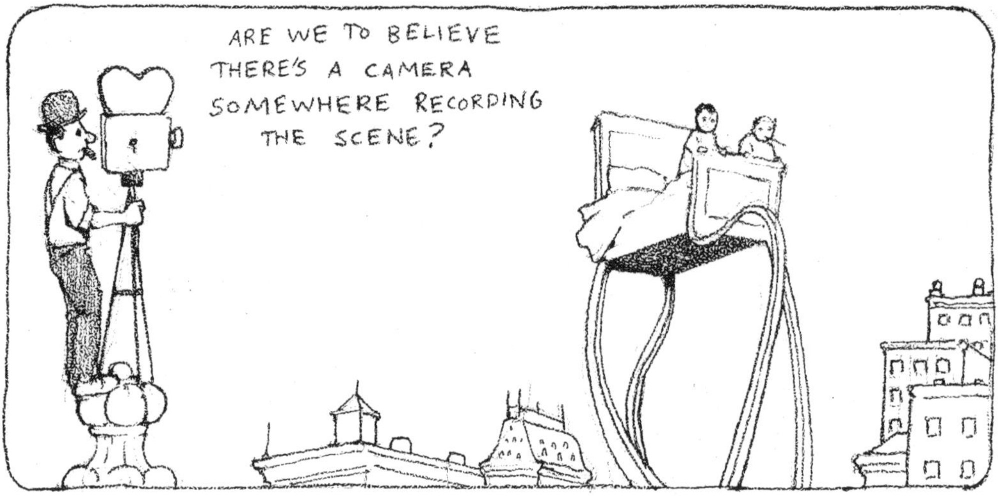
ARE WE TO BELIEVE THERE'S A CAMERA SOMEWHERE RECORDING THE SCENE?

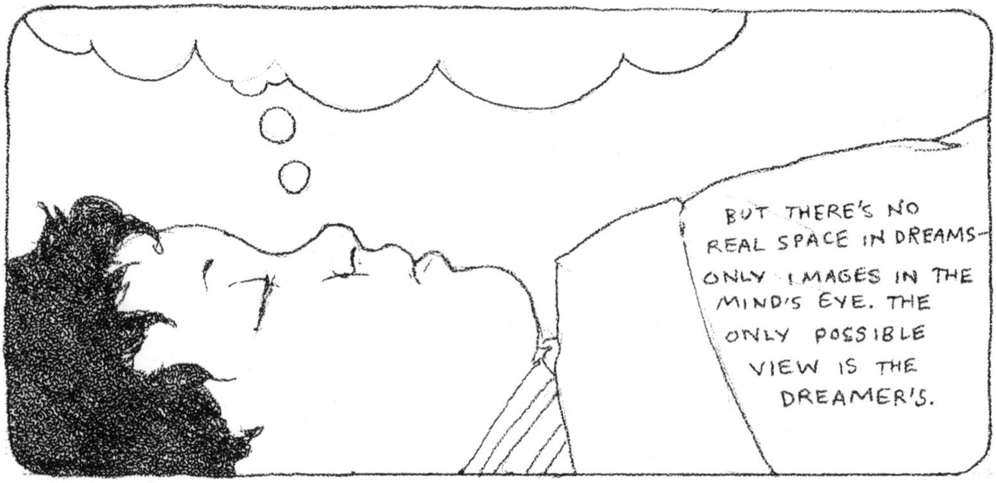
BUT THERE'S NO REAL SPACE IN DREAMS— ONLY IMAGES IN THE MIND'S EYE. THE ONLY POSSIBLE VIEW IS THE DREAMER'S.

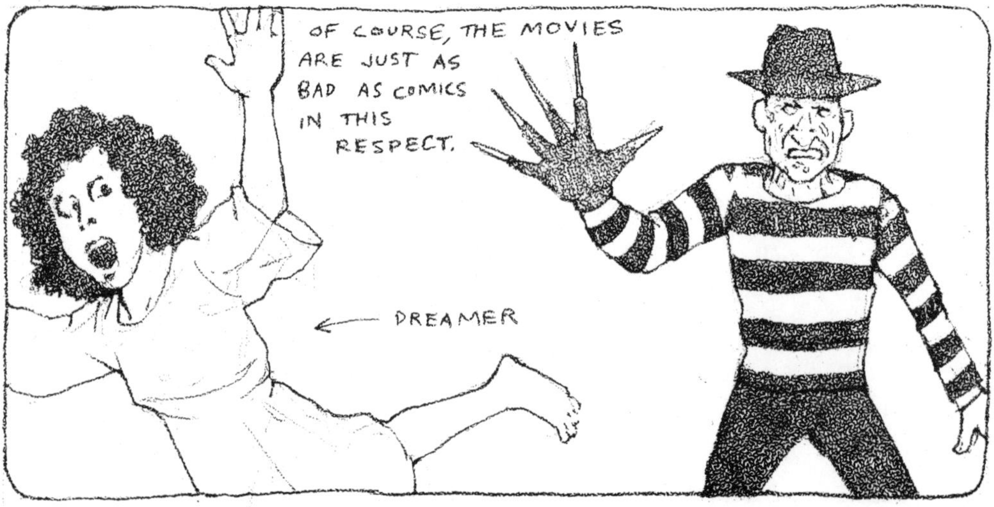
OF COURSE, THE MOVIES ARE JUST AS BAD AS COMICS IN THIS RESPECT.
DREAMER

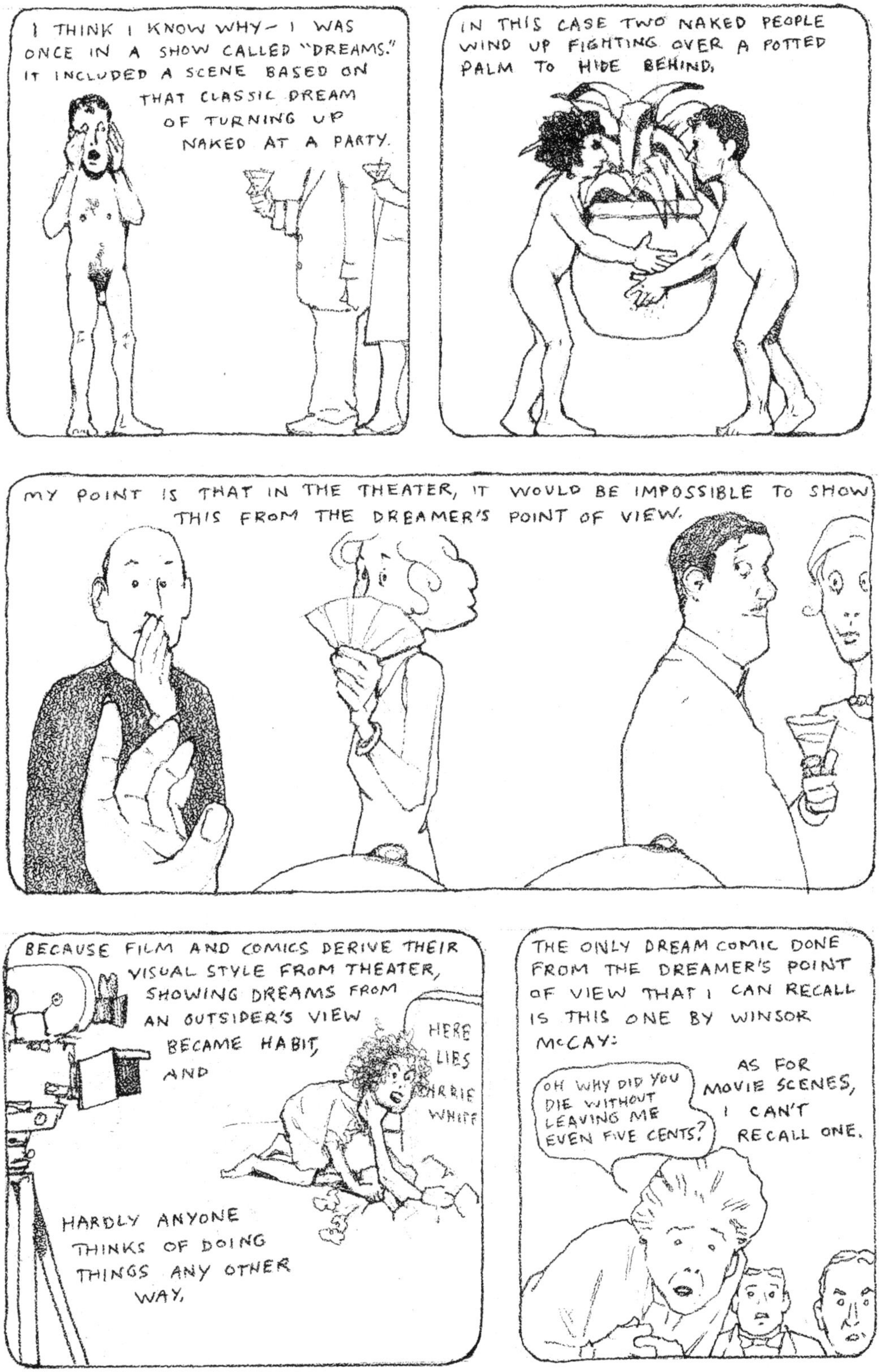
I THINK I KNOW WHY— I WAS ONCE IN A SHOW CALLED "DREAMS." IT INCLUDED A SCENE BASED ON THAT CLASSIC DREAM OF TURNING UP NAKED AT A PARTY.
IN THIS CASE TWO NAKED PEOPLE WIND UP FIGHTING OVER A POTTED PALM TO HIDE BEHIND.
MY POINT IS THAT IN THE THEATER, IT WOULD BE IMPOSSIBLE TO SHOW THIS FROM THE DREAMER'S POINT OF VIEW.
BECAUSE FILM AND COMICS DERIVE THEIR VISUAL STYLE FROM THEATER, SHOWING DREAMS FROM AN OUTSIDER'S VIEW BECAME HABIT, AND
HERE LIES
HARDLY ANYONE THINKS OF DOING THINGS ANY OTHER WAY.
THE ONLY DREAM COMIC DONE FROM THE DREAMER'S POINT OF VIEW THAT I CAN RECALL IS THIS ONE BY WINSOR McCAY:
OH WHY DID YOU DIE WITHOUT LEAVING ME EVEN FIVE CENTS?
AS FOR MOVIE SCENES, I CAN'T RECALL ONE.

I'LL GIVE A QUICK HIGH-FIVE TO TWO DEPICTIONS OF DREAMS THAT I THINK GET IT MORE OR LESS RIGHT.

THE HITCH IS THAT NEITHER ONE CALLS ITSELF A DREAM SCENE IN SO MANY WORDS.

ONE IS A RICK GEARY COMIC WHERE A GUY COMES BACK TO HIS CHILDHOOD HOME TO FIND BIZARRE CHANGES— HIS FOLKS HAVE ADDED A CHAPEL TO THE HOUSE AND HIS MOM IS WEARING AN EYEPATCH.

TELLINGLY, THE GUY COMING HOME IS NEVER SHOWN.

THE OTHER IS THE "FIND THE FISH" SCENE FROM "MONTY PYTHON'S THE MEANING OF LIFE."

IT WENT WHEREVER I DID GO!

IN A QUIET WAY I'VE BEEN TRYING TO PUT THIS IDEA IN PRACTICE IN SHORT STRIPS DRAWN ON MY PALM PILOT.

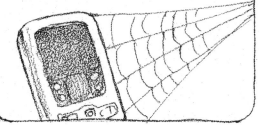

I'VE DONE ABOUT THIRTY—SHORT SCENES FROM LIFE, SOME DREAM STRIPS, ALL "SUBJECTIVE CAMERA." SOME OF THEM HAVE BEEN UP ON JOHN WEEKS'S WEBSITE. I HAVEN'T DONE ANY IN A WHILE, THOUGH. WHO HAS TIME?

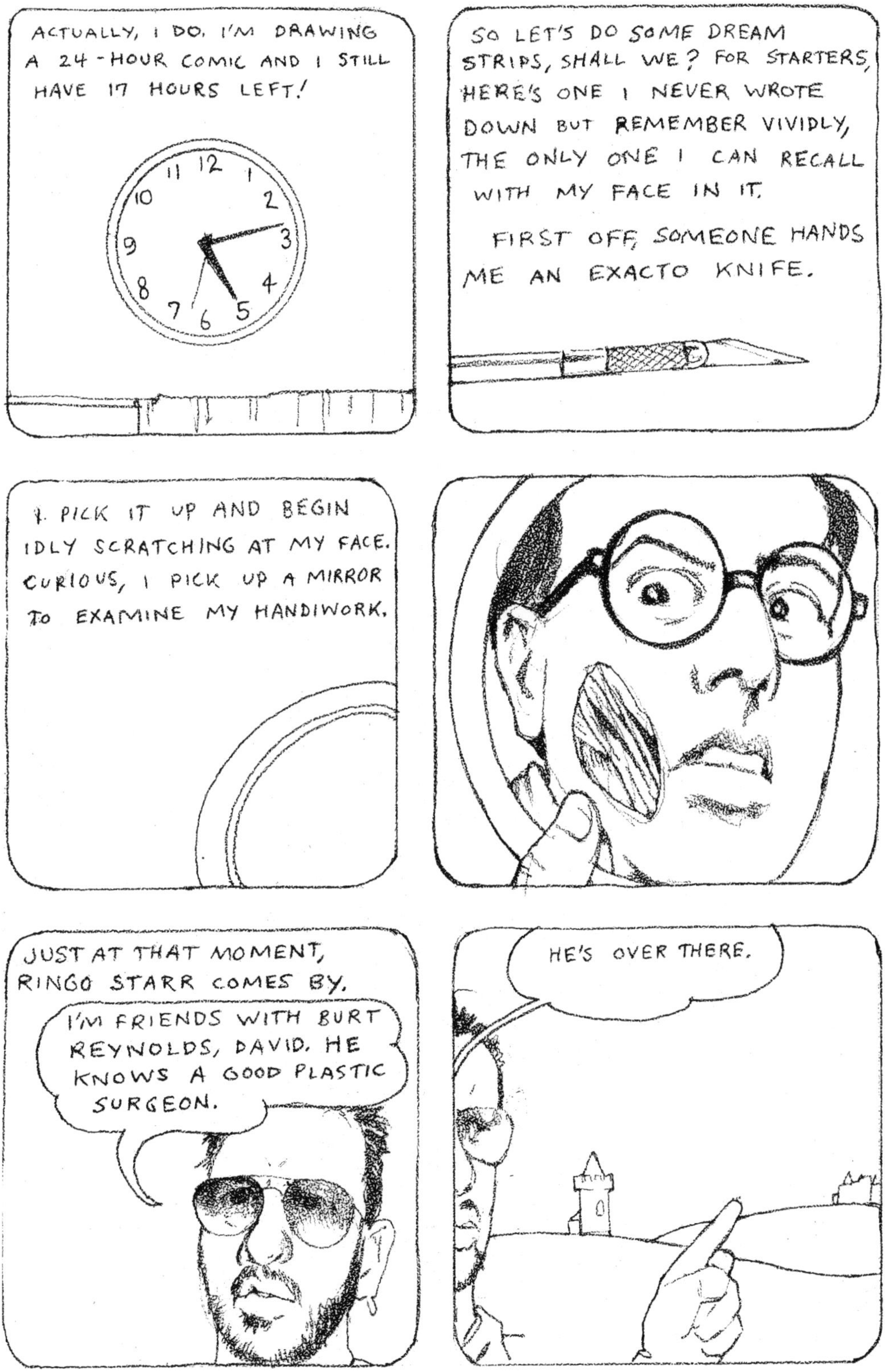
ACTUALLY, I DO. I'M DRAWING A 24-HOUR COMIC AND I STILL HAVE 17 HOURS LEFT!
12
1
2
3
4
5
6
7
8
9
10
11
SO LET'S DO SOME DREAM STRIPS, SHALL WE? FOR STARTERS, HERE'S ONE I NEVER WROTE DOWN BUT REMEMBER VIVIDLY, THE ONLY ONE I CAN RECALL WITH MY FACE IN IT.
FIRST OFF, SOMEONE HANDS ME AN EXACTO KNIFE.
I PICK IT UP AND BEGIN IDLY SCRATCHING AT MY FACE. CURIOUS, I PICK UP A MIRROR TO EXAMINE MY HANDIWORK.
JUST AT THAT MOMENT, RINGO STARR COMES BY.
I'M FRIENDS WITH BURT REYNOLDS, DAVID. HE KNOWS A GOOD PLASTIC SURGEON.
HE'S OVER THERE.

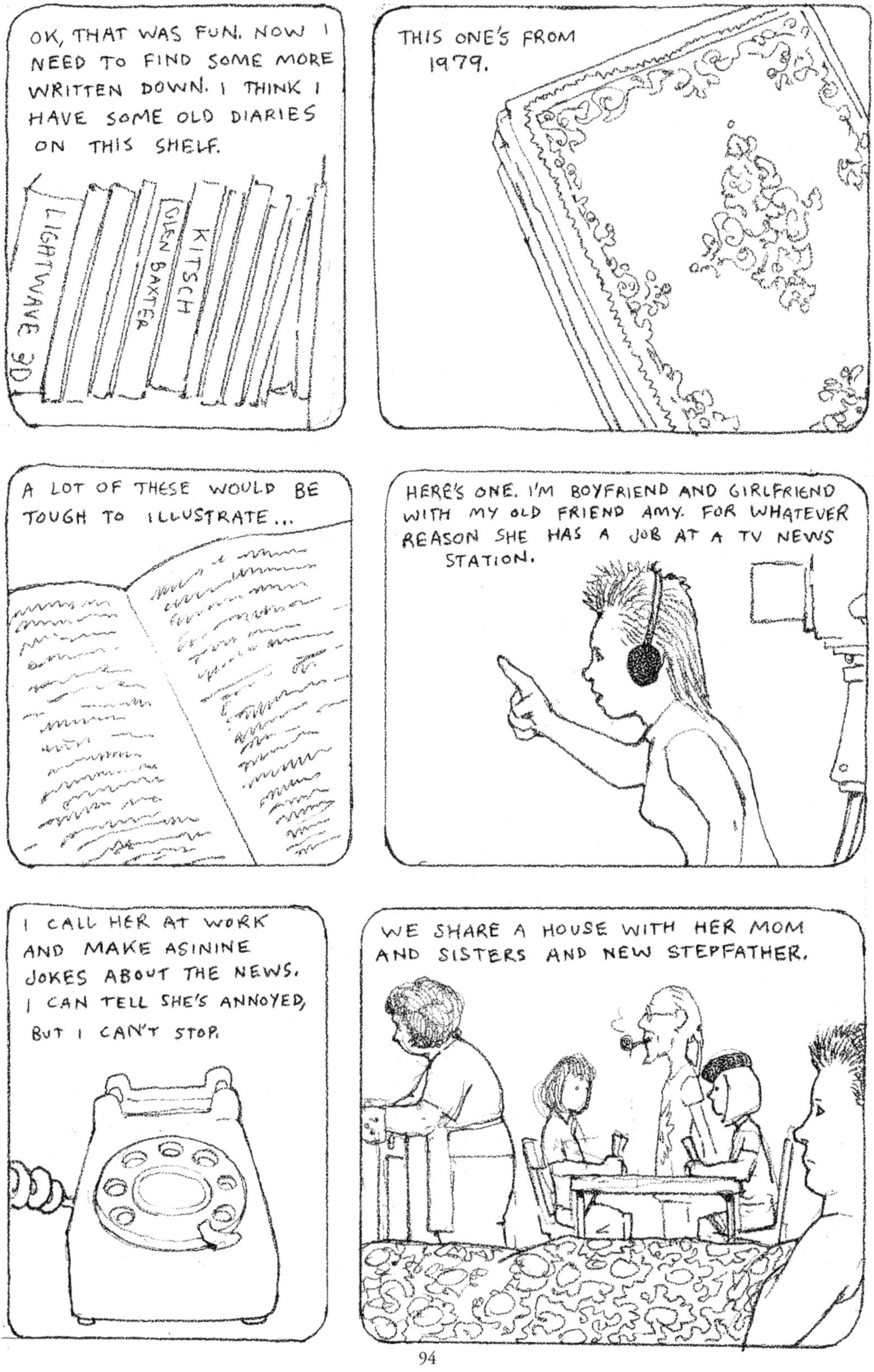
OK, THAT WAS FUN. NOW I NEED TO FIND SOME MORE WRITTEN DOWN. I THINK I HAVE SOME OLD DIARIES ON THIS SHELF.
LIGHTWAVE 3D
GLEN BAXTER
KITSCH
THIS ONE'S FROM 1979.
A LOT OF THESE WOULD BE TOUGH TO ILLUSTRATE...
HERE'S ONE. I'M BOYFRIEND AND GIRLFRIEND WITH MY OLD FRIEND AMY. FOR WHATEVER REASON SHE HAS A JOB AT A TV NEWS STATION.
I CALL HER AT WORK AND MAKE ASININE JOKES ABOUT THE NEWS. I CAN TELL SHE'S ANNOYED, BUT I CAN'T STOP.
WE SHARE A HOUSE WITH HER MOM AND SISTERS AND NEW STEPFATHER.

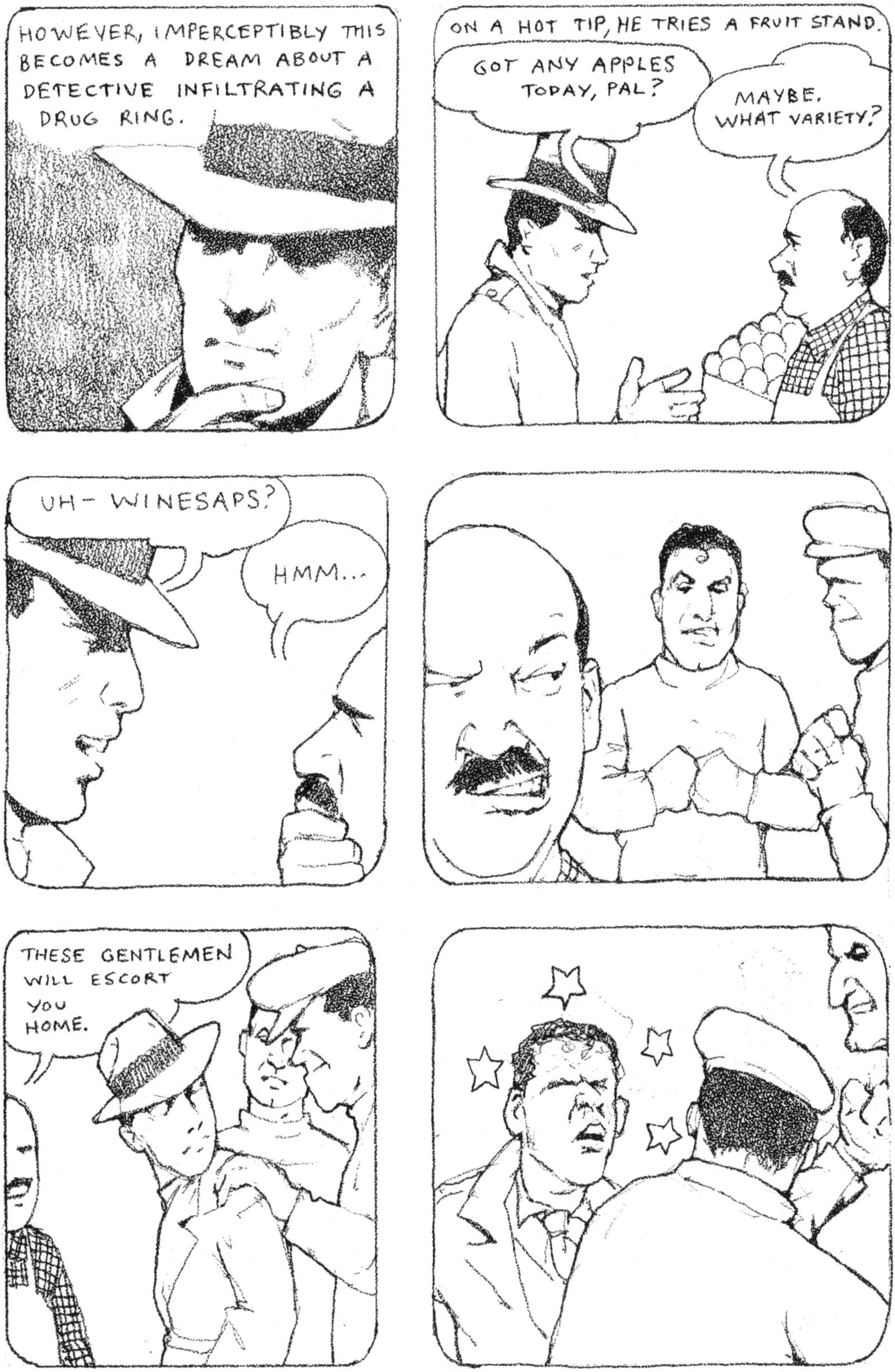
HOWEVER, IMPERCEPTIBLY THIS BECOMES A DREAM ABOUT A DETECTIVE INFILTRATING A DRUG RING.
ON A HOT TIP, HE TRIES A FRUIT STAND.
GOT ANY APPLES TODAY, PAL?
MAYBE. WHAT VARIETY?
UH- WINESAPS?
HMM...
THESE GENTLEMEN WILL ESCORT YOU HOME.

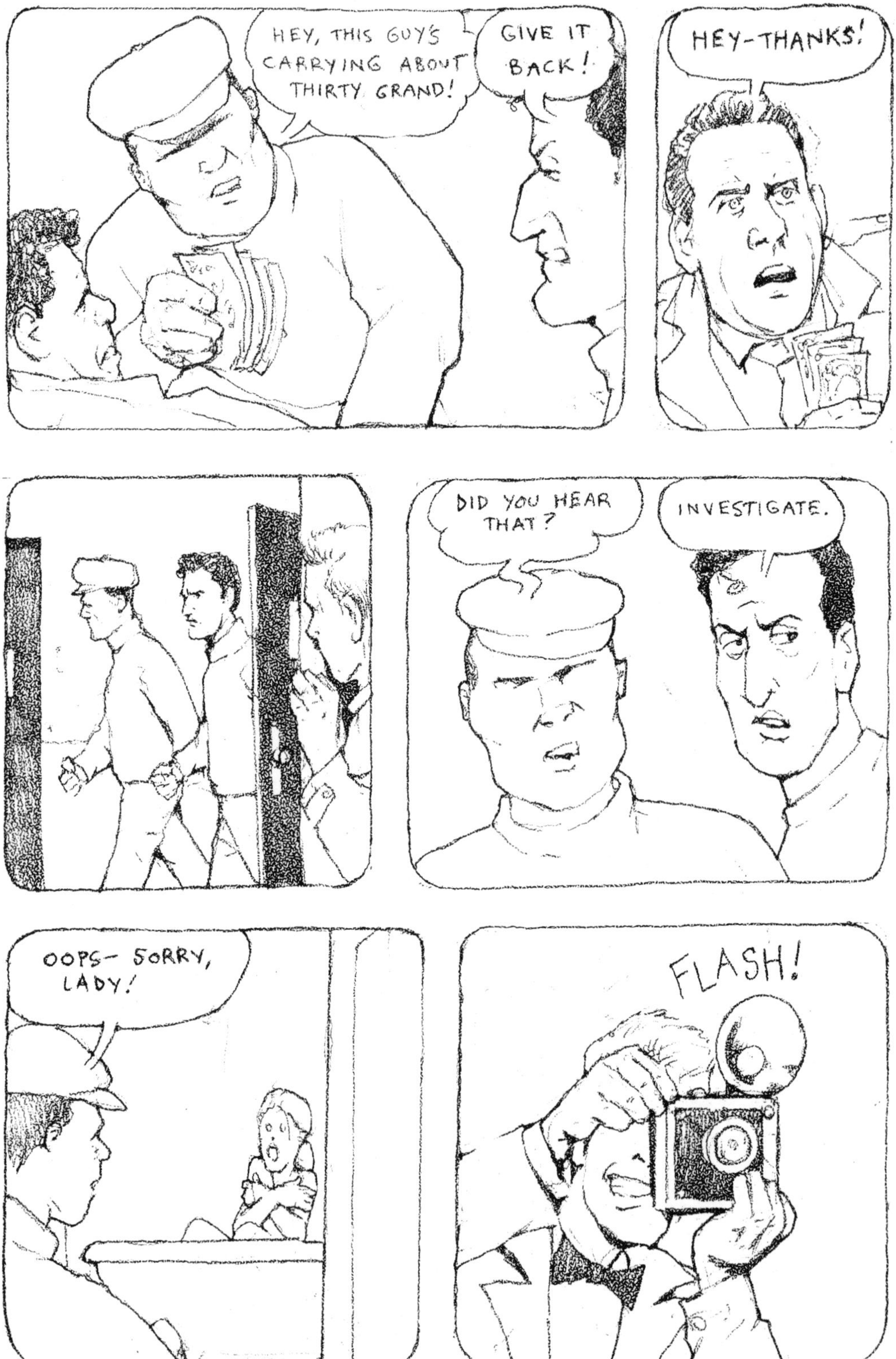
HEY, THIS GUY'S CARRYING ABOUT THIRTY GRAND!
GIVE IT BACK!
HEY-THANKS!
DID YOU HEAR THAT?
INVESTIGATE.
OOPS- SORRY, LADY!
FLASH!

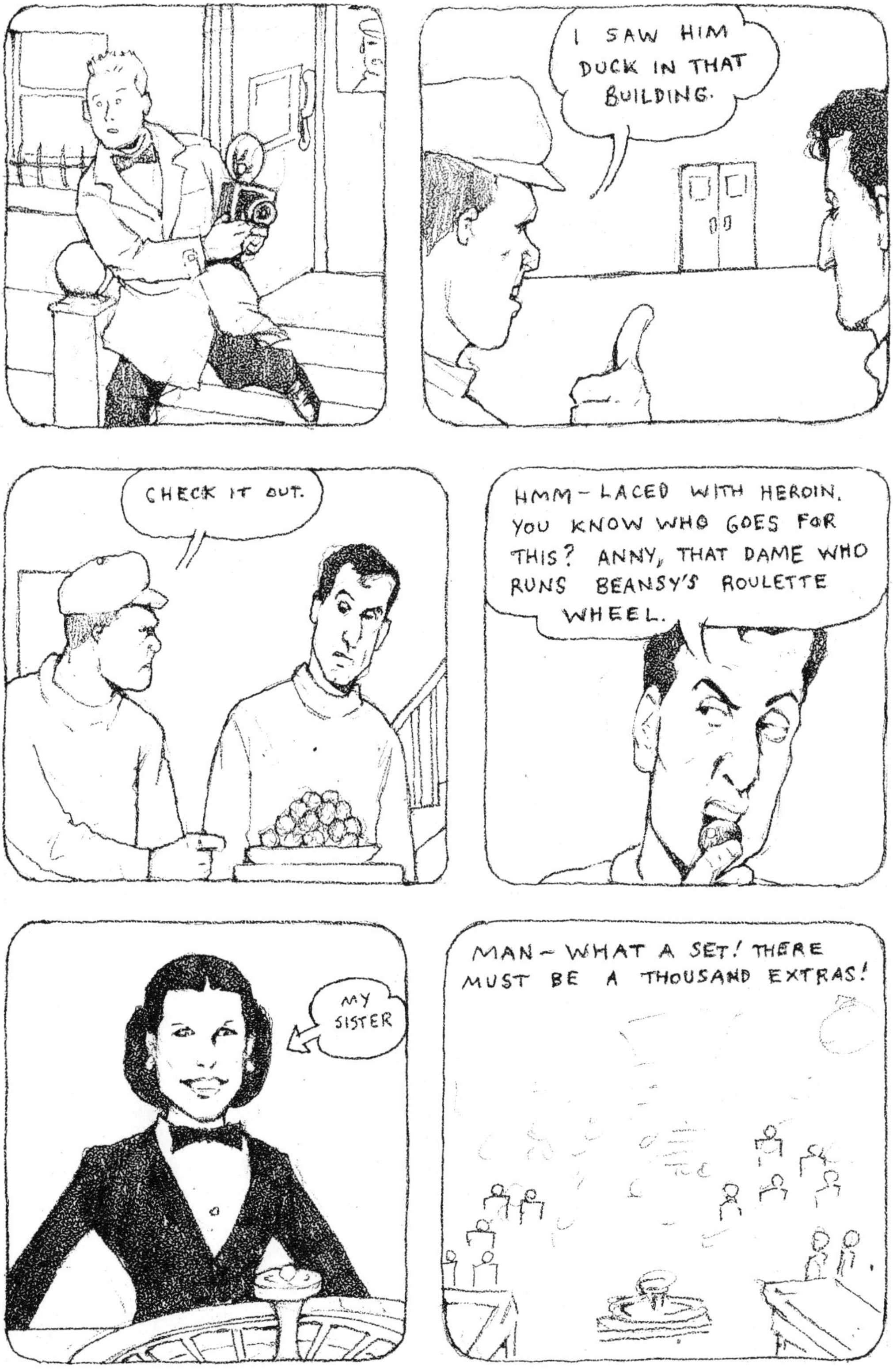
I SAW HIM DUCK IN THAT BUILDING.
CHECK IT OUT.
HMM — LACED WITH HEROIN. YOU KNOW WHO GOES FOR THIS? ANNY, THAT DAME WHO RUNS BEANSY'S ROULETTE WHEEL.
MY SISTER
MAN — WHAT A SET! THERE MUST BE A THOUSAND EXTRAS!

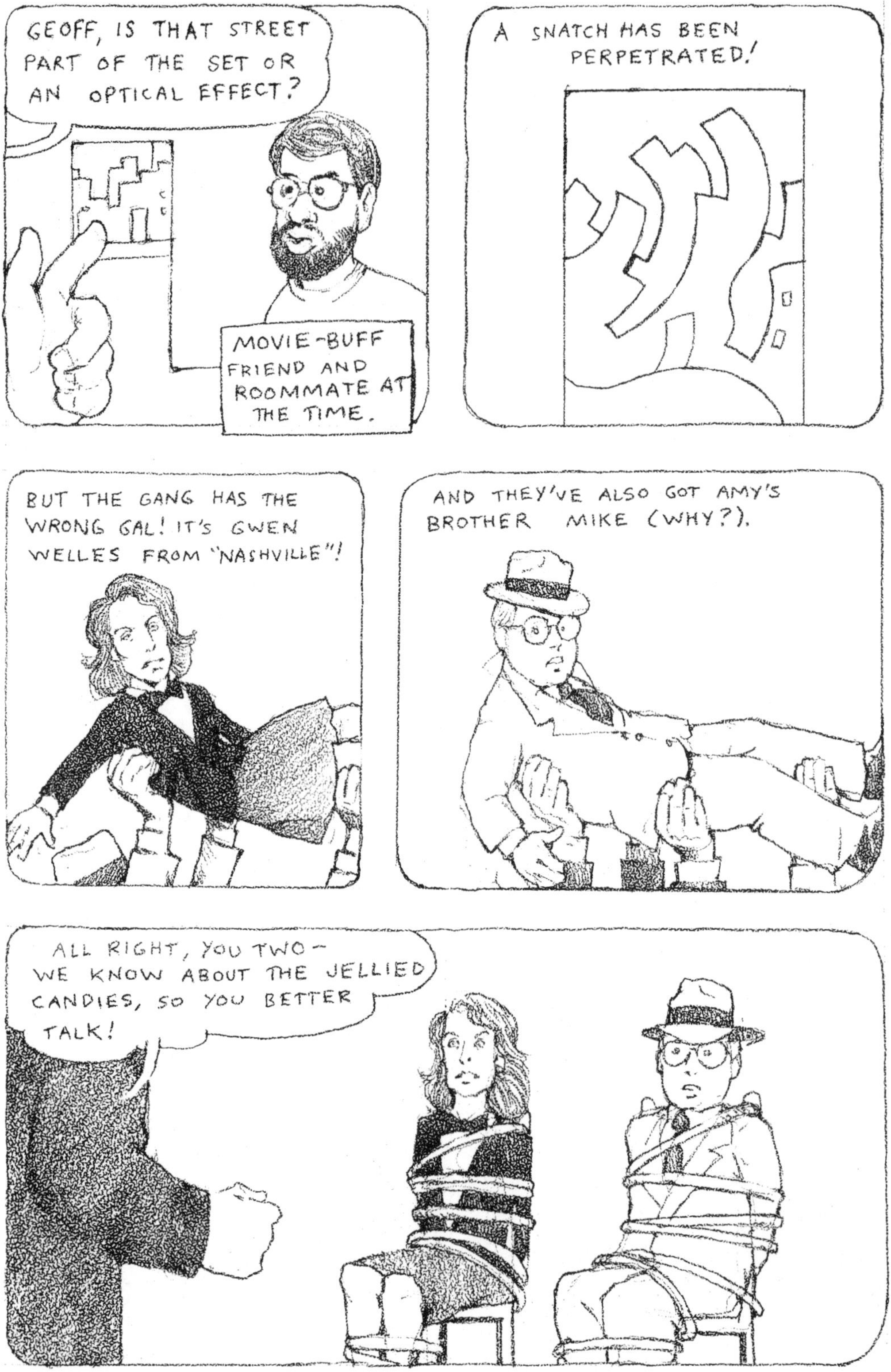
GEOFF, IS THAT STREET PART OF THE SET OR AN OPTICAL EFFECT?
MOVIE-BUFF FRIEND AND ROOMMATE AT THE TIME.
A SNATCH HAS BEEN PERPETRATED!
BUT THE GANG HAS THE WRONG GAL! IT'S GWEN WELLES FROM "NASHVILLE"!
AND THEY'VE ALSO GOT AMY'S BROTHER MIKE (WHY?).
ALL RIGHT, YOU TWO— WE KNOW ABOUT THE JELLIED CANDIES, SO YOU BETTER TALK!

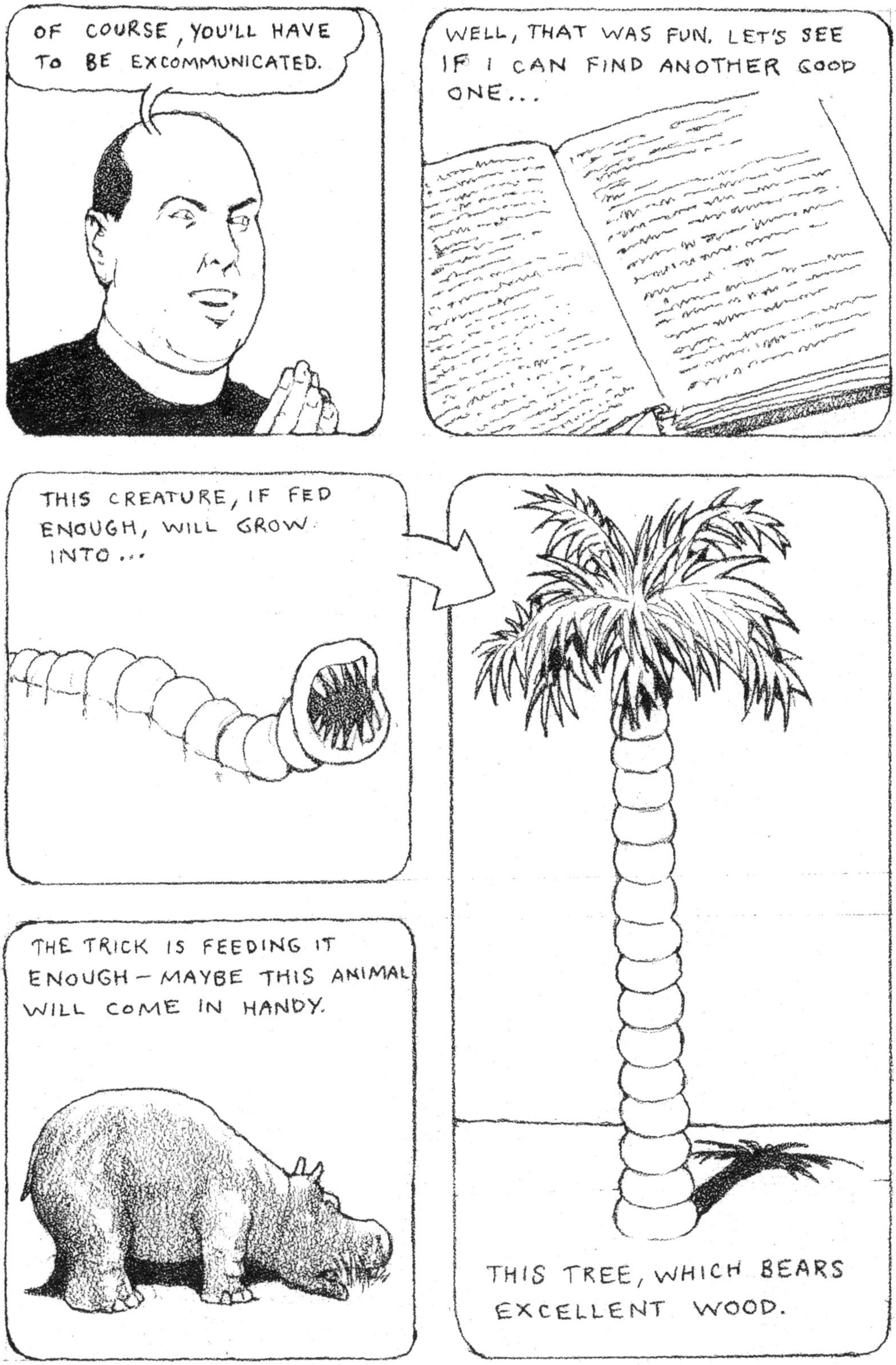
OF COURSE, YOU'LL HAVE TO BE EXCOMMUNICATED.
WELL, THAT WAS FUN. LET'S SEE IF I CAN FIND ANOTHER GOOD ONE...
THIS CREATURE, IF FED ENOUGH, WILL GROW INTO...
THIS TREE, WHICH BEARS EXCELLENT WOOD.
THE TRICK IS FEEDING IT ENOUGH — MAYBE THIS ANIMAL WILL COME IN HANDY.

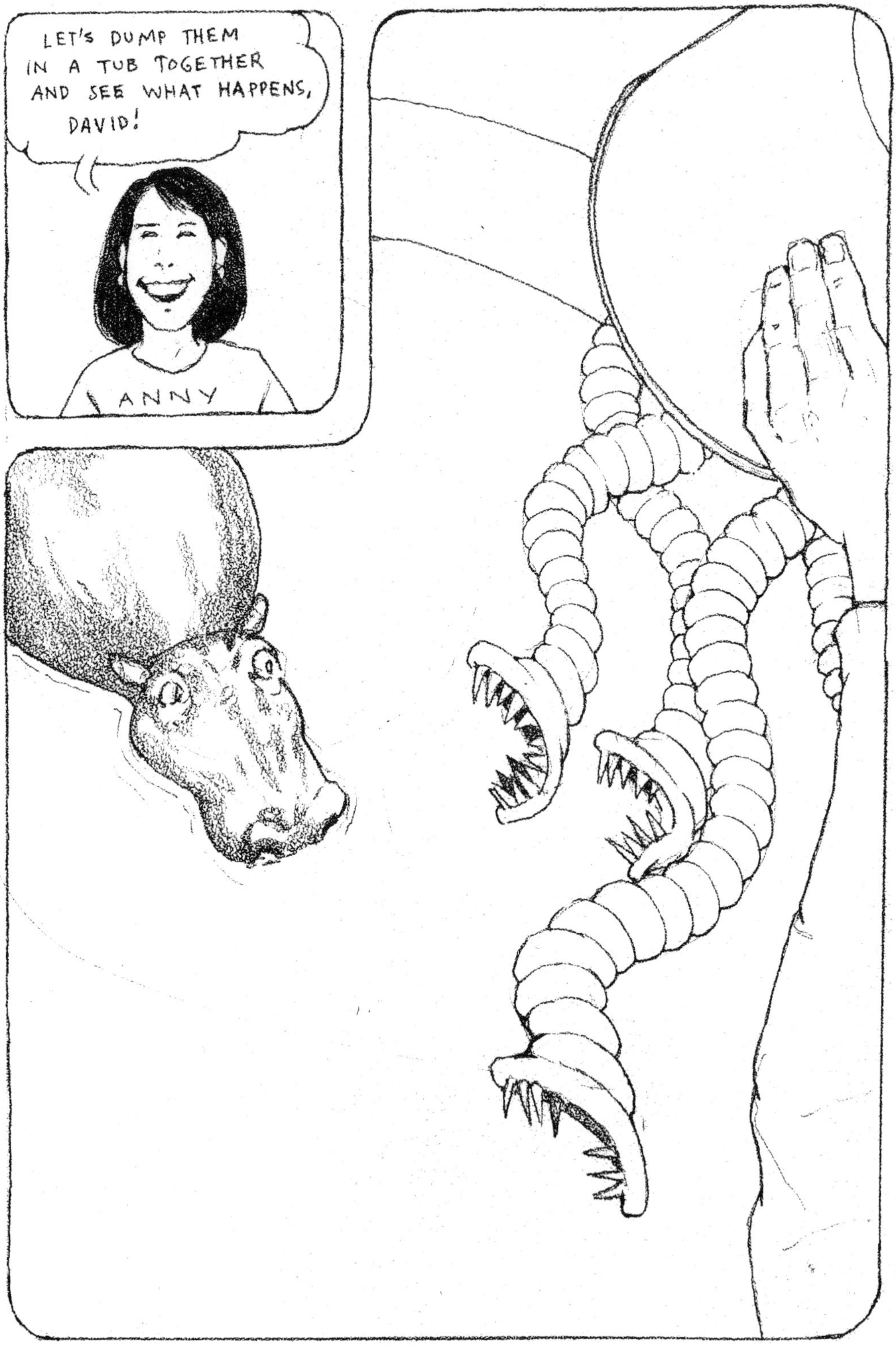
LET'S DUMP THEM IN A TUB TOGETHER AND SEE WHAT HAPPENS, DAVID!
ANNY

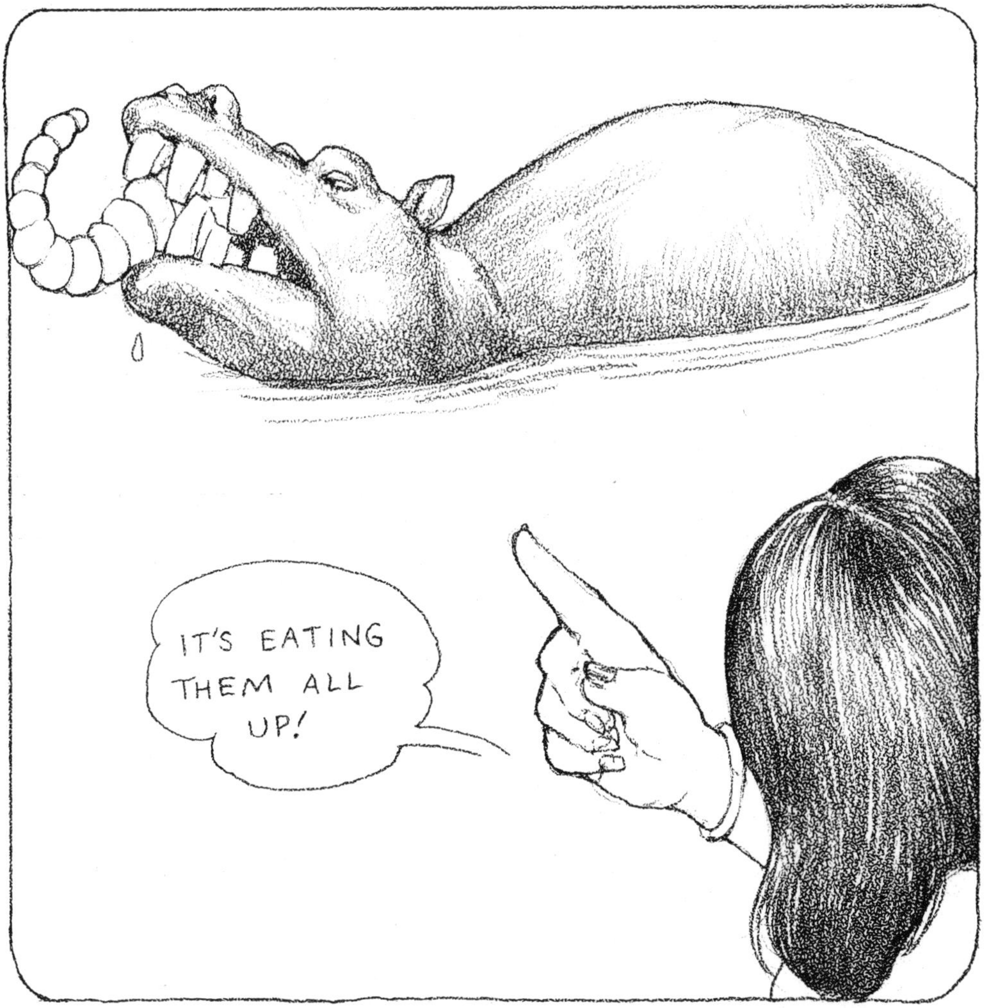
IT'S EATING THEM ALL UP!

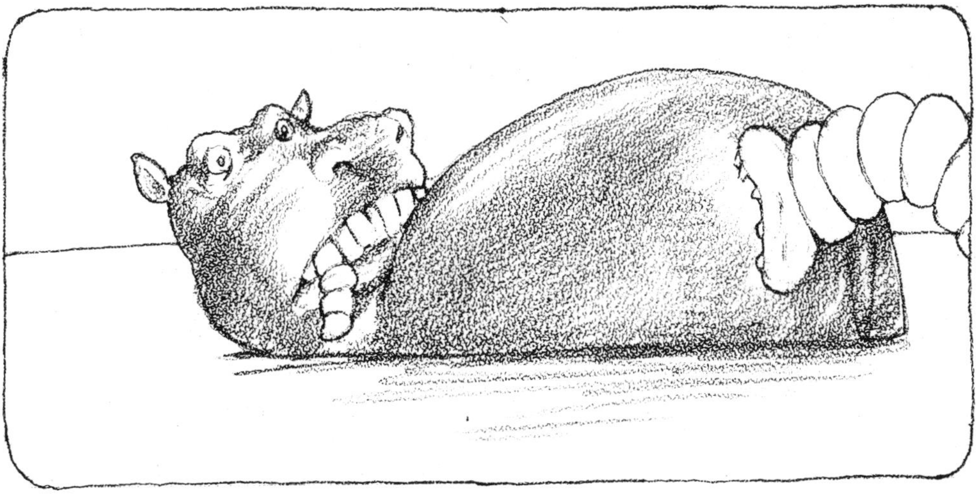

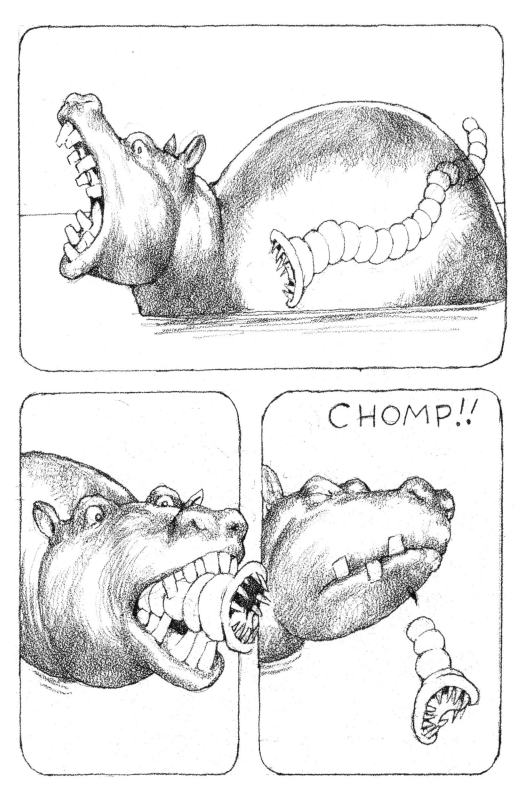

CHOMP!!

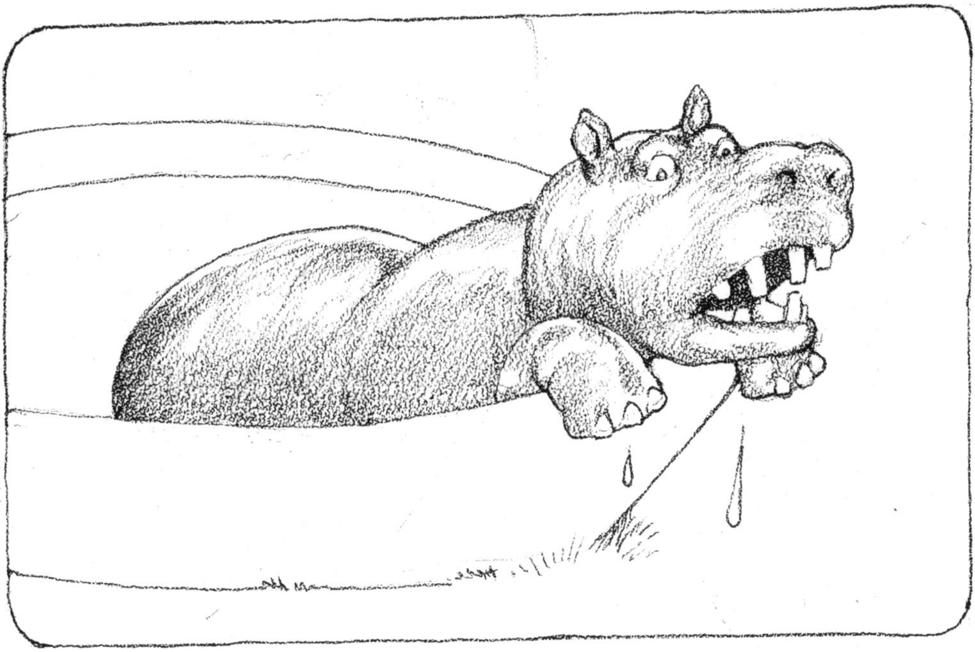

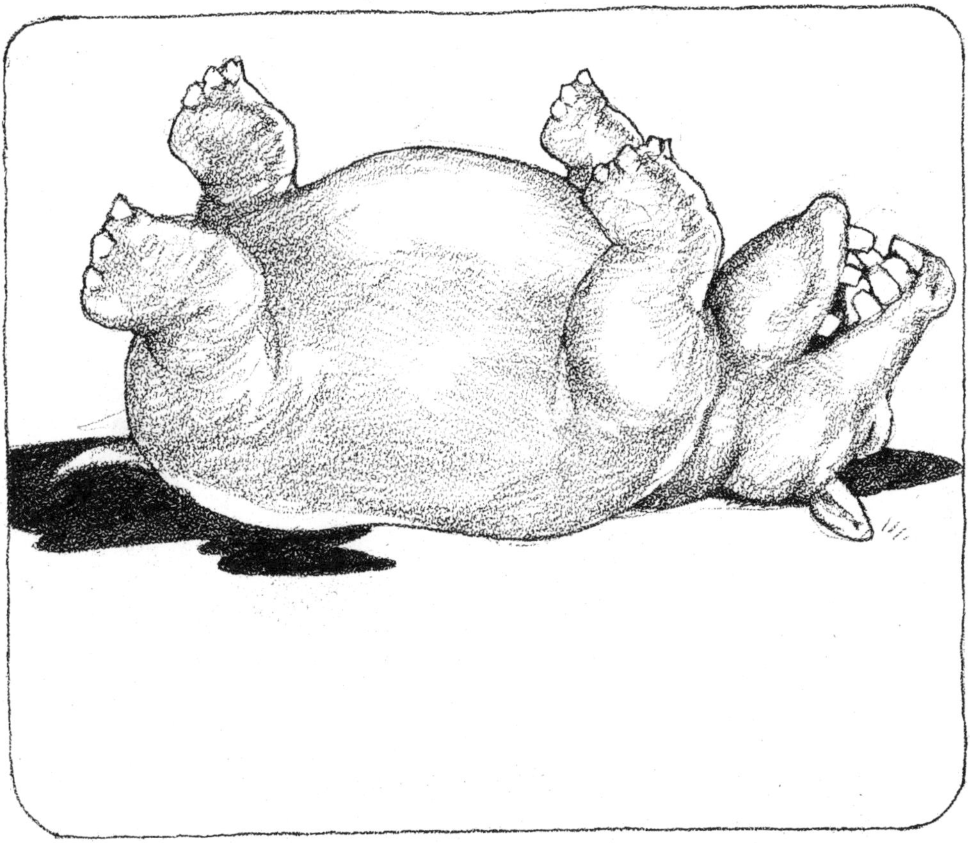

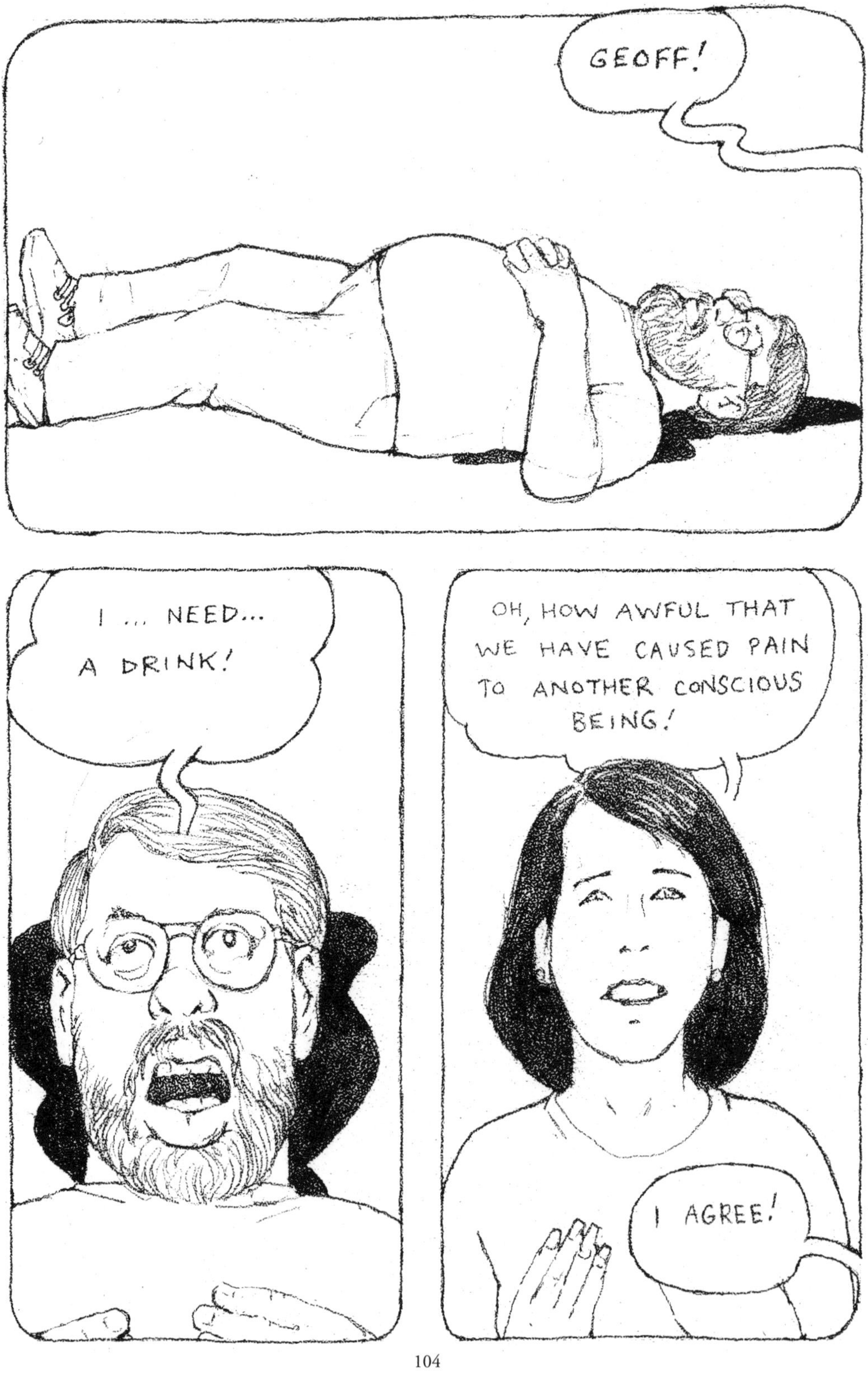
GEOFF!
I ... NEED... A DRINK!
OH, HOW AWFUL THAT WE HAVE CAUSED PAIN TO ANOTHER CONSCIOUS BEING!
I AGREE!

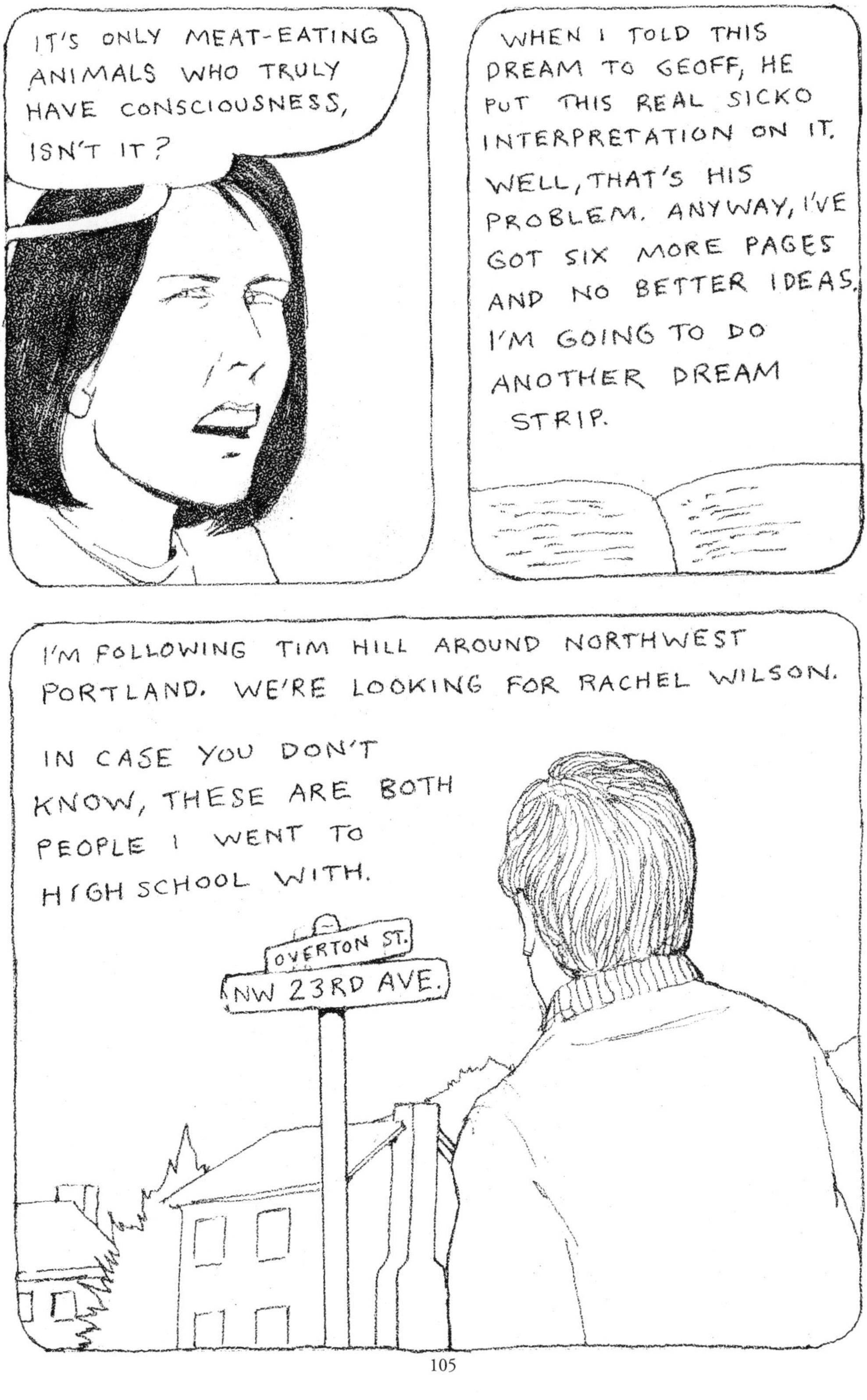
IT'S ONLY MEAT-EATING ANIMALS WHO TRULY HAVE CONSCIOUSNESS, ISN'T IT?
WHEN I TOLD THIS DREAM TO GEOFF, HE PUT THIS REAL SICKO INTERPRETATION ON IT. WELL, THAT'S HIS PROBLEM. ANYWAY, I'VE GOT SIX MORE PAGES AND NO BETTER IDEAS. I'M GOING TO DO ANOTHER DREAM STRIP.
I'M FOLLOWING TIM HILL AROUND NORTHWEST PORTLAND. WE'RE LOOKING FOR RACHEL WILSON.
IN CASE YOU DON'T KNOW, THESE ARE BOTH PEOPLE I WENT TO HIGH SCHOOL WITH.
OVERTON ST.
NW 23RD AVE.

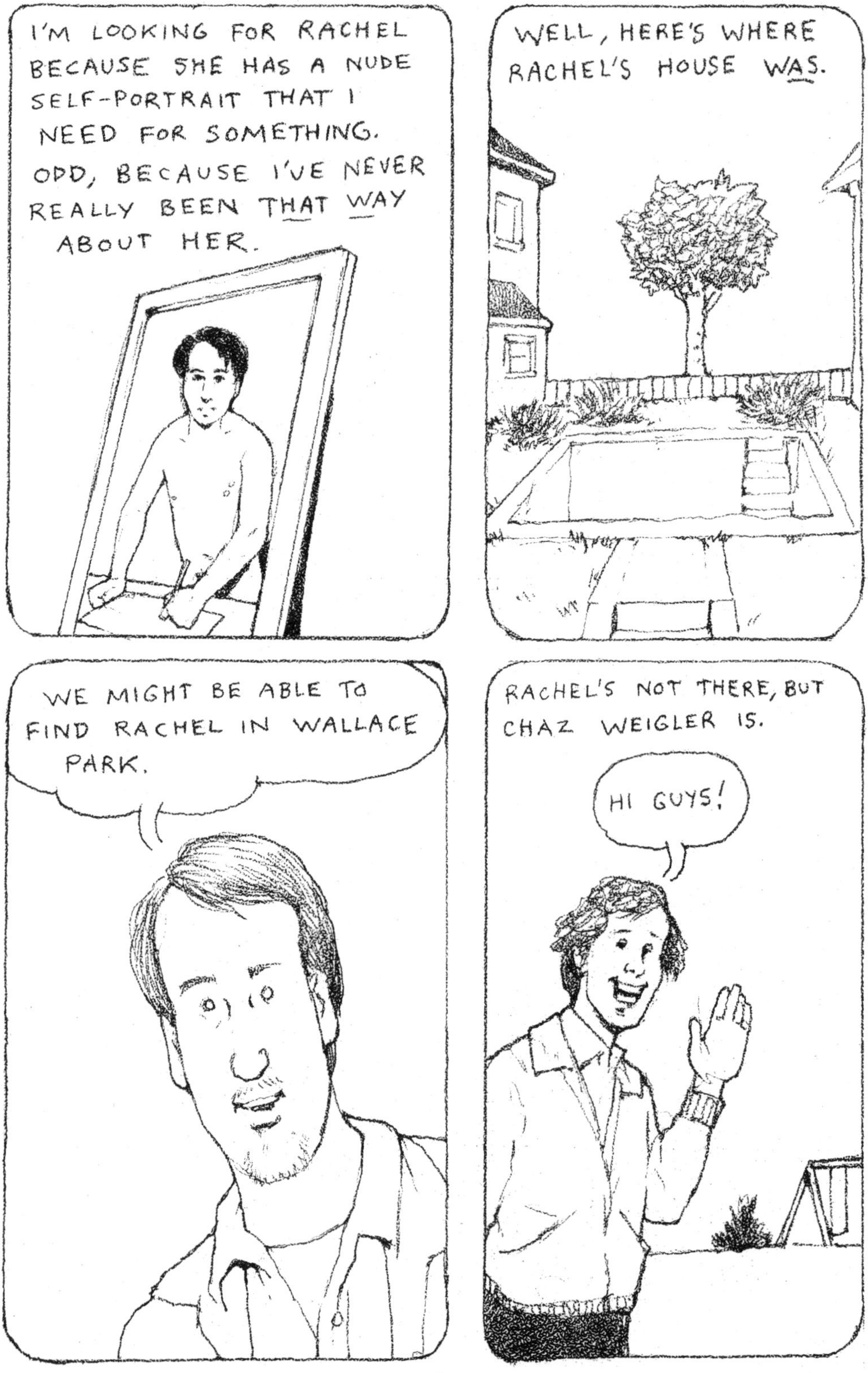
I'M LOOKING FOR RACHEL BECAUSE SHE HAS A NUDE SELF-PORTRAIT THAT I NEED FOR SOMETHING.
ODD, BECAUSE I'VE NEVER REALLY BEEN THAT WAY ABOUT HER.
WELL, HERE'S WHERE RACHEL'S HOUSE WAS.
WE MIGHT BE ABLE TO FIND RACHEL IN WALLACE PARK.
RACHEL'S NOT THERE, BUT CHAZ WEIGLER IS.
HI GUYS!

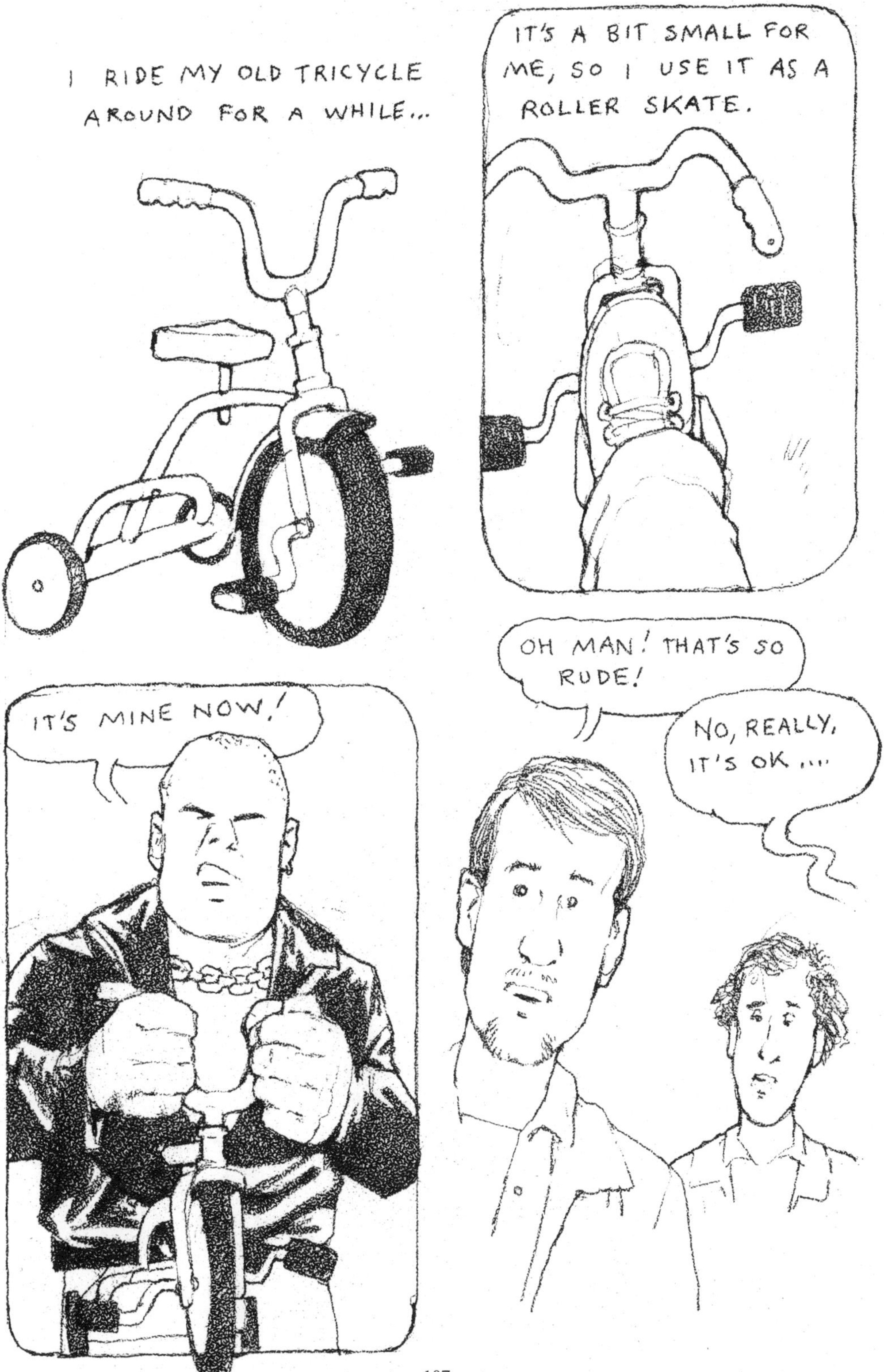
I RIDE MY OLD TRICYCLE AROUND FOR A WHILE...
IT'S A BIT SMALL FOR ME, SO I USE IT AS A ROLLER SKATE.
IT'S MINE NOW!
OH MAN! THAT'S SO RUDE!
NO, REALLY, IT'S OK....

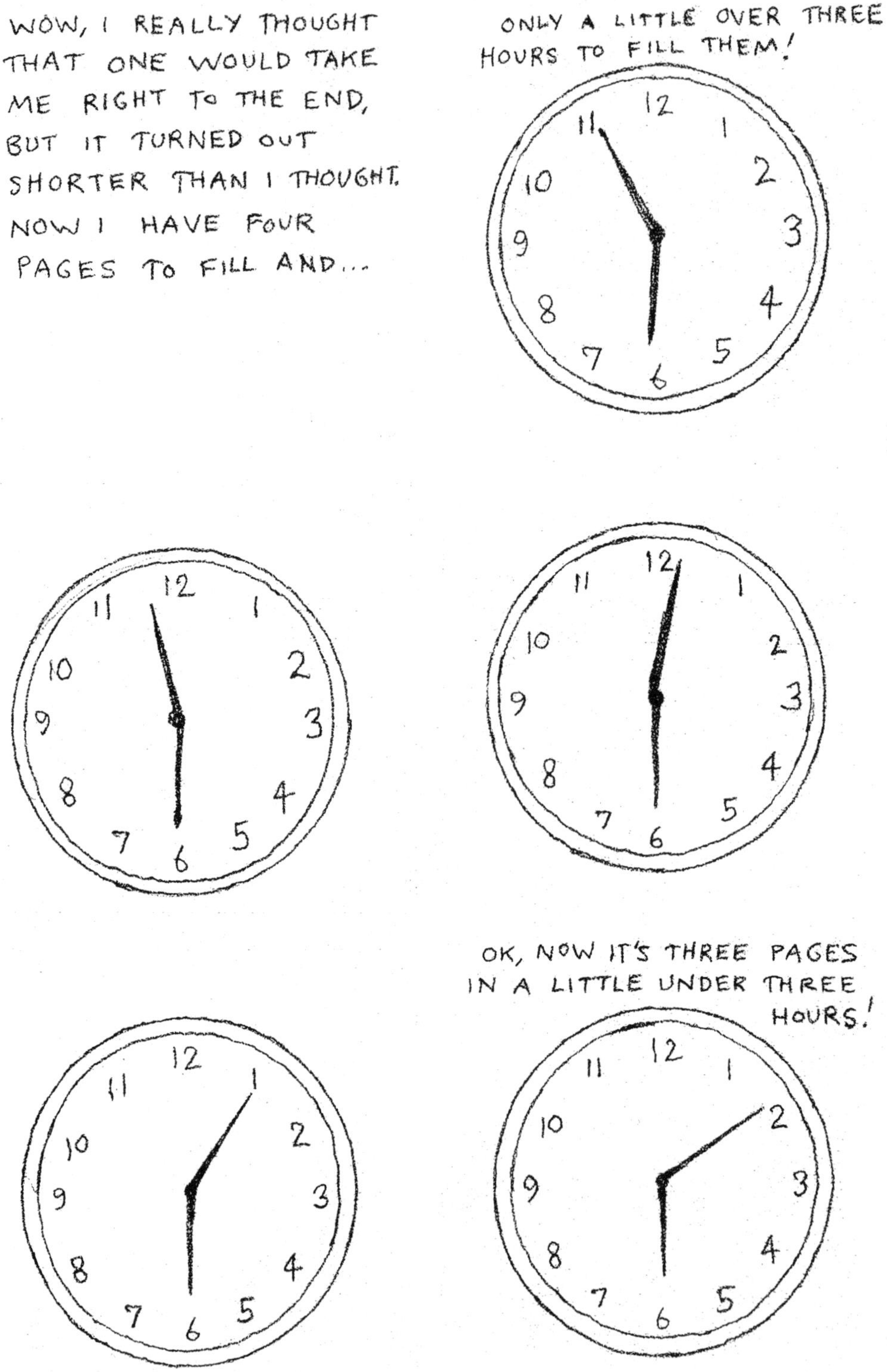
WOW, I REALLY THOUGHT THAT ONE WOULD TAKE ME RIGHT TO THE END, BUT IT TURNED OUT SHORTER THAN I THOUGHT. NOW I HAVE FOUR PAGES TO FILL AND...
ONLY A LITTLE OVER THREE HOURS TO FILL THEM!
OK, NOW IT'S THREE PAGES IN A LITTLE UNDER THREE HOURS!

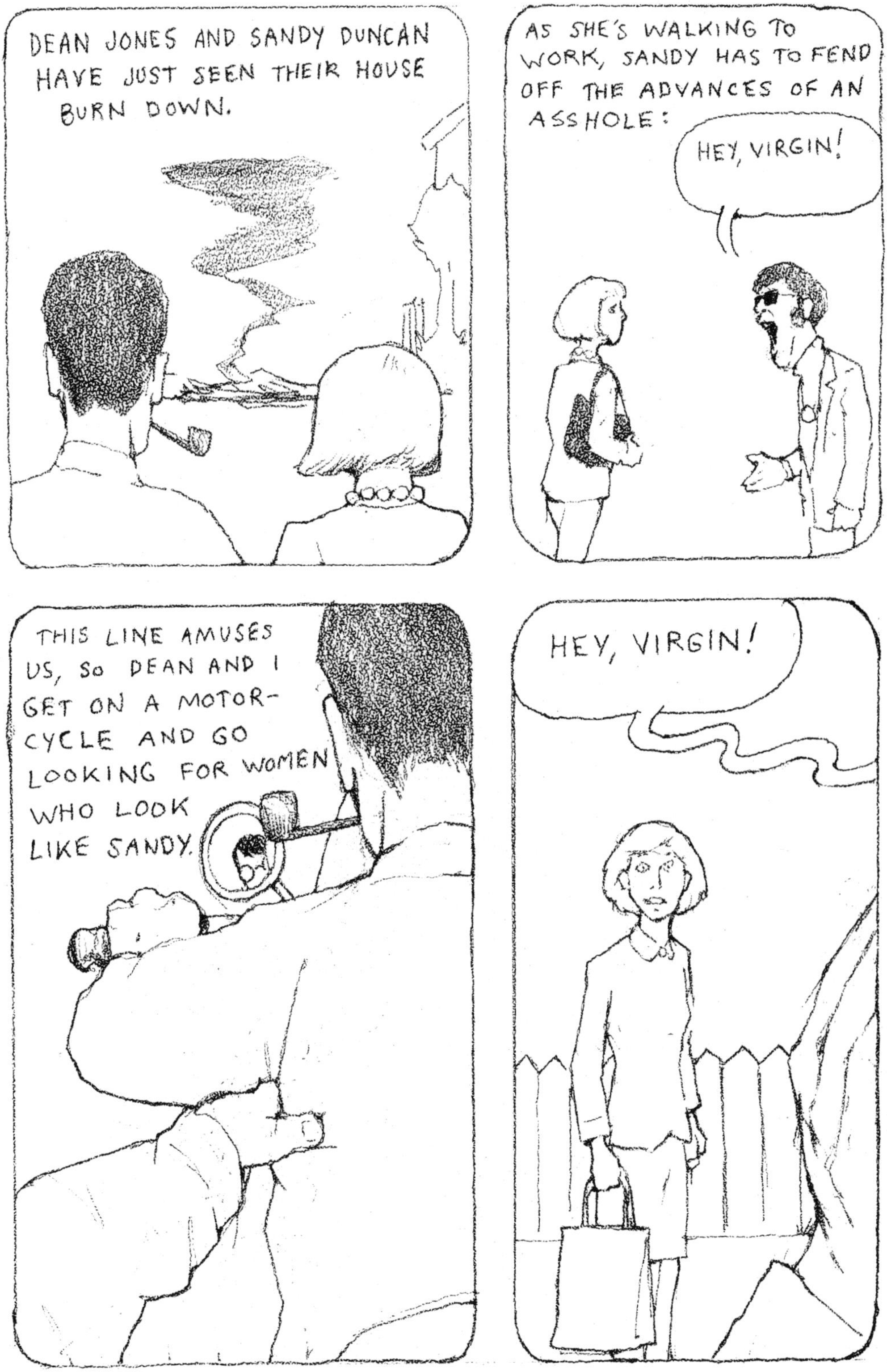
DEAN JONES AND SANDY DUNCAN HAVE JUST SEEN THEIR HOUSE BURN DOWN.
AS SHE'S WALKING TO WORK, SANDY HAS TO FEND OFF THE ADVANCES OF AN ASSHOLE:
HEY, VIRGIN!
THIS LINE AMUSES US, SO DEAN AND I GET ON A MOTOR-CYCLE AND GO LOOKING FOR WOMEN WHO LOOK LIKE SANDY.
HEY, VIRGIN!

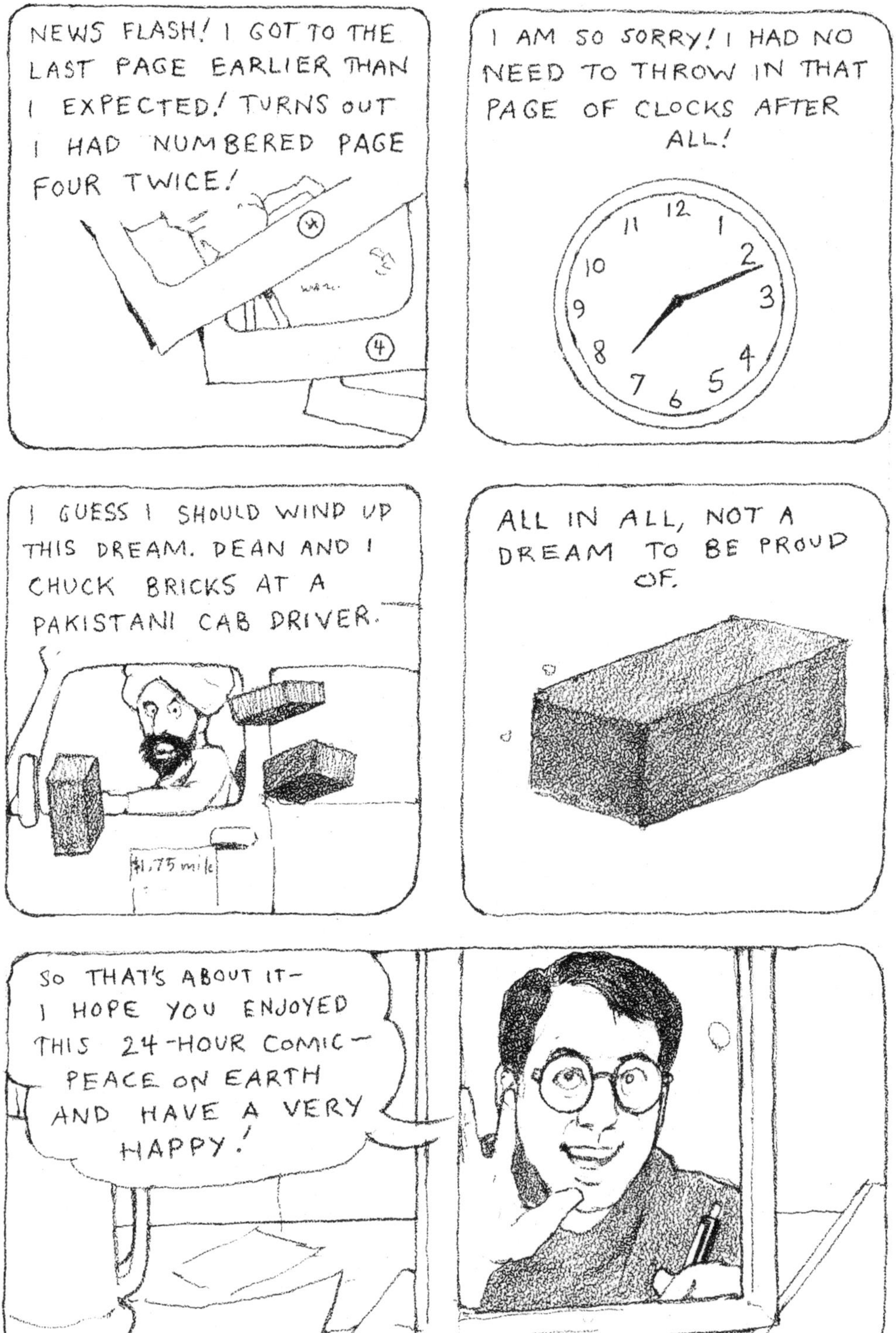
NEWS FLASH! I GOT TO THE LAST PAGE EARLIER THAN I EXPECTED! TURNS OUT I HAD NUMBERED PAGE FOUR TWICE!
I AM SO SORRY! I HAD NO NEED TO THROW IN THAT PAGE OF CLOCKS AFTER ALL!
I GUESS I SHOULD WIND UP THIS DREAM. DEAN AND I CHUCK BRICKS AT A PAKISTANI CAB DRIVER.
$1.75 mile
ALL IN ALL, NOT A DREAM TO BE PROUD OF.
SO THAT'S ABOUT IT– I HOPE YOU ENJOYED THIS 24-HOUR COMIC– PEACE ON EARTH AND HAVE A VERY HAPPY!

BINGO THE CAT

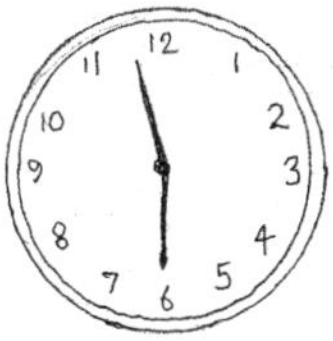

NOTES ON "BINGO THE CAT"

Purely an exercise in trying to be funny without using words. Our pet cat goes through the looking glass, à la Alice. As in "The Harold Project," I drew over preprinted perspective grids.

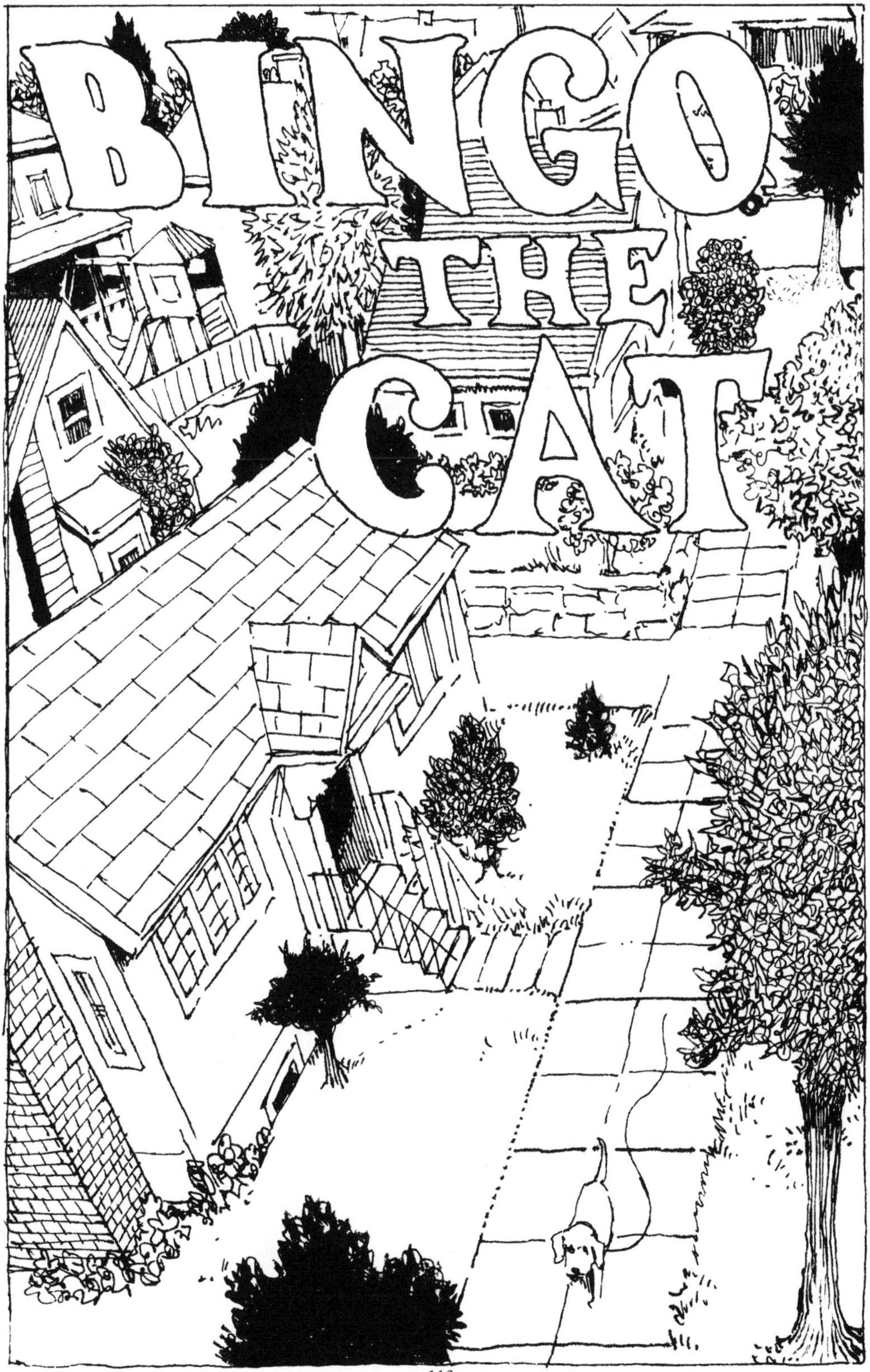
BINGO
THE
CAT

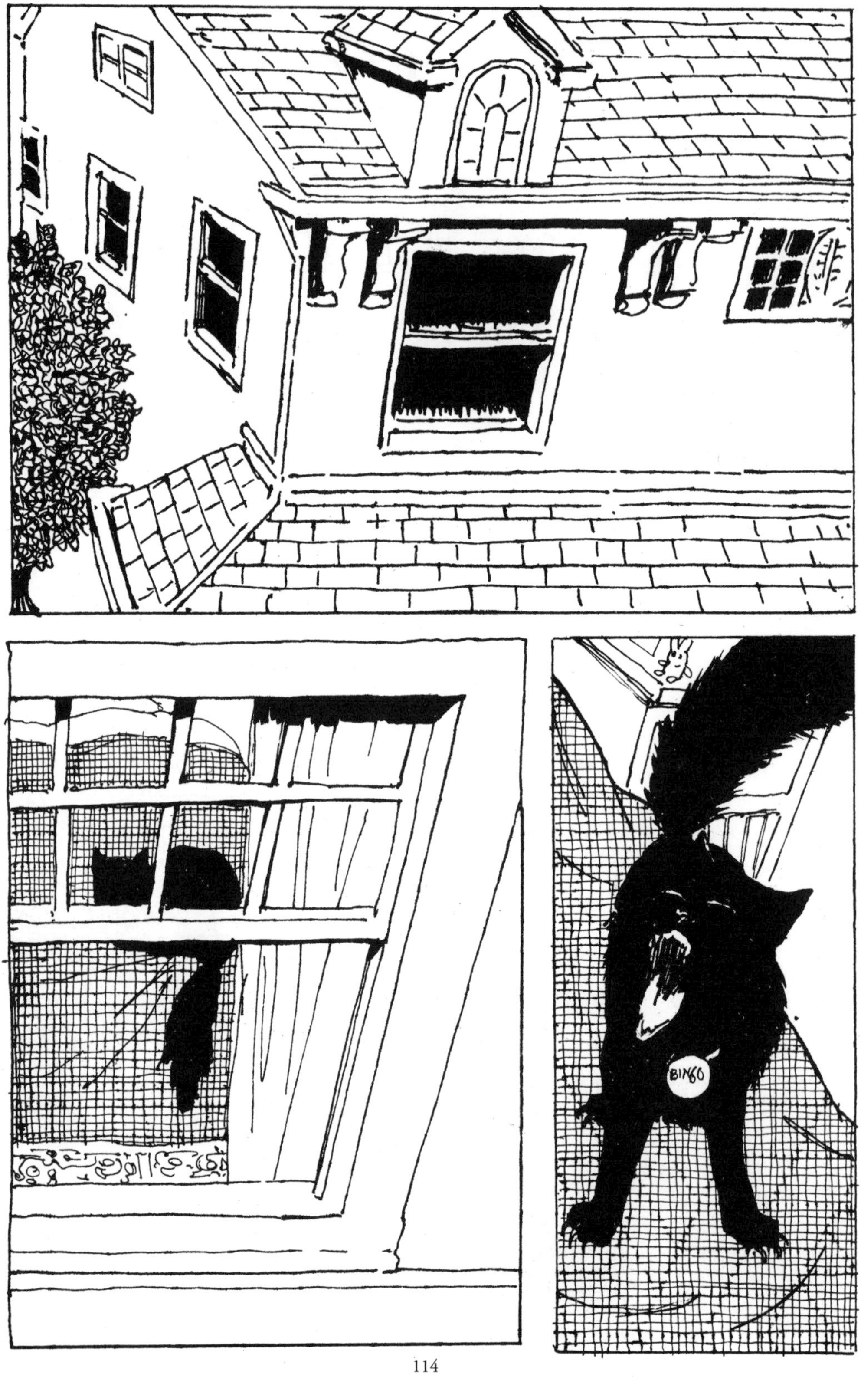
BINGO

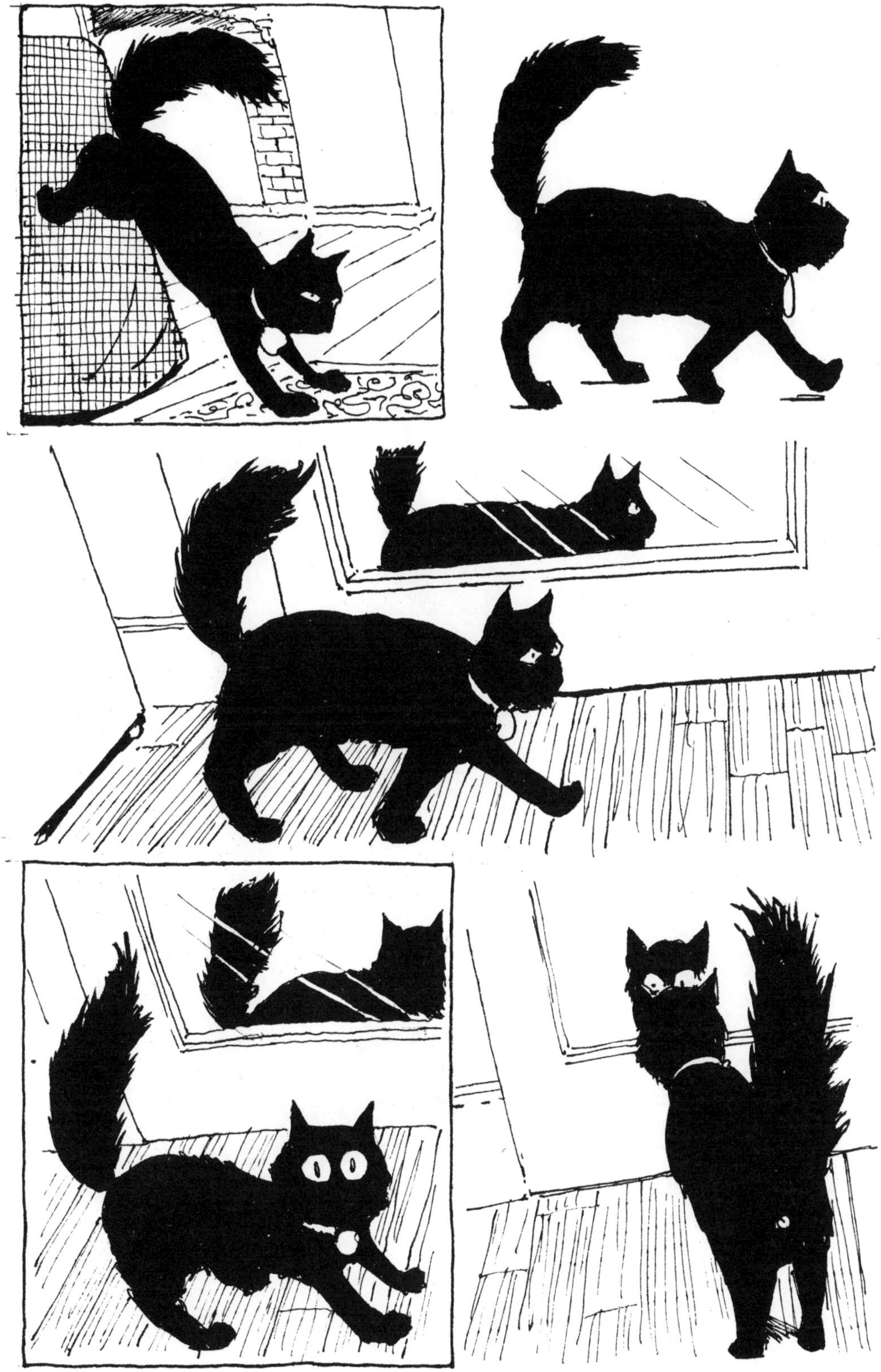

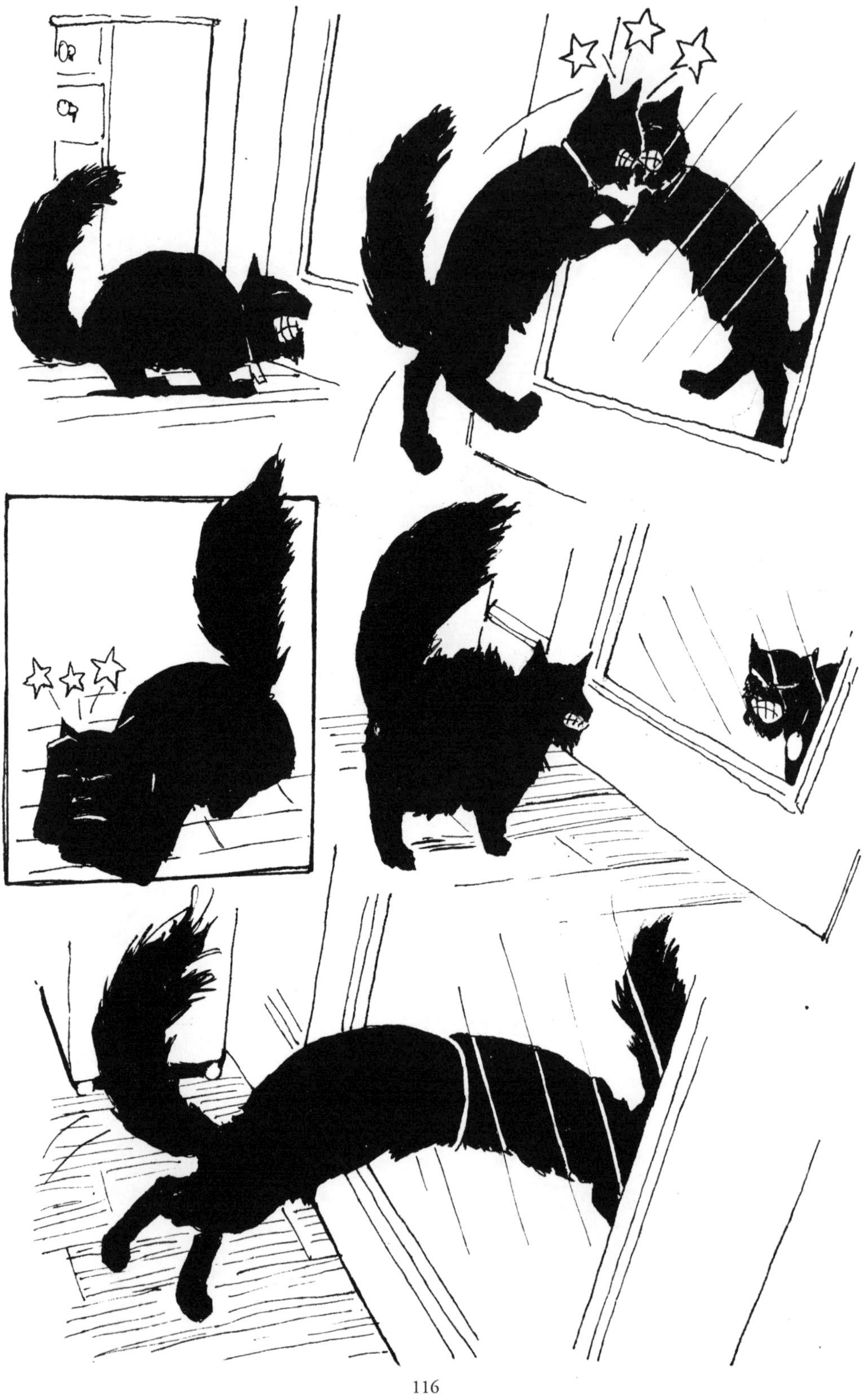

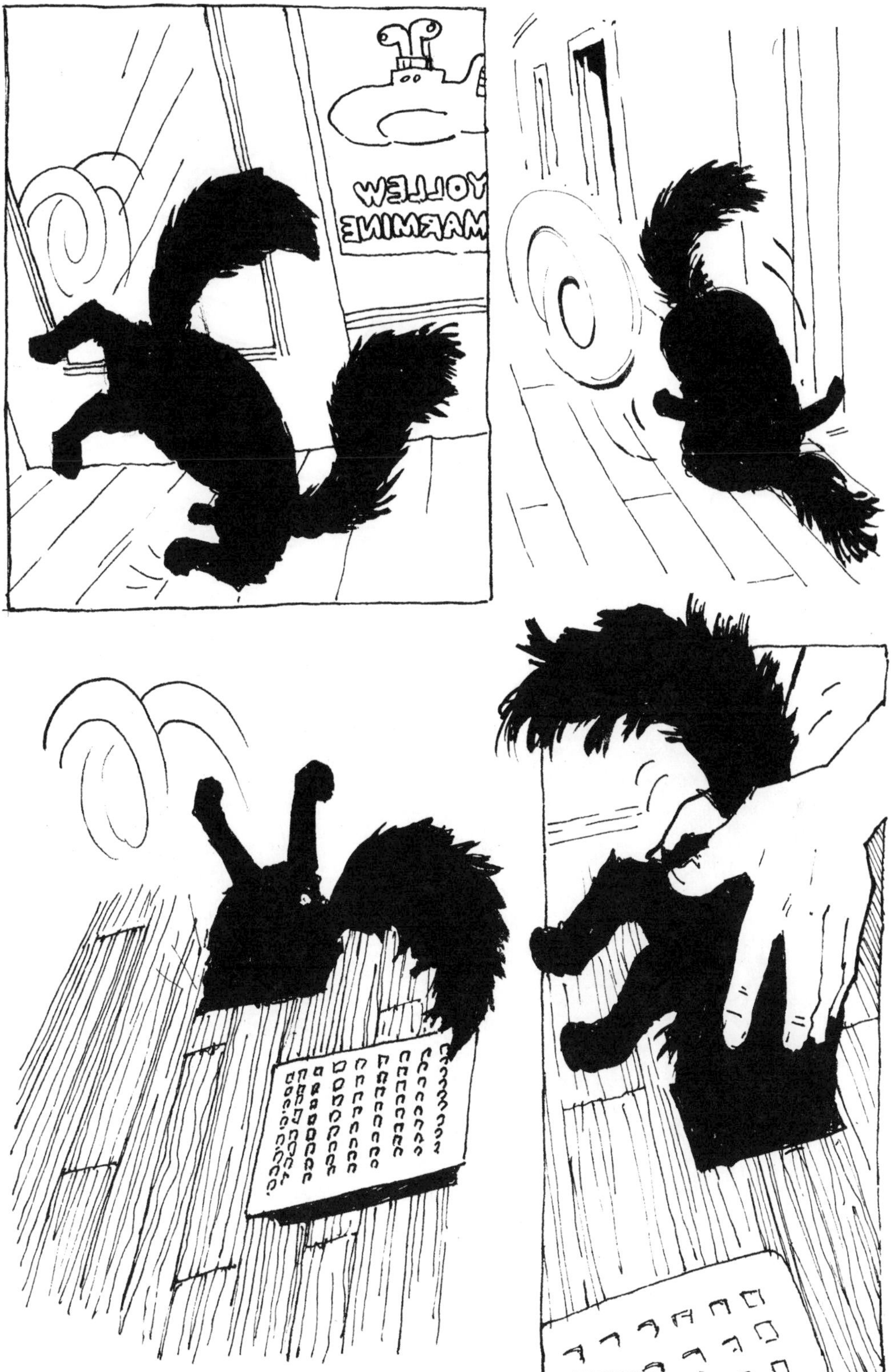

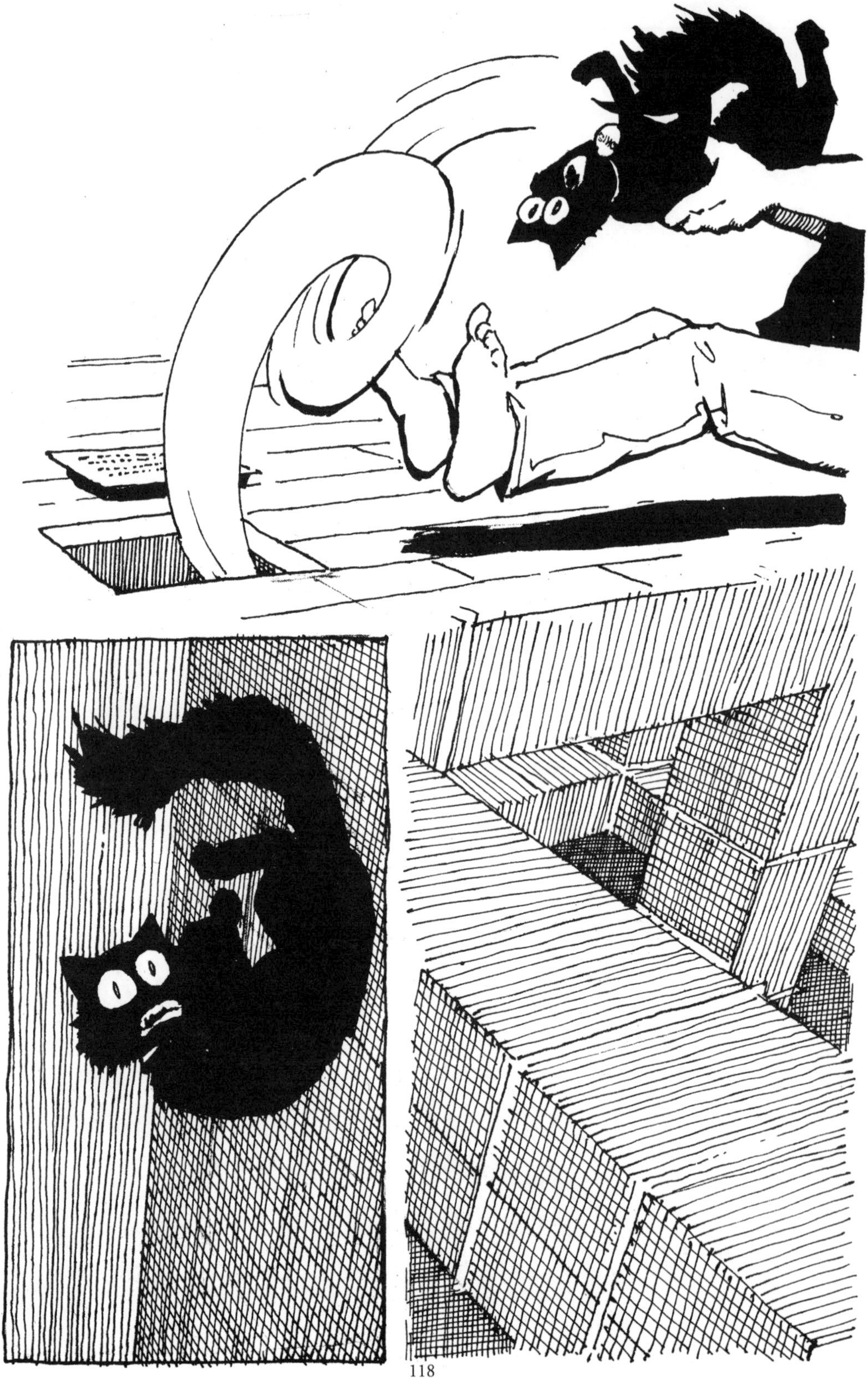

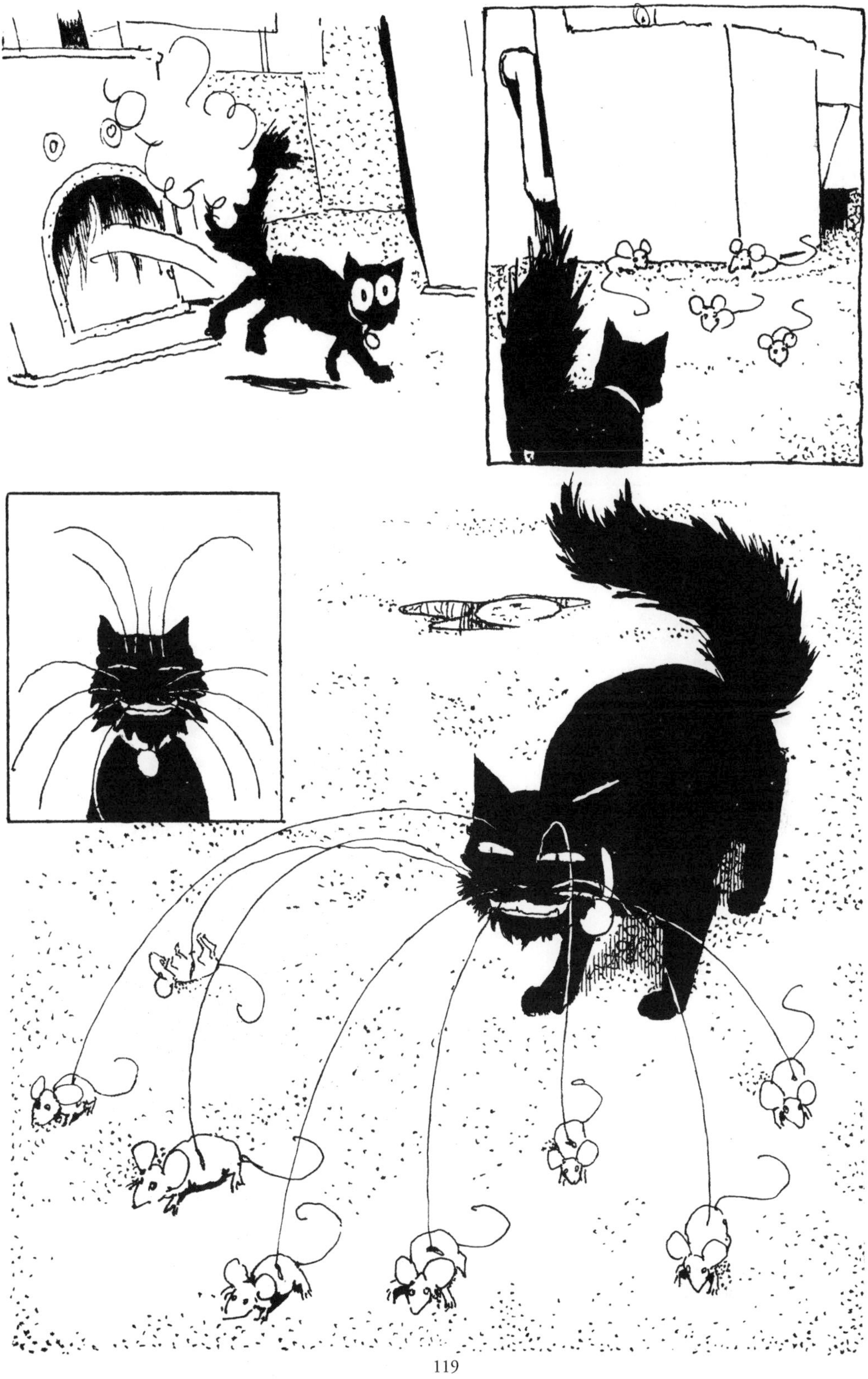

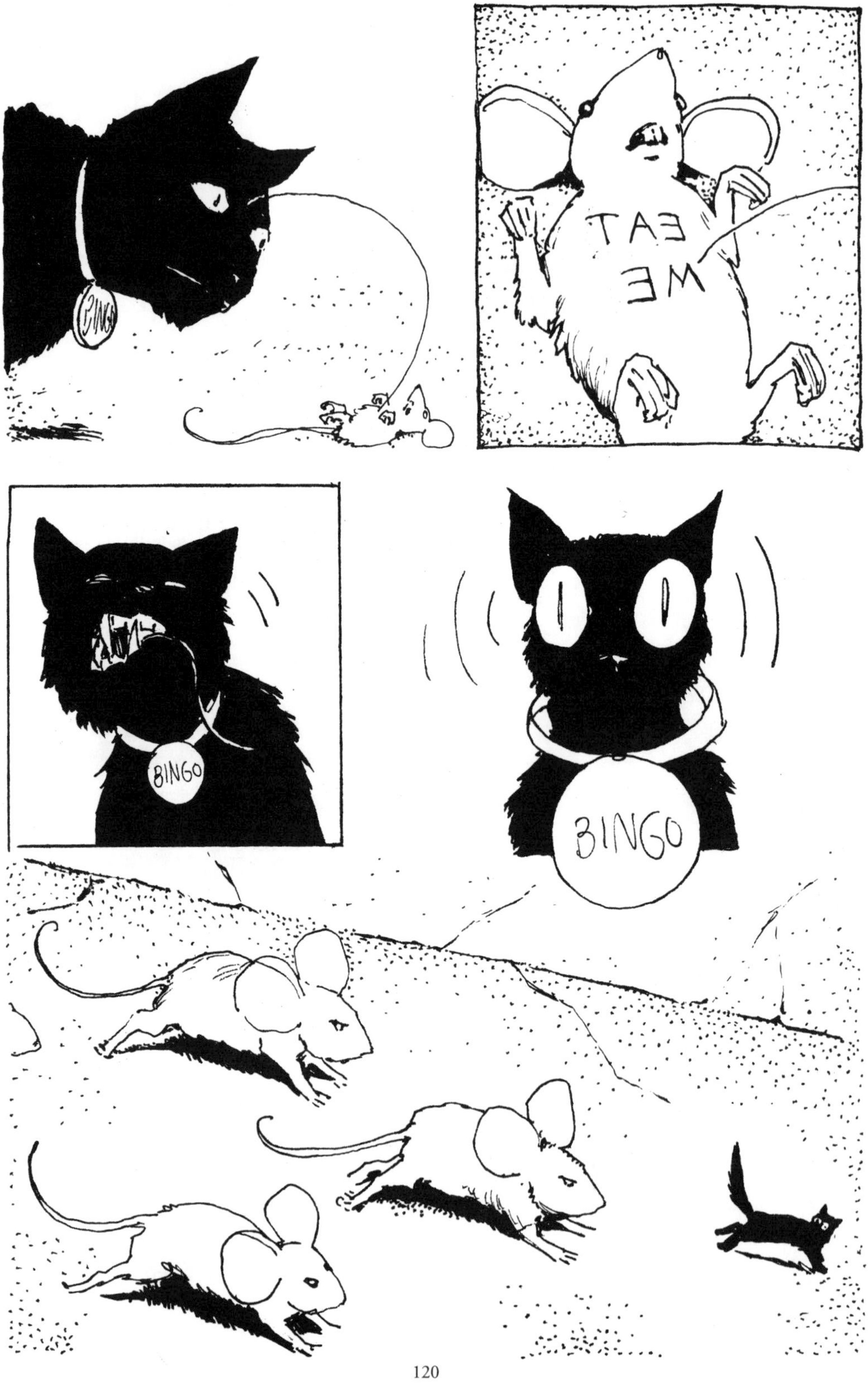
BINGO
EAT ME
BINGO
BINGO

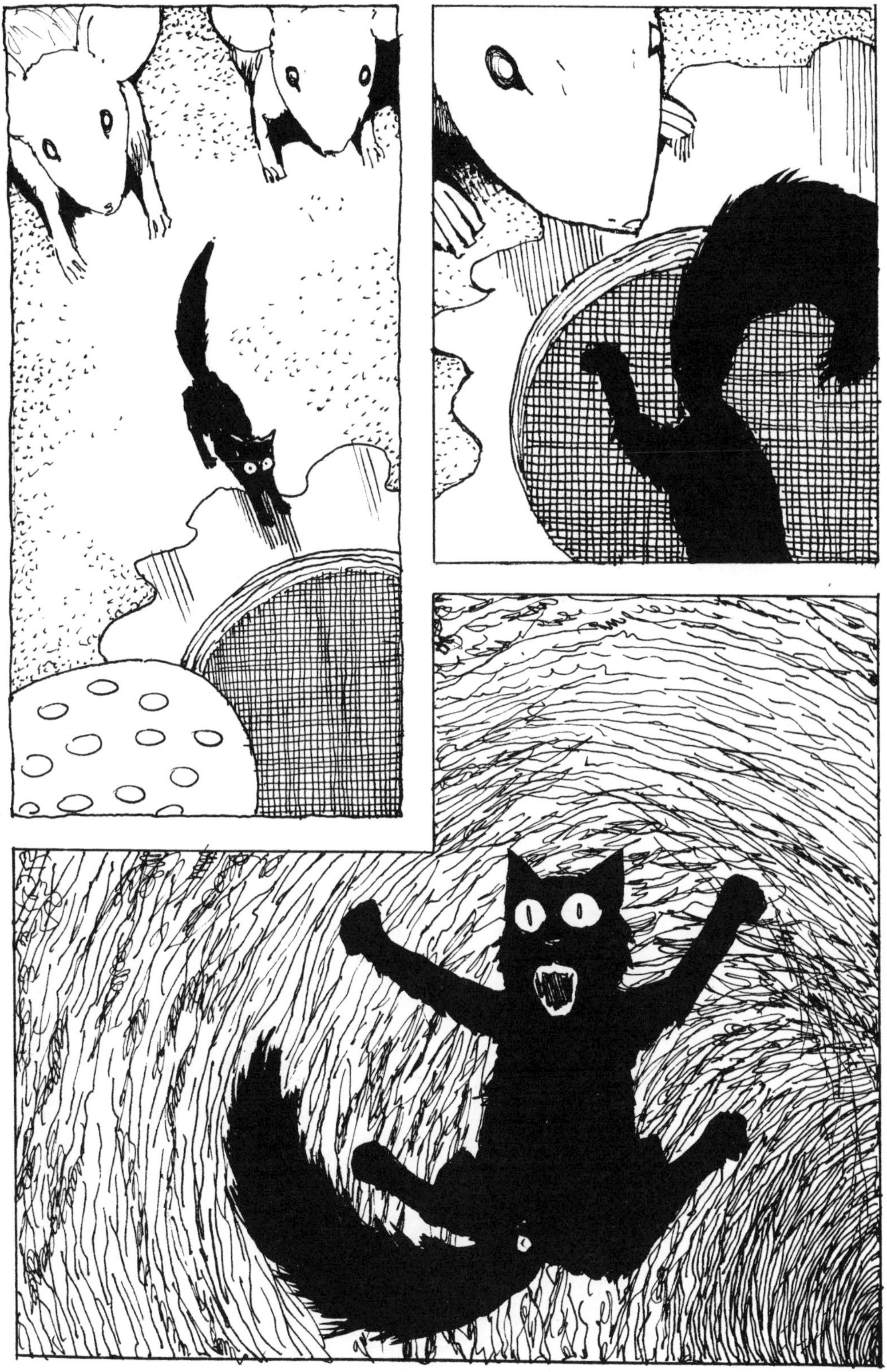

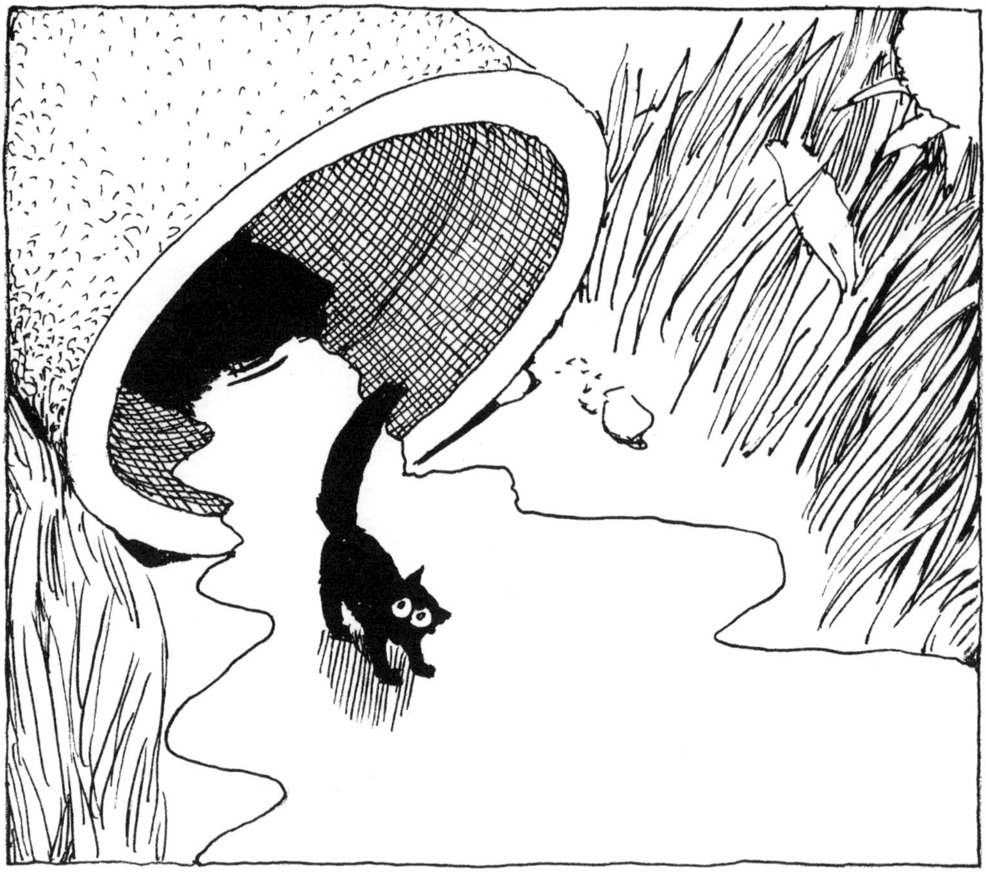

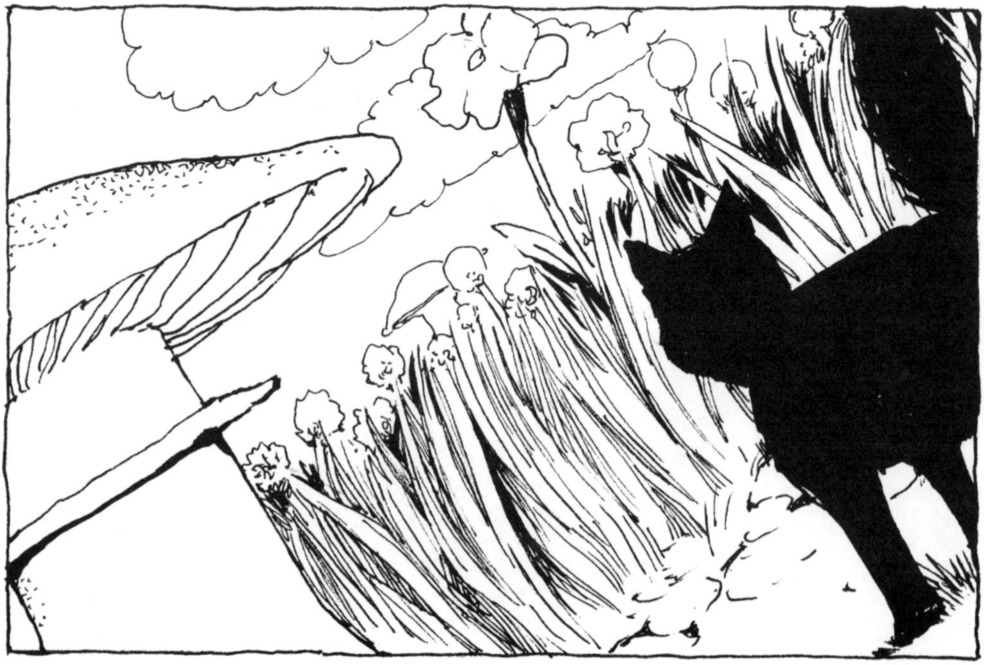

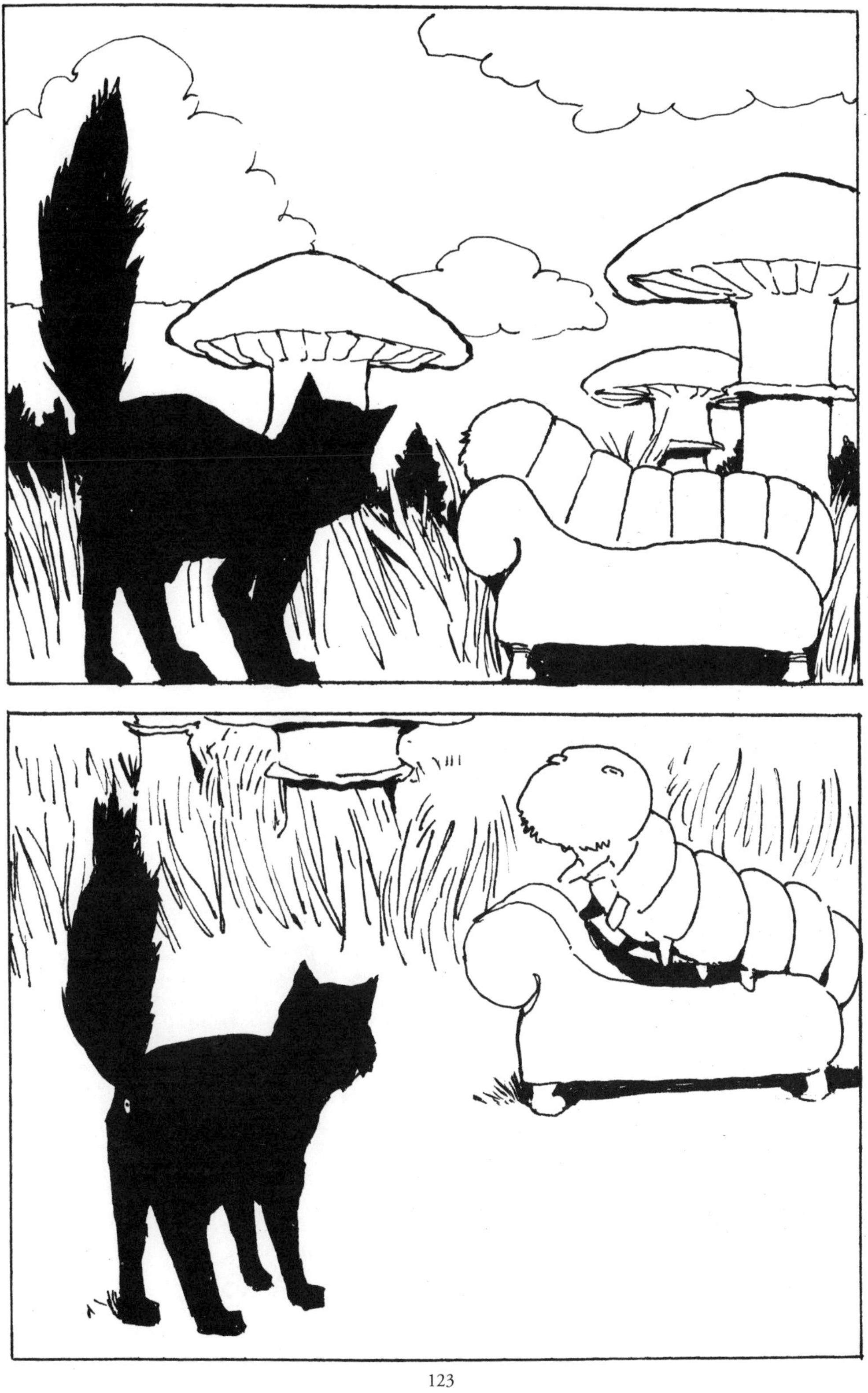

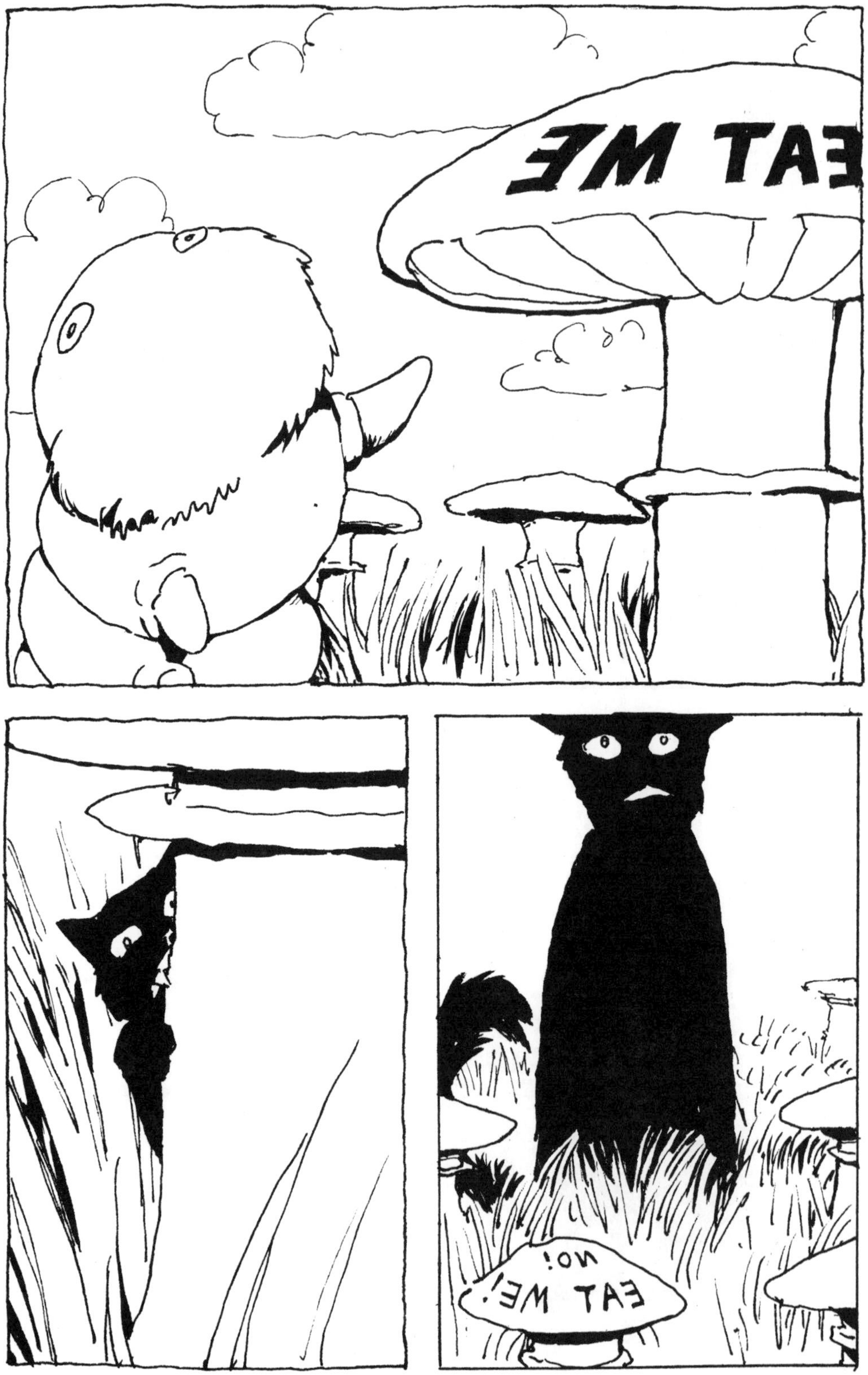
EAT ME
NO! EAT ME!

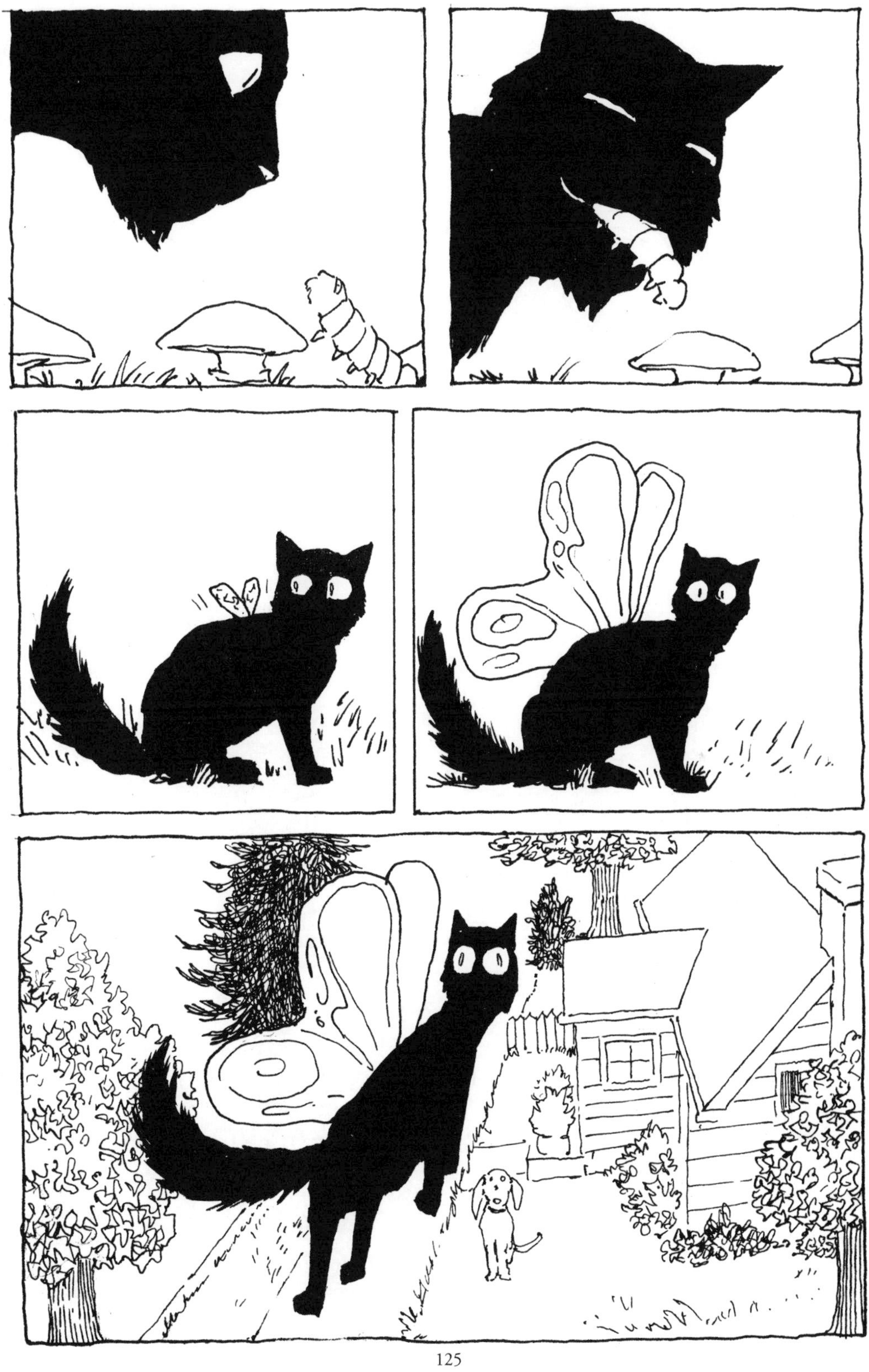

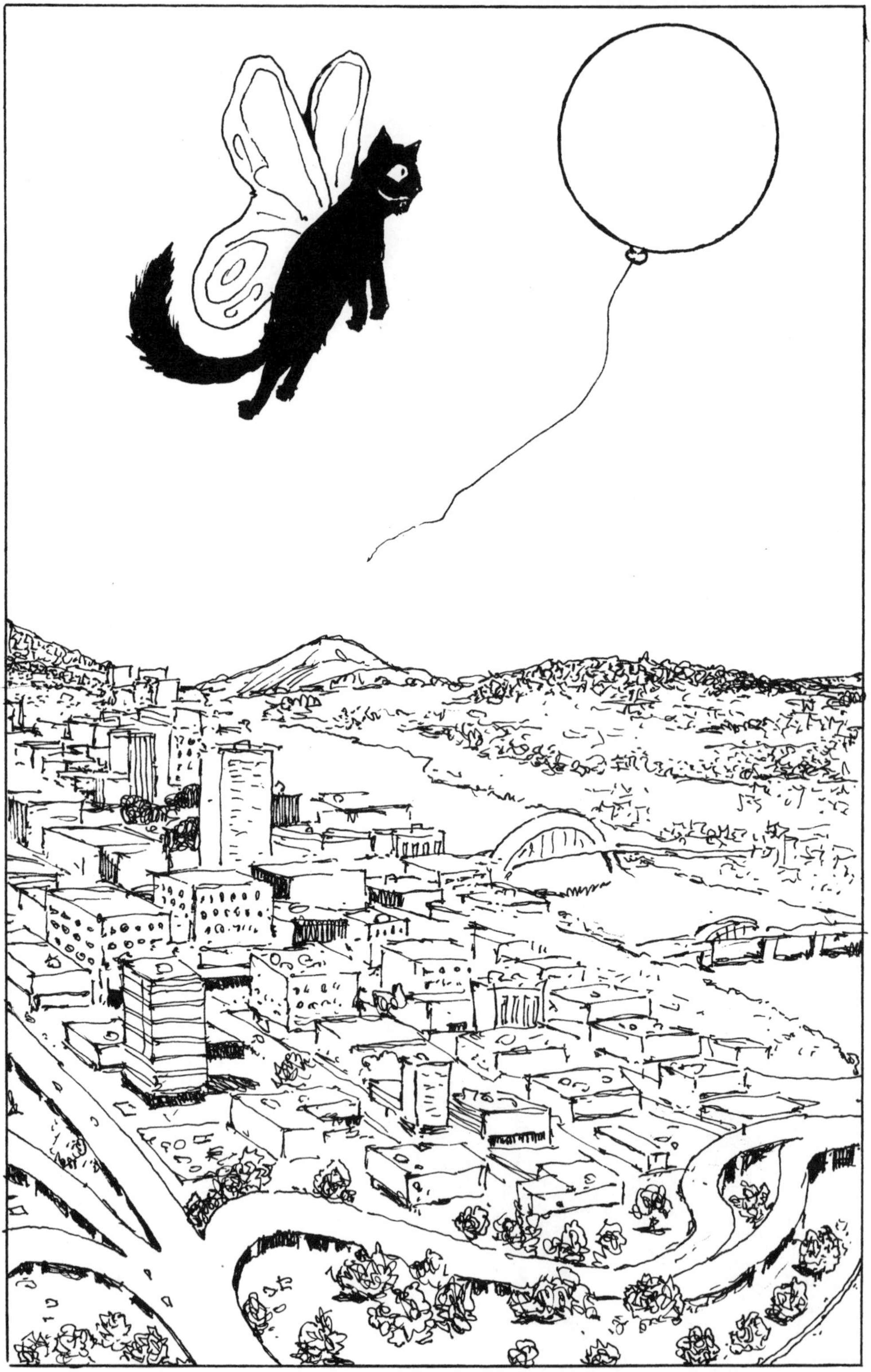

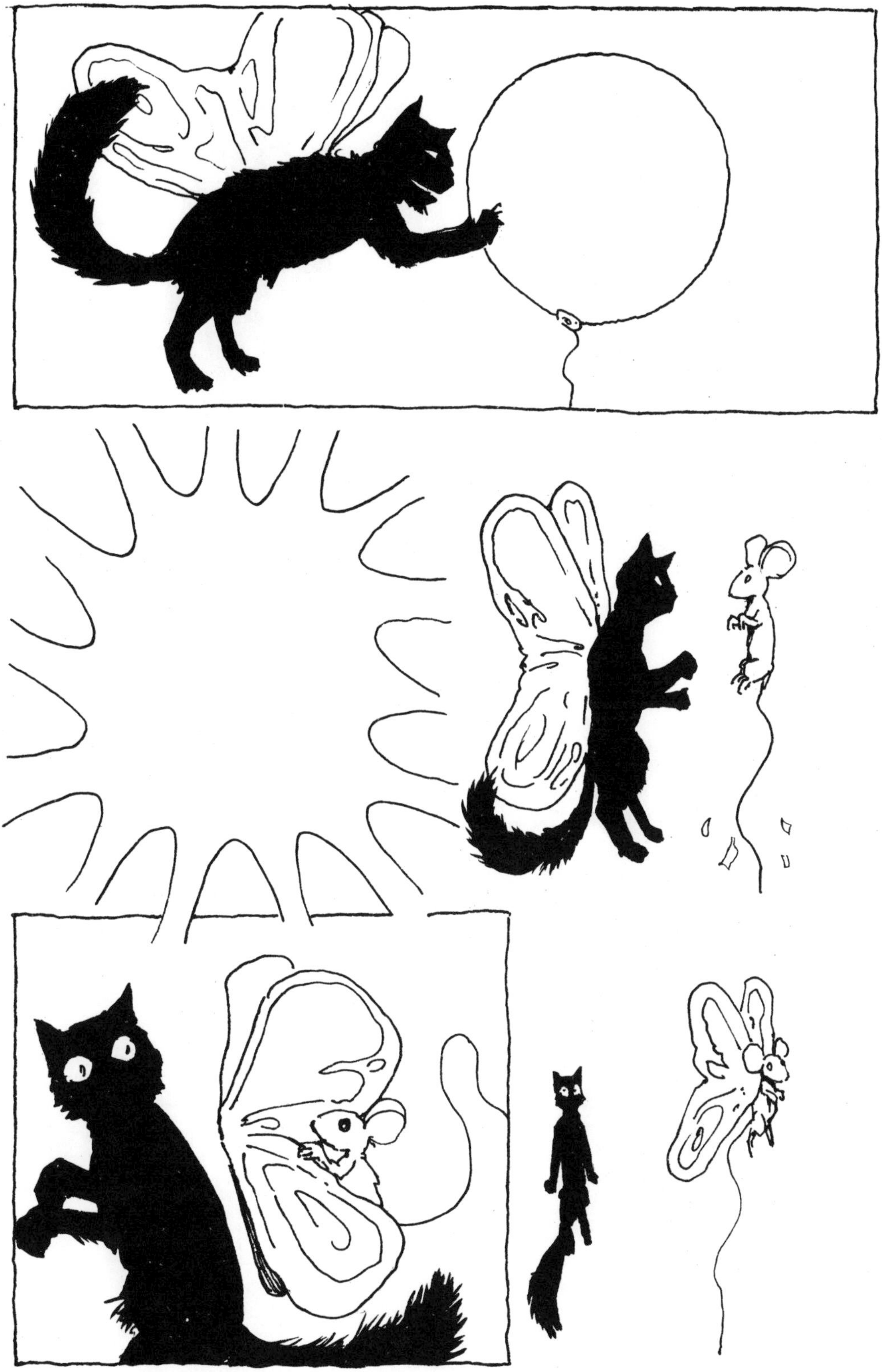

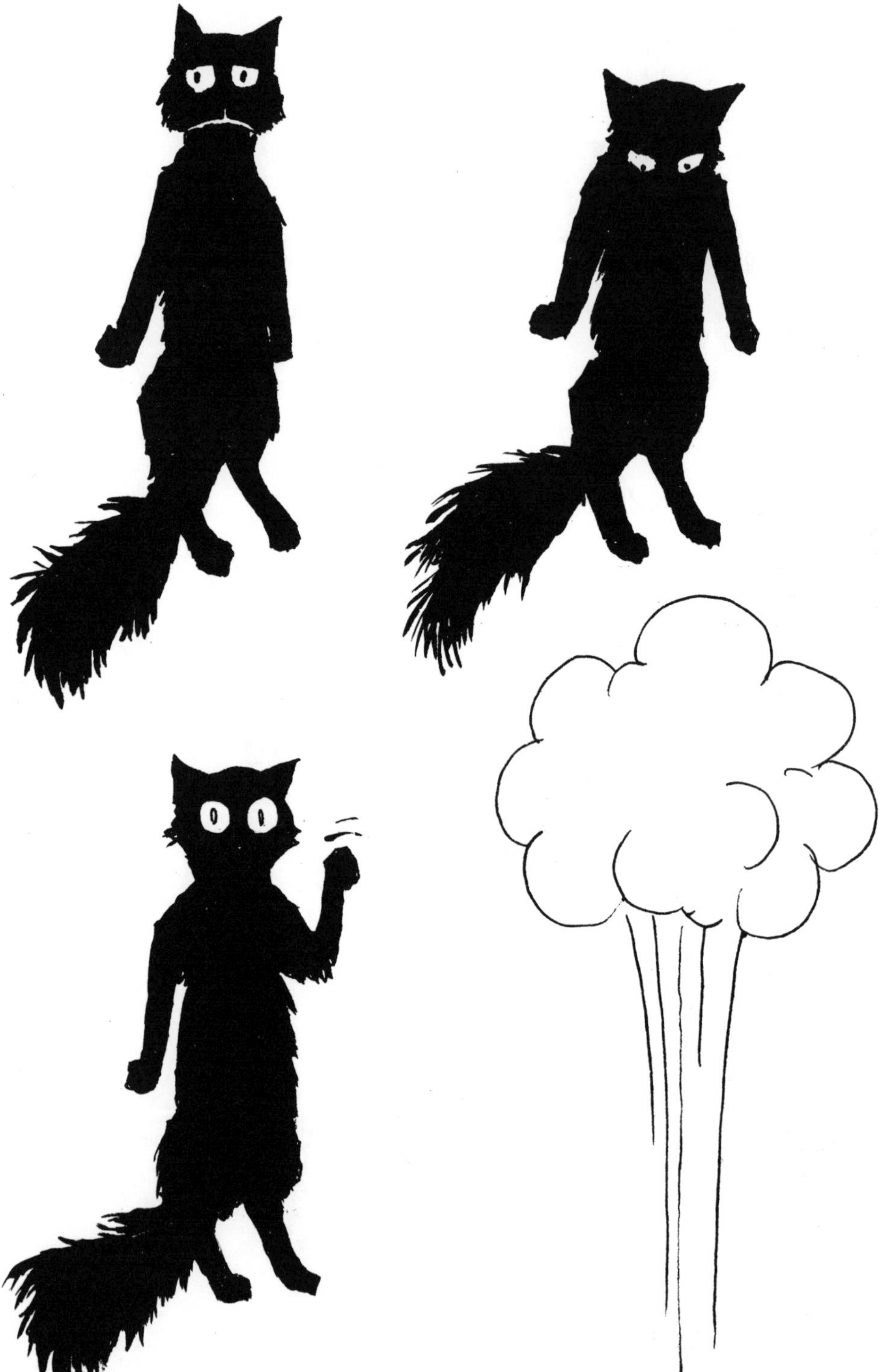

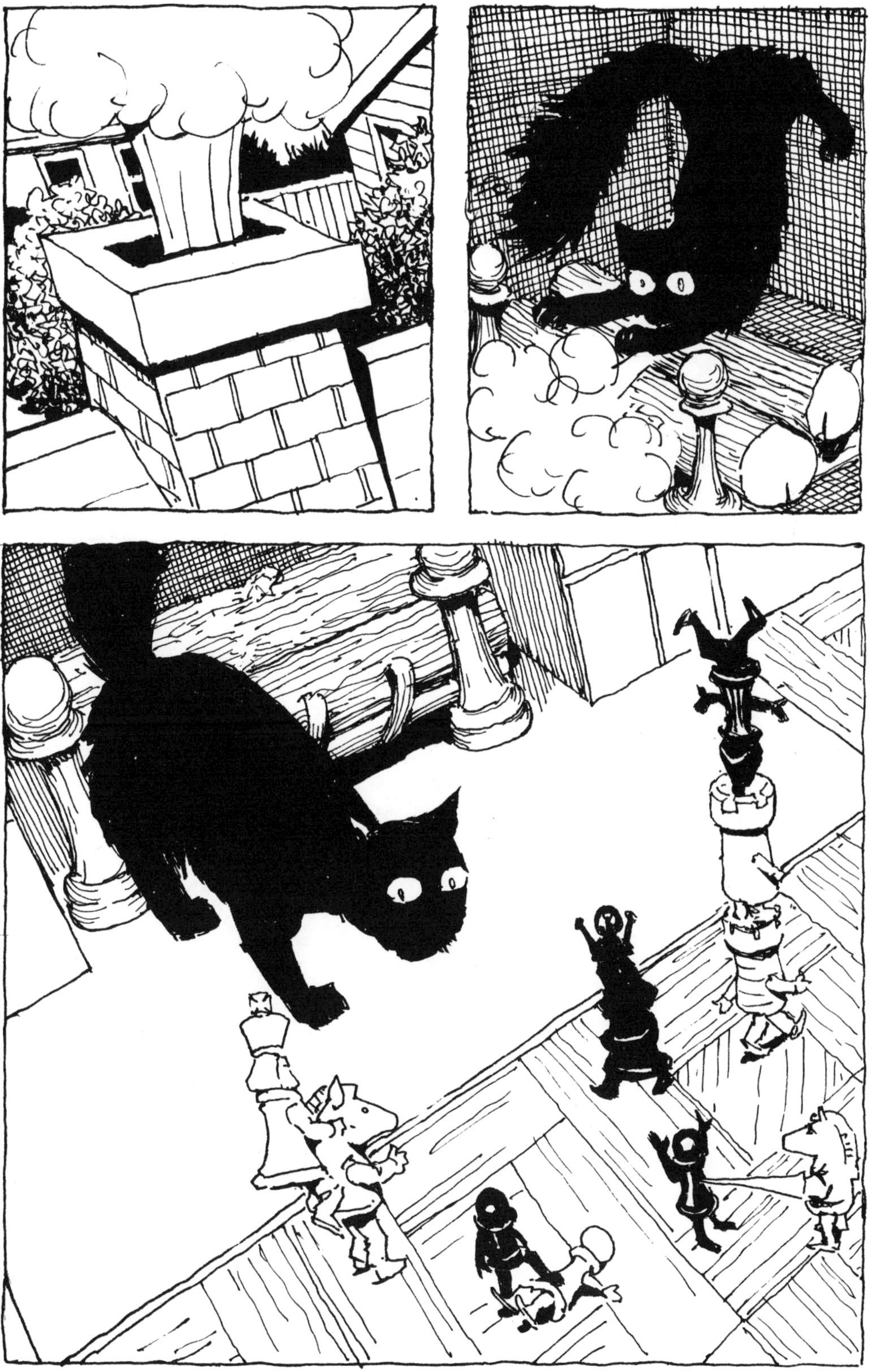

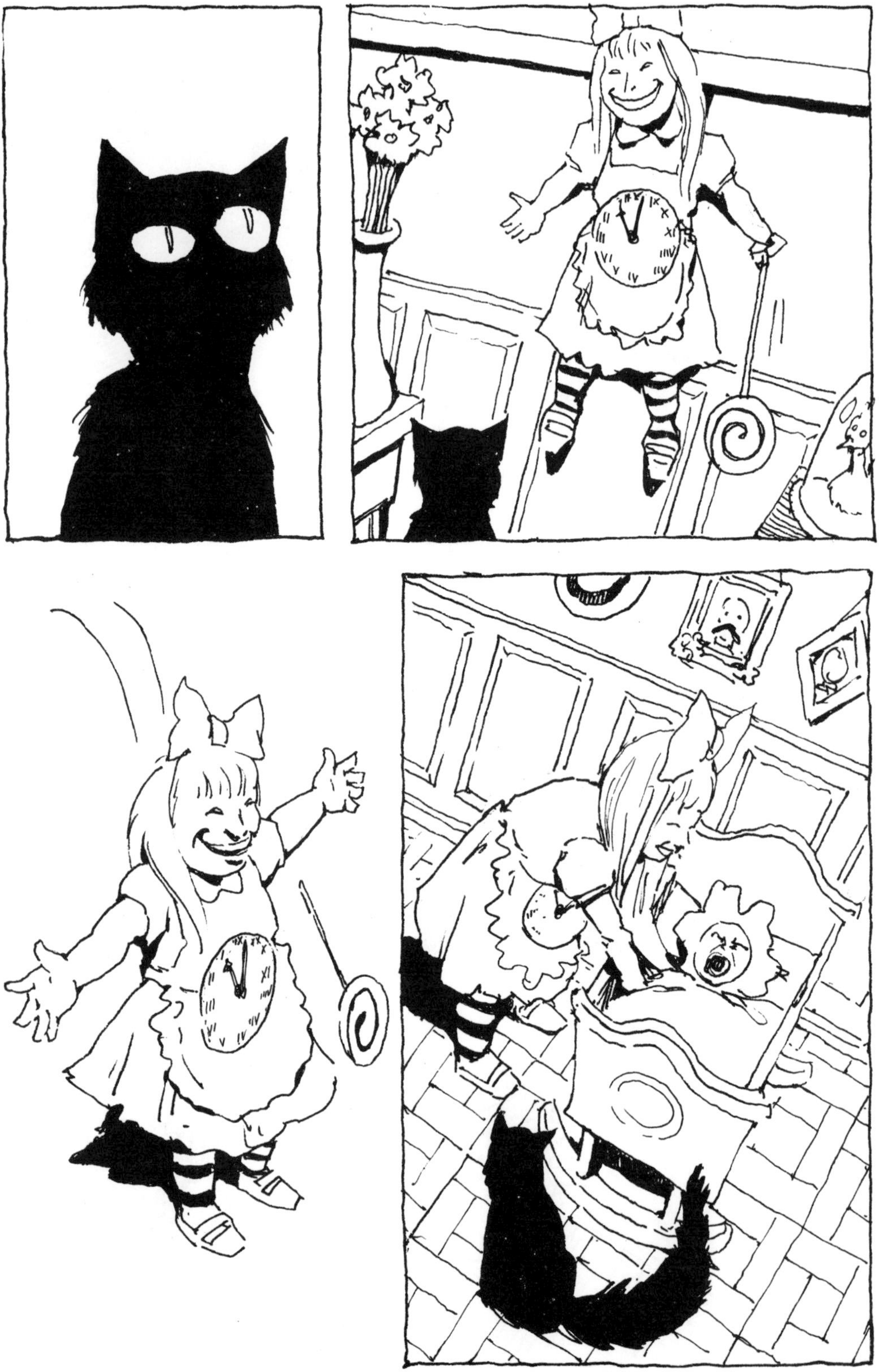

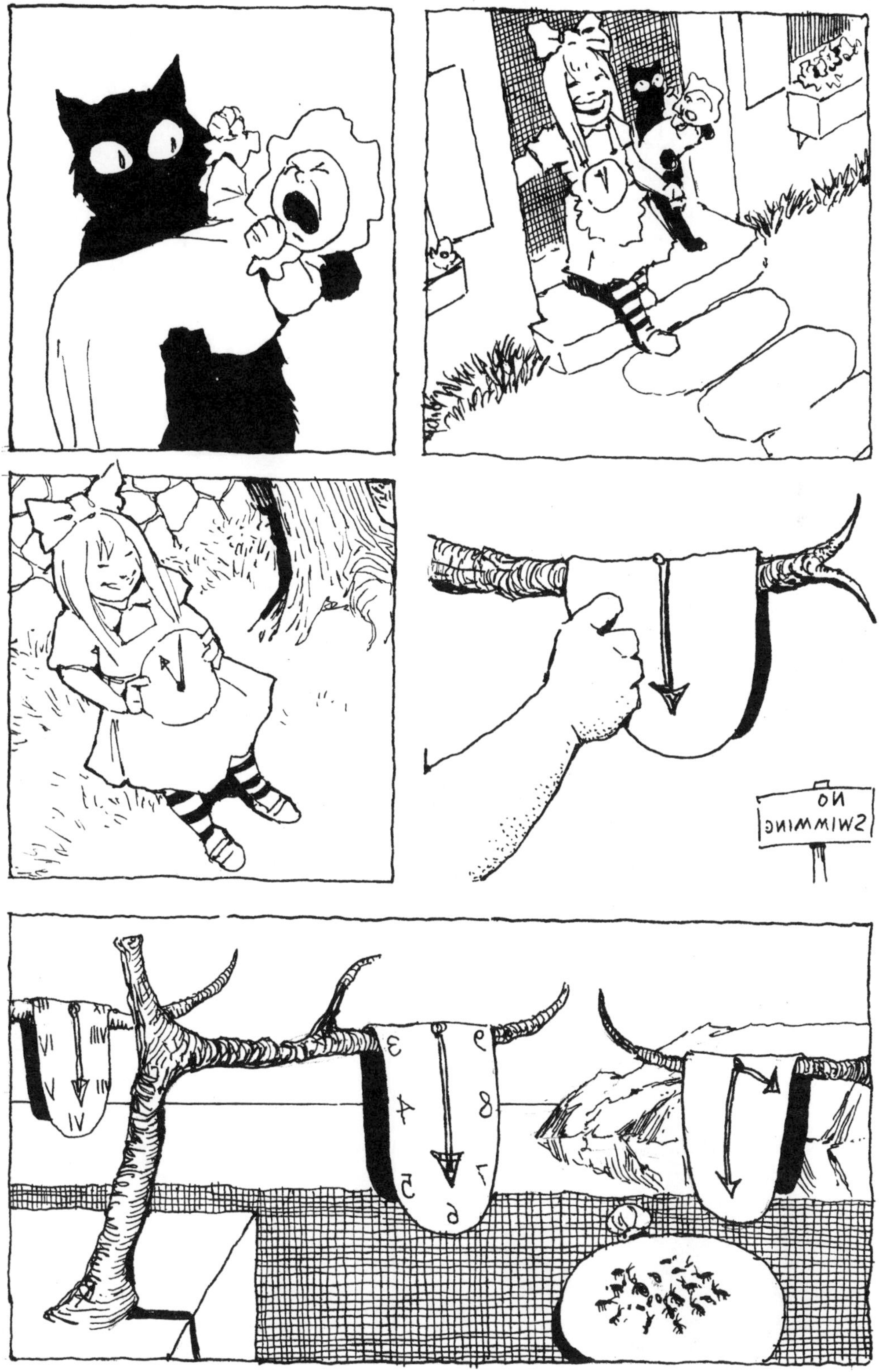
NO SWIMMING

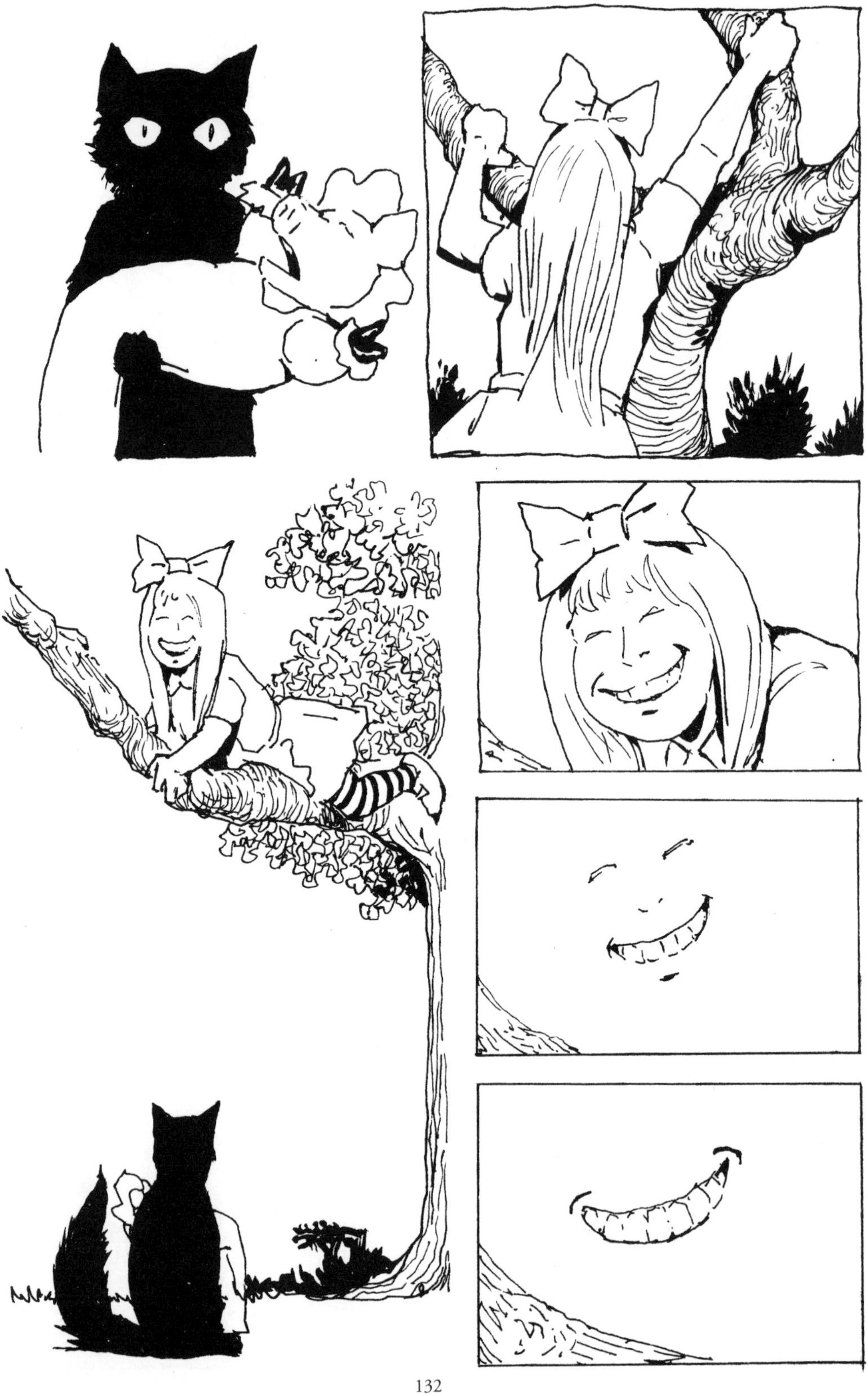

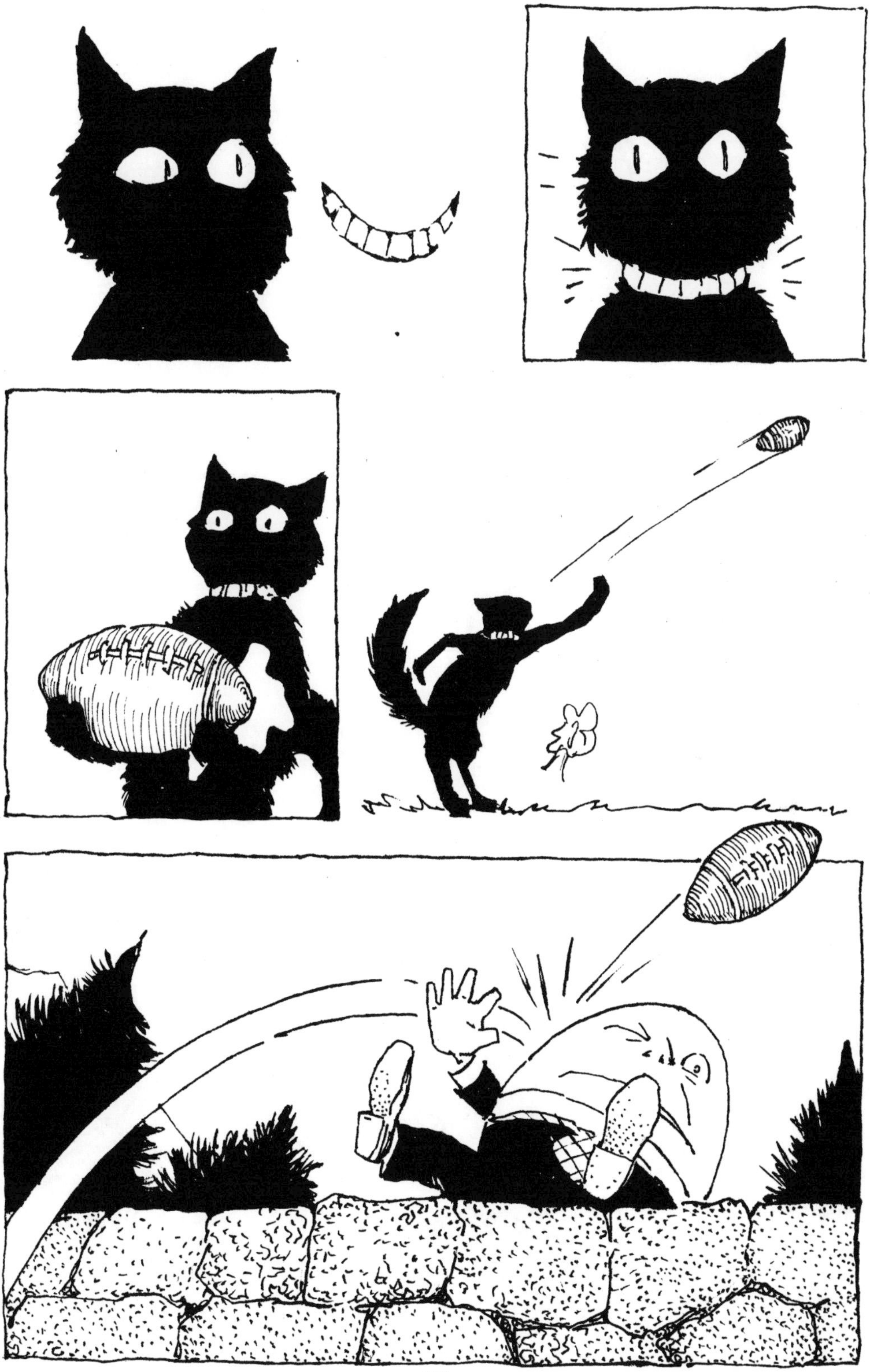

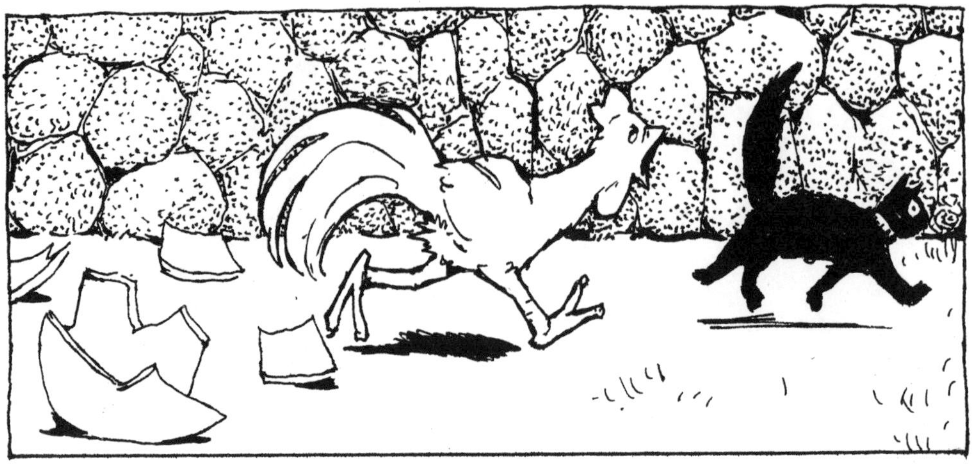

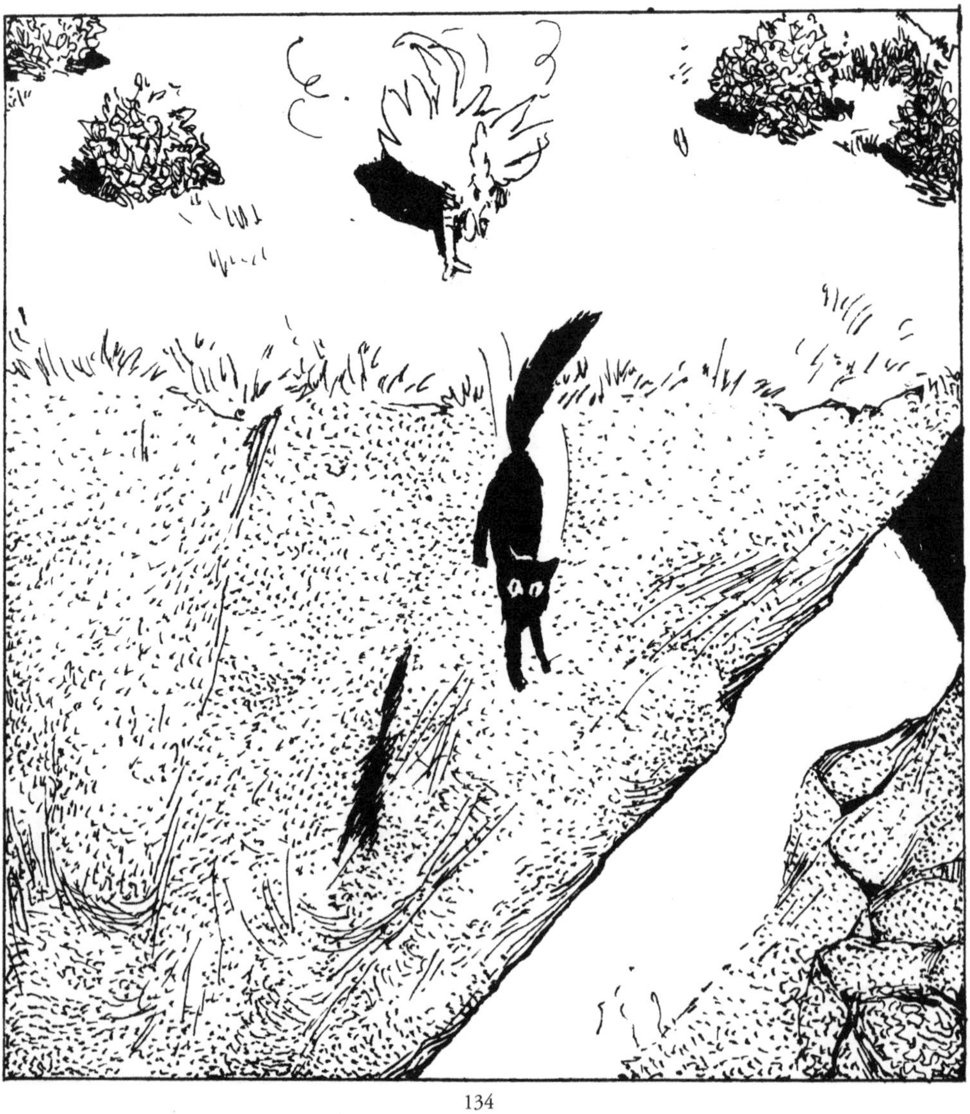

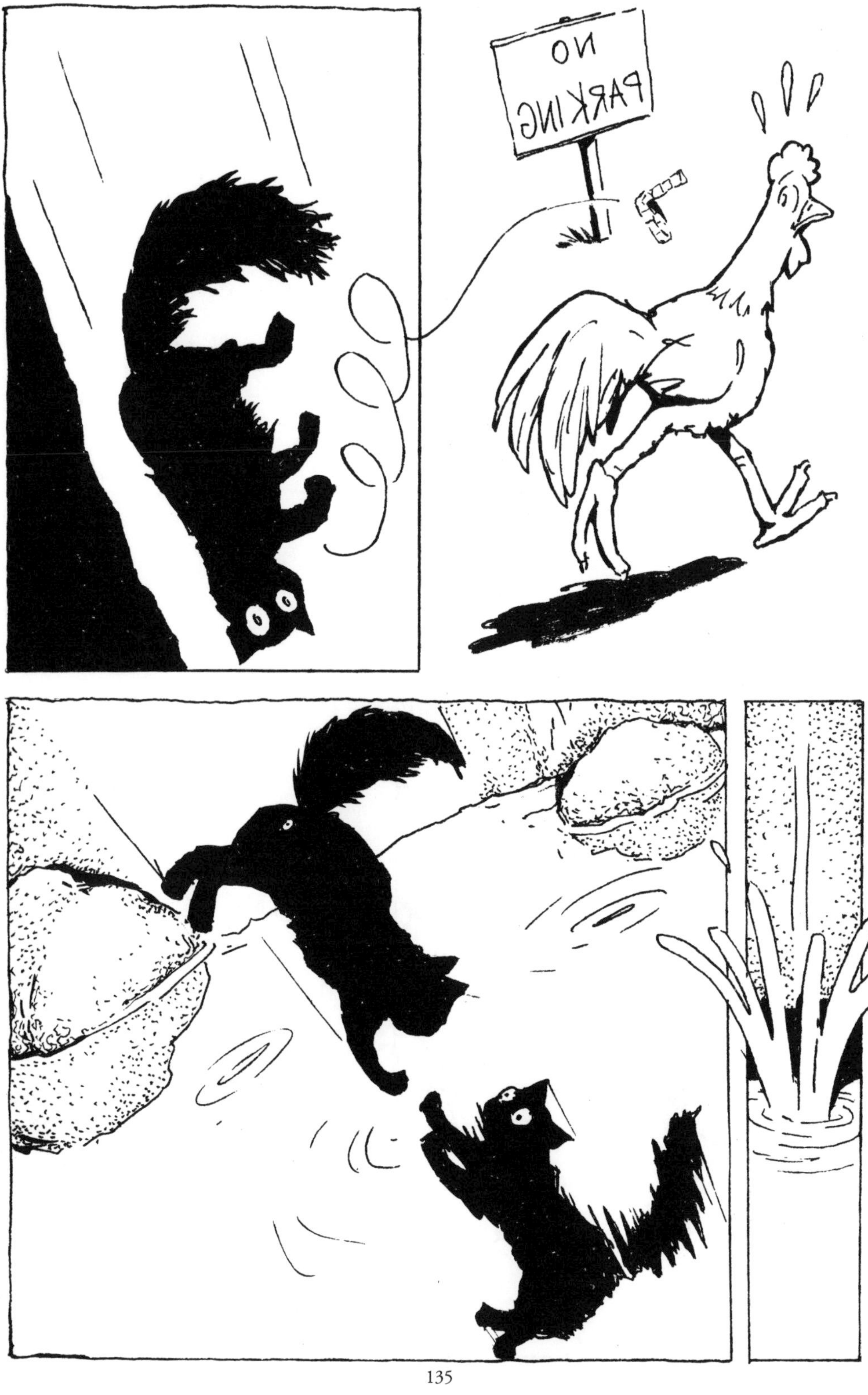
NO PARKING

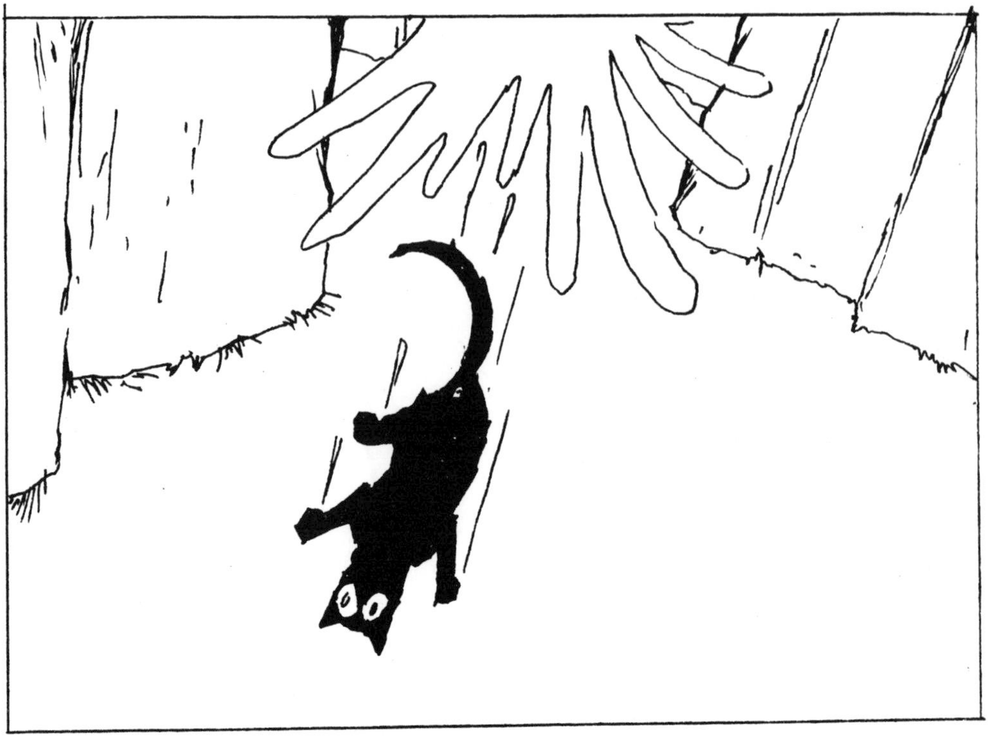

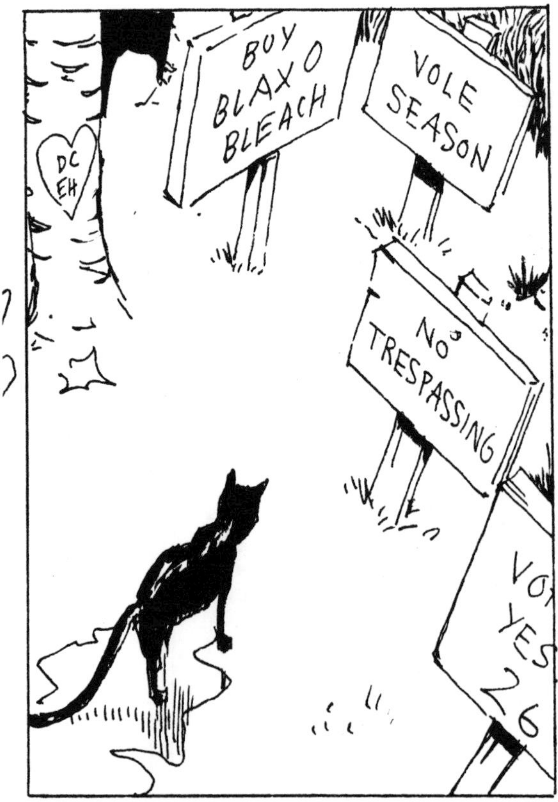
DC
EH
BUY
BLAXO
BLEACH
VOLE
SEASON
NO
TRESPASSING
VO
YES
26

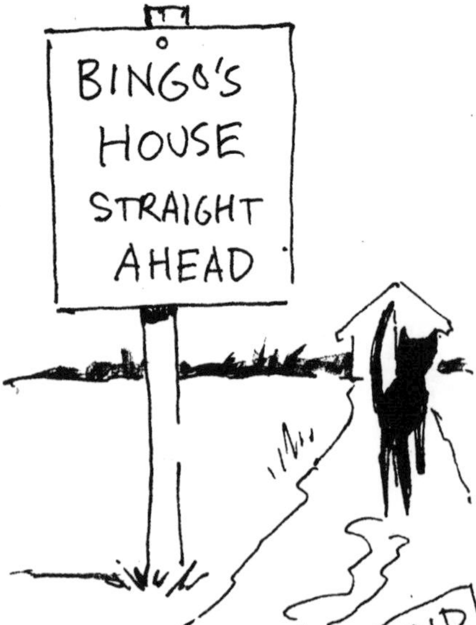
BINGO'S
HOUSE
STRAIGHT
AHEAD
END

FROM AN INFINITE DISTANCE

NOTES ON "FROM AN INFINITE DISTANCE"

Not that much to say about this one. Mostly, I was trying to see how fast I could possibly get to twenty-four pages. To do so, I did this session entirely alone in my studio (when I invite others over, I feel compelled to stay awake to keep the slower participants company), used the simple vertical oblique drawing method rather than perspective, and worked insanely small—four by six inches. As a result, I was able to finish work in seventeen hours rather than the usual twenty-four, and actually get to sleep before dawn.

The story itself is almost completely random, once again directed by scraps of reference pulled from a sack (rampaging cow, library, etc.). I was later able to use a reworked version of the opening explanation of vertical oblique in the chapter on parallel drawing methods in my book *Extreme Perspective!* The reference to Al Gore definitely dates this one. We were still mired in the Bush presidency, and pining for Hope and Change. Remarkable what four years with a Democratic president has done to solve global warming, isn't it?

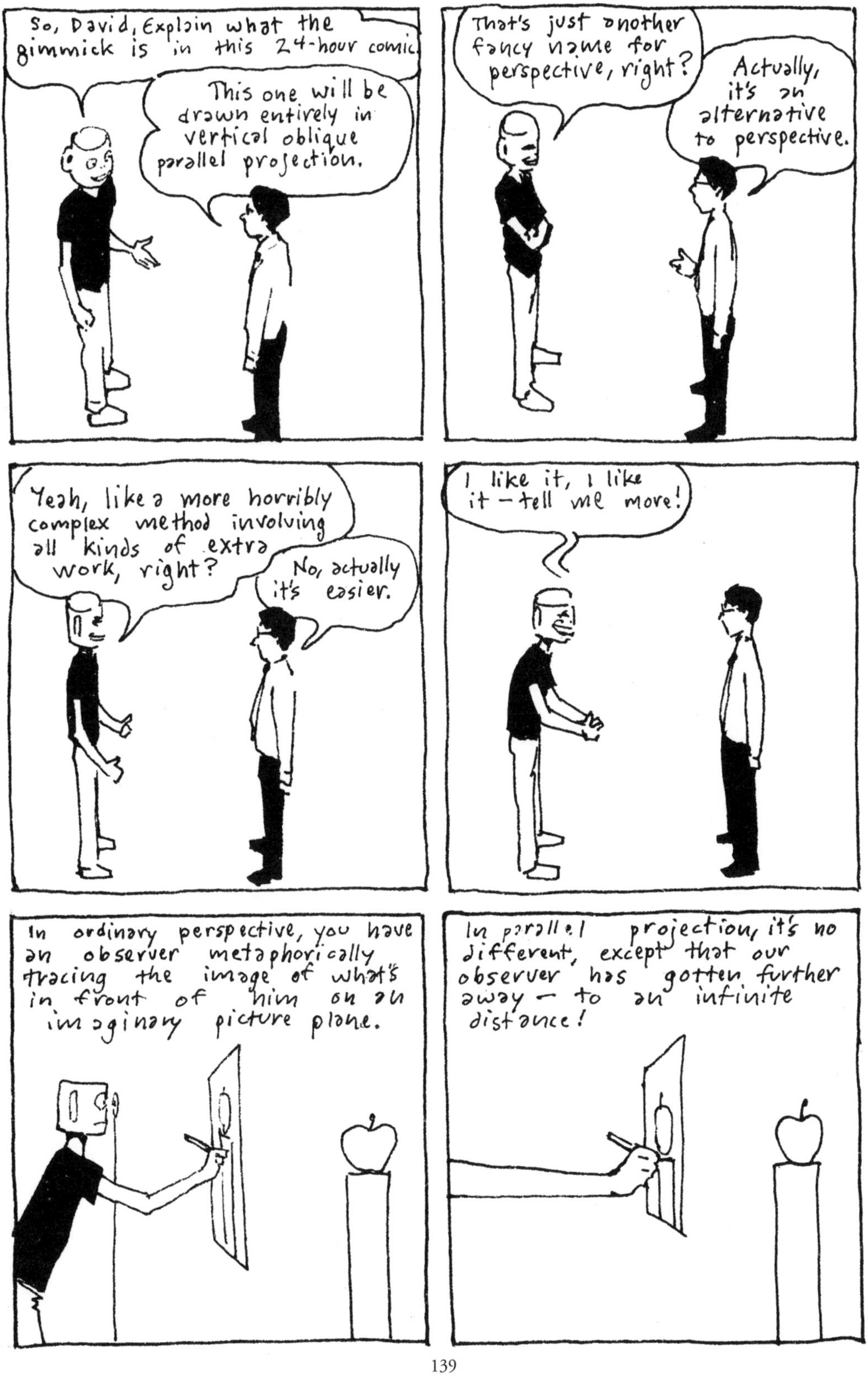
So, David, Explain what the gimmick is in this 24-hour comic.
This one will be drawn entirely in vertical oblique parallel projection.
That's just another fancy name for perspective, right?
Actually, it's an alternative to perspective.
Yeah, like a more horribly complex method involving all kinds of extra work, right?
No, actually it's easier.
I like it, I like it - tell me more!
In ordinary perspective, you have an observer metaphorically tracing the image of what's in front of him on an imaginary picture plane.
In parallel projection, it's no different, except that our observer has gotten further away - to an infinite distance!

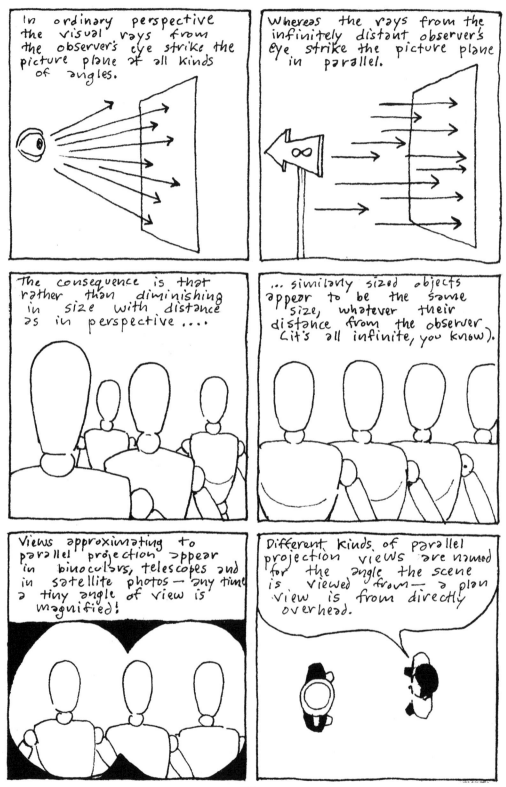

In ordinary perspective the visual rays from the observer's eye strike the picture plane at all kinds of angles.

Whereas the rays from the infinitely distant observer's eye strike the picture plane in parallel.

The consequence is that rather than diminishing in size with distance as in perspective....

.. similarly sized objects appear to be the same size, whatever their distance from the observer (it's all infinite, you know).

Views approximating to parallel projection appear in binoculars, telescopes and in satellite photos — any time a tiny angle of view is magnified!

Different kinds of parallel projection views are named for the angle the scene is viewed from — a plan view is from directly overhead.

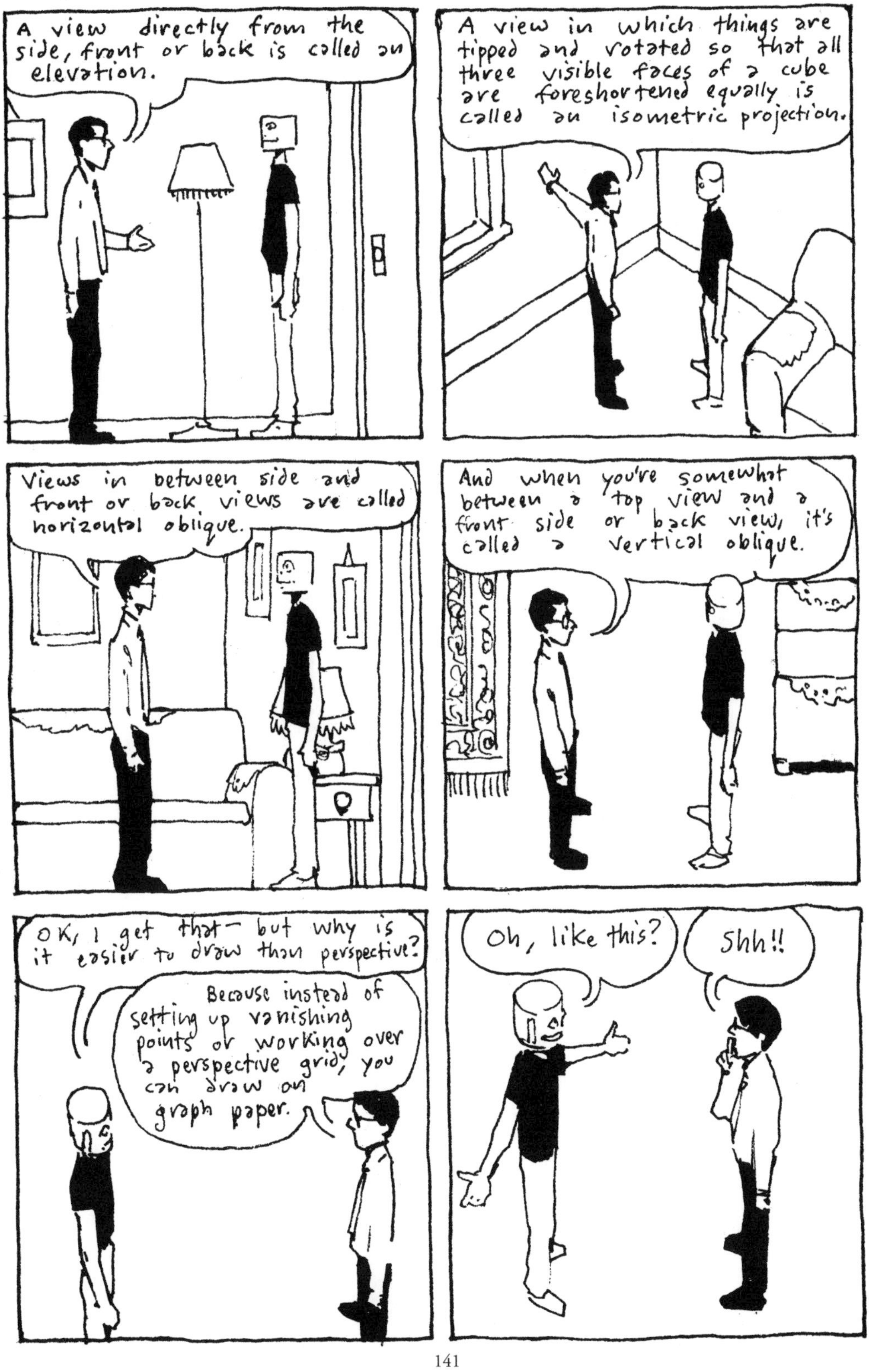
A view directly from the side, front or back is called an elevation.
A view in which things are tipped and rotated so that all three visible faces of a cube are foreshortened equally is called an isometric projection.
Views in between side and front or back views are called horizontal oblique.
And when you're somewhat between a top view and a front side or back view, it's called a vertical oblique.
OK, I get that— but why is it easier to draw than perspective?
Because instead of setting up vanishing points or working over a perspective grid, you can draw on graph paper.
Oh, like this?
Shh!!

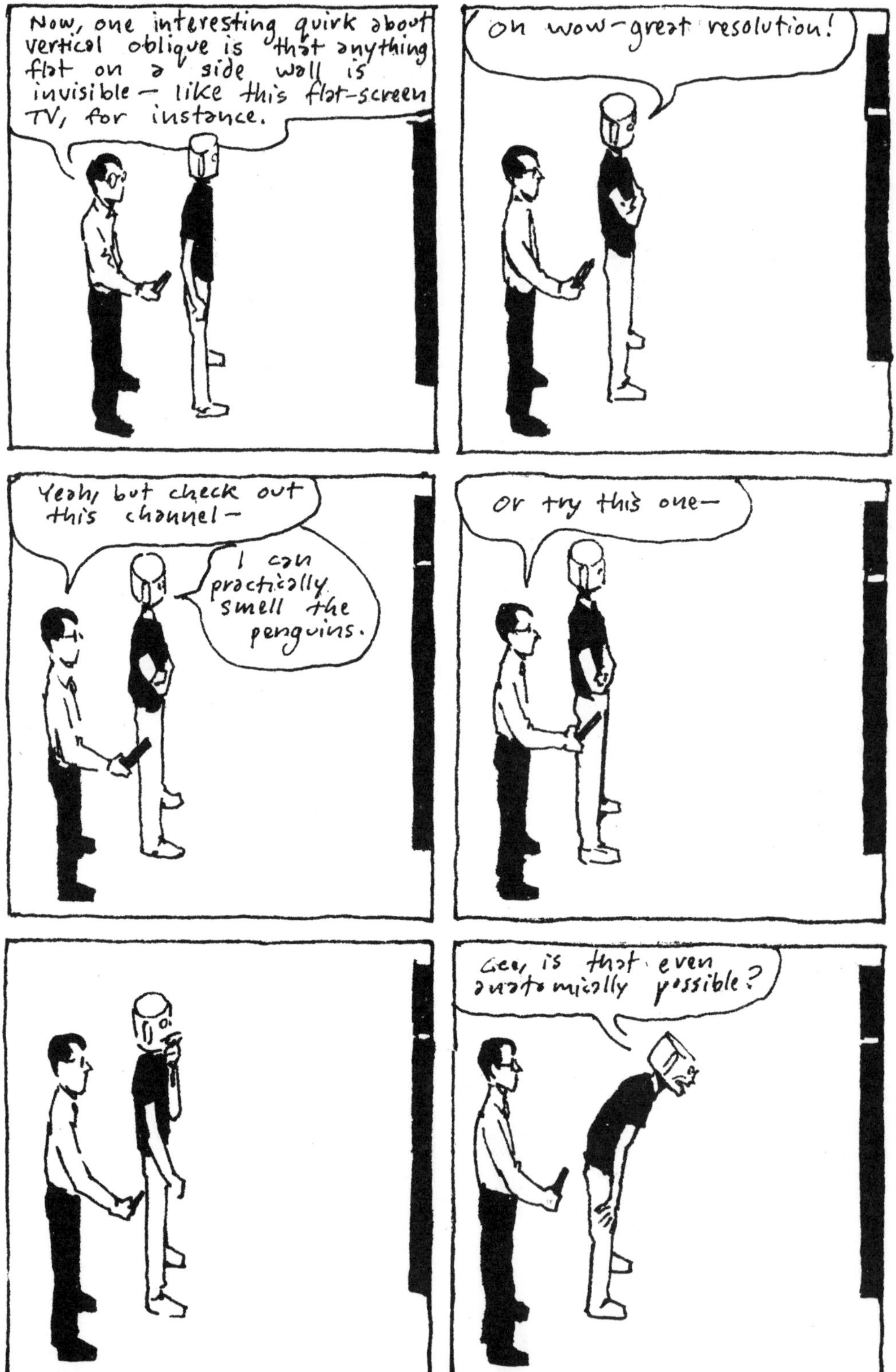
Now, one interesting quirk about vertical oblique is that anything flat on a side wall is invisible — like this flat-screen TV, for instance.
Oh wow — great resolution!
Yeah, but check out this channel —
I can practically smell the penguins.
Or try this one —
Gee, is that even anatomically possible?

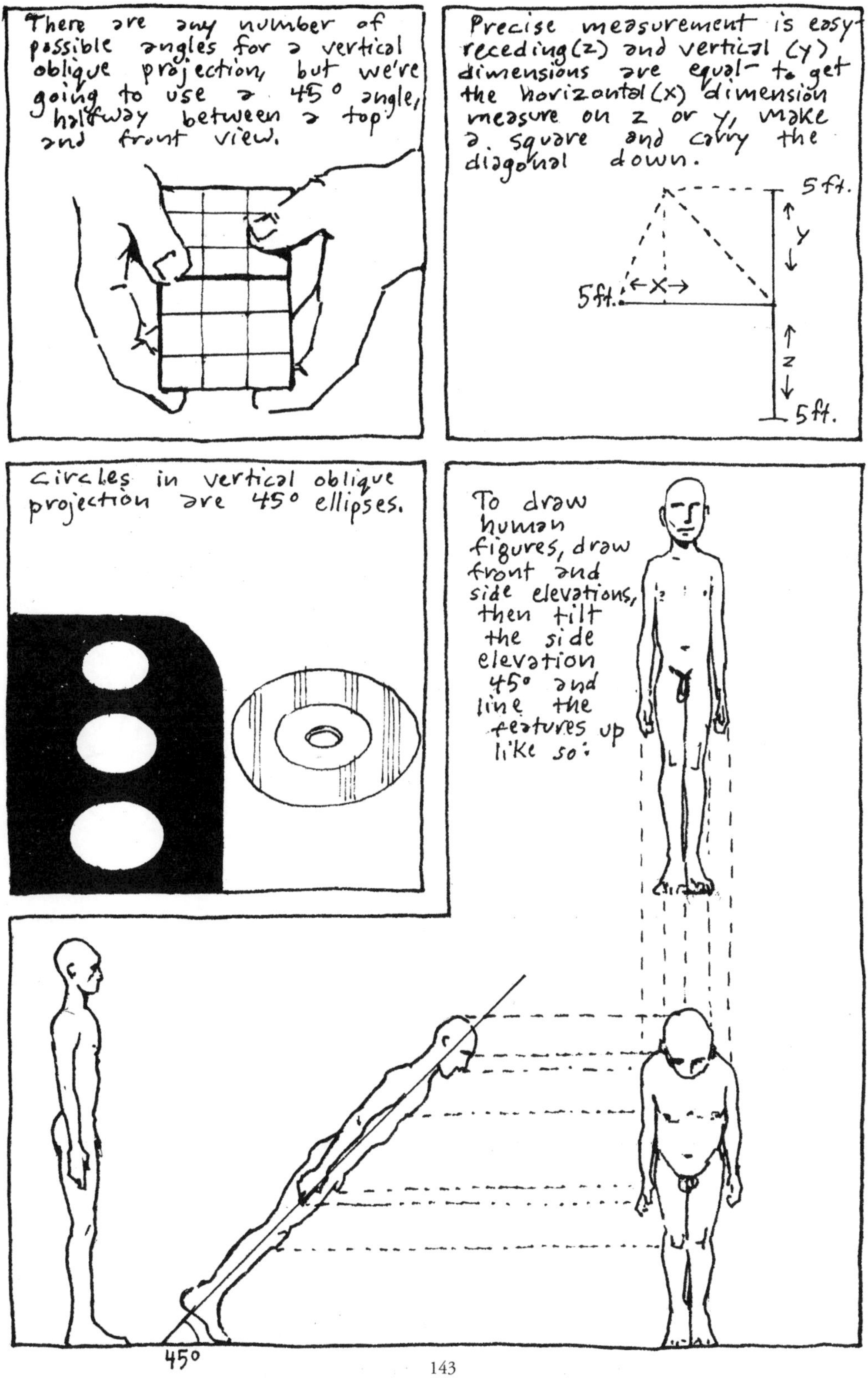
There are any number of possible angles for a vertical oblique projection, but we're going to use a 45° angle, halfway between a top and front view.
Precise measurement is easy- receding(z) and vertical (y) dimensions are equal- to get the horizontal(x) dimension measure on z or y, make a square and carry the diagonal down.
5ft.
y
5ft.
←x→
z
5ft.
Circles in vertical oblique projection are 45° ellipses.
To draw human figures, draw front and side elevations, then tilt the side elevation 45° and line the features up like so:
45°

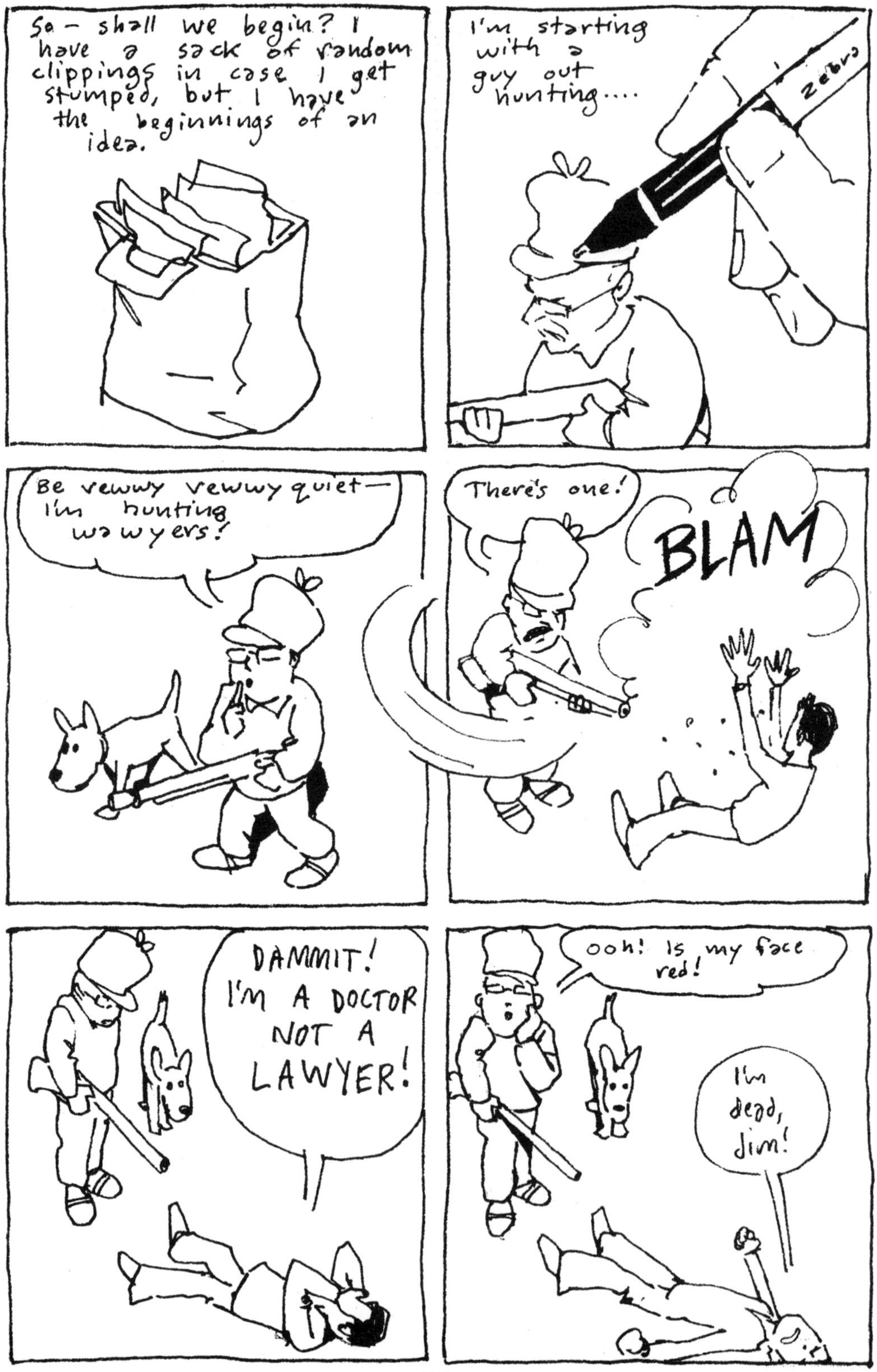
So - shall we begin? I have a sack of random clippings in case I get stumped, but I have the beginnings of an idea.
I'm starting with a guy out hunting....
zebra
Be vewwy vewwy quiet— I'm hunting wawyers!
There's one!
BLAM
DAMMIT! I'M A DOCTOR NOT A LAWYER!
ooh! Is my face red!
I'm dead, Jim!

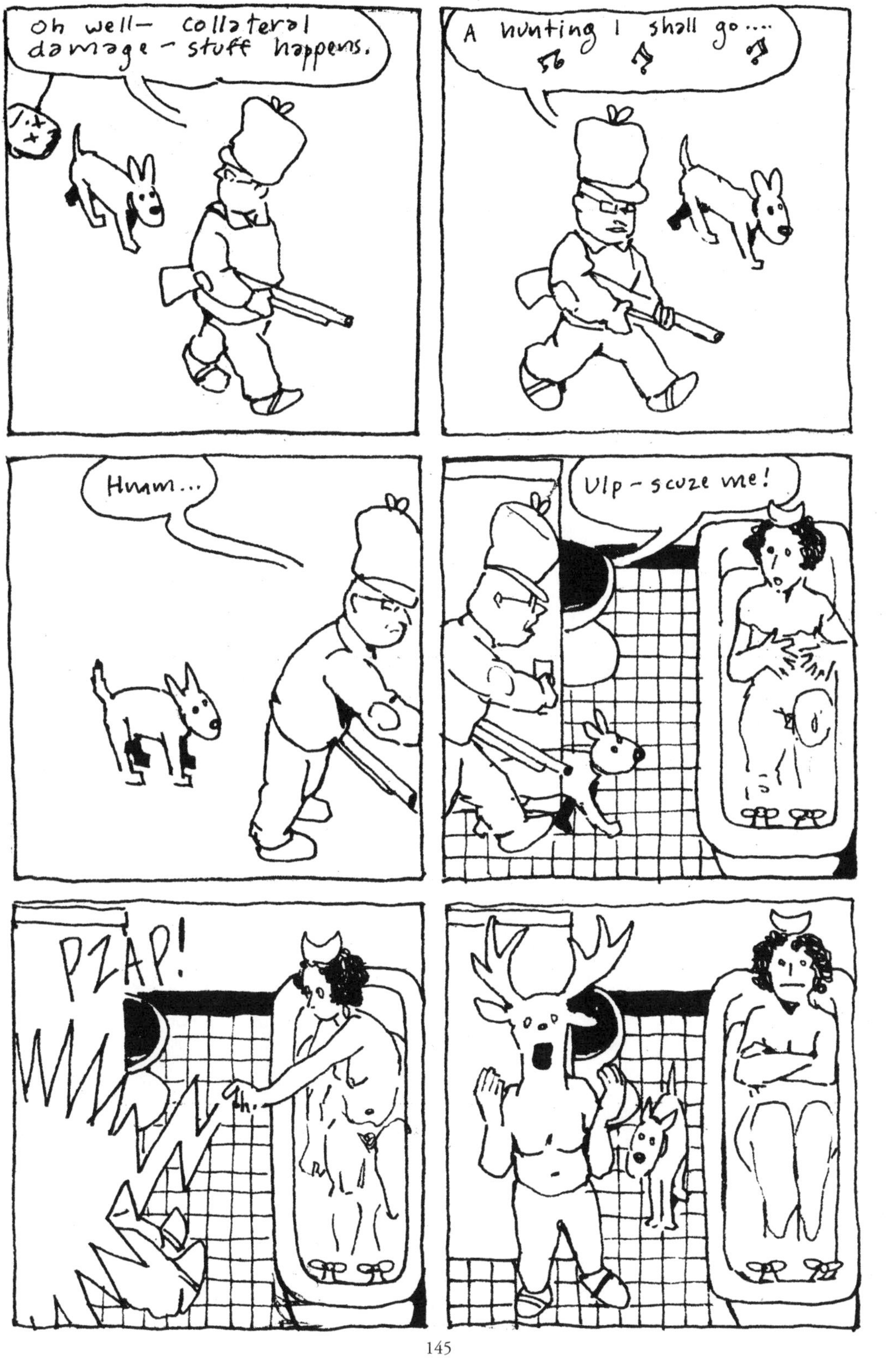
Oh well— collateral damage - stuff happens.
A hunting I shall go....
Hmm...
Ulp - scuze me!
PZAP!

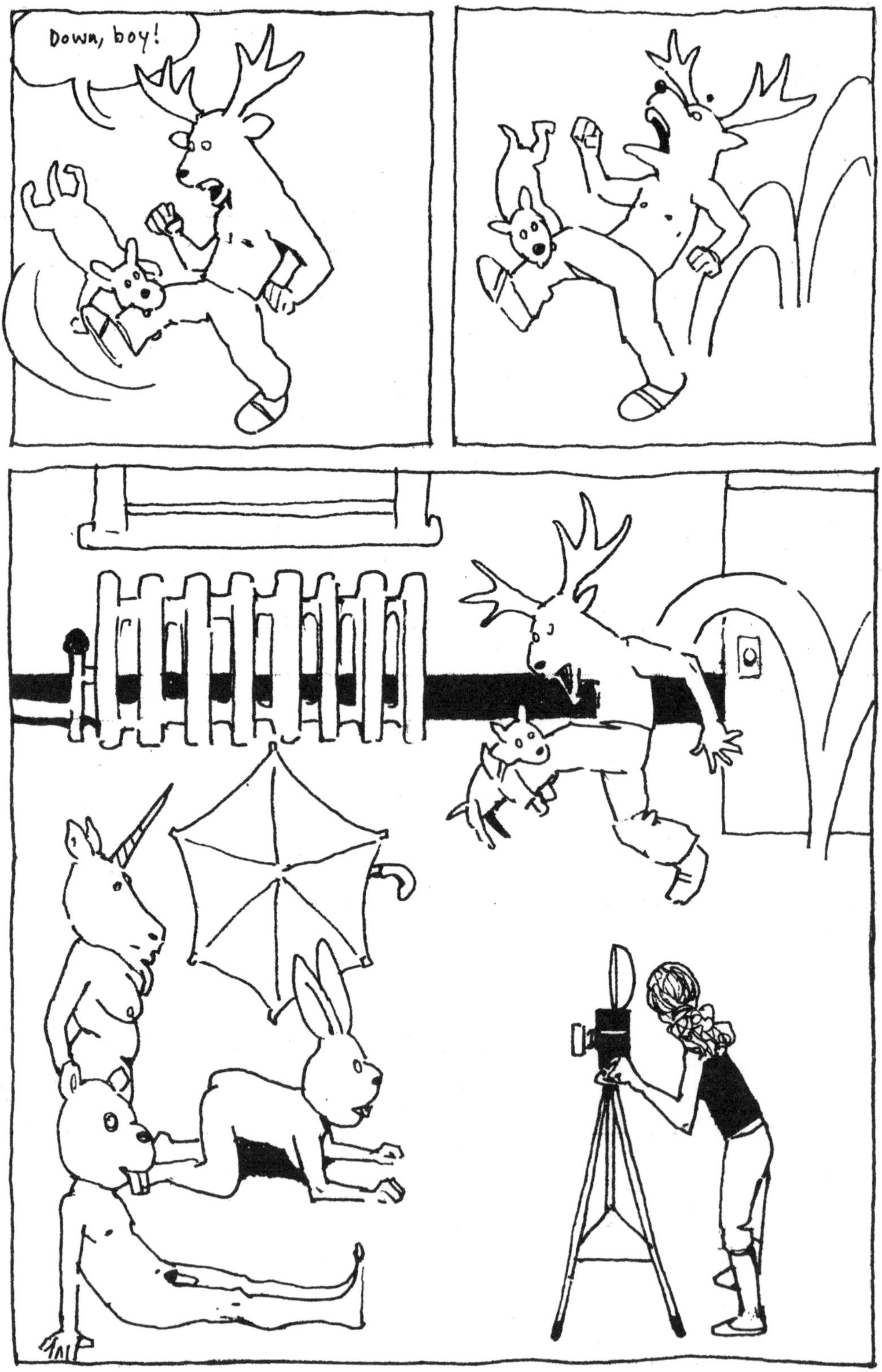
Down, boy!

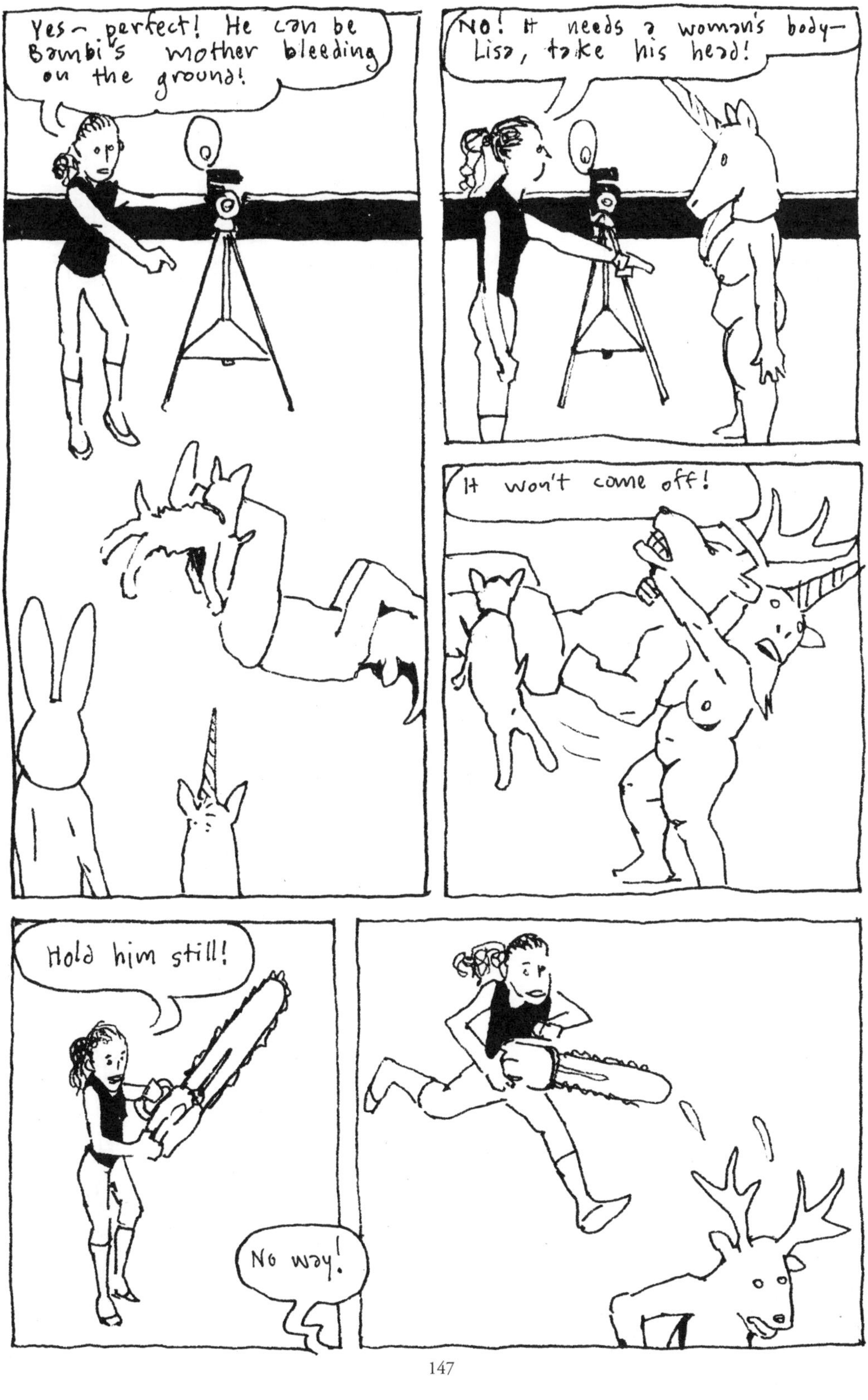
Yes- perfect! He can be Bambi's mother bleeding on the ground!
NO! It needs a woman's body- Lisa, take his head!
It won't come off!
Hold him still!
No way!

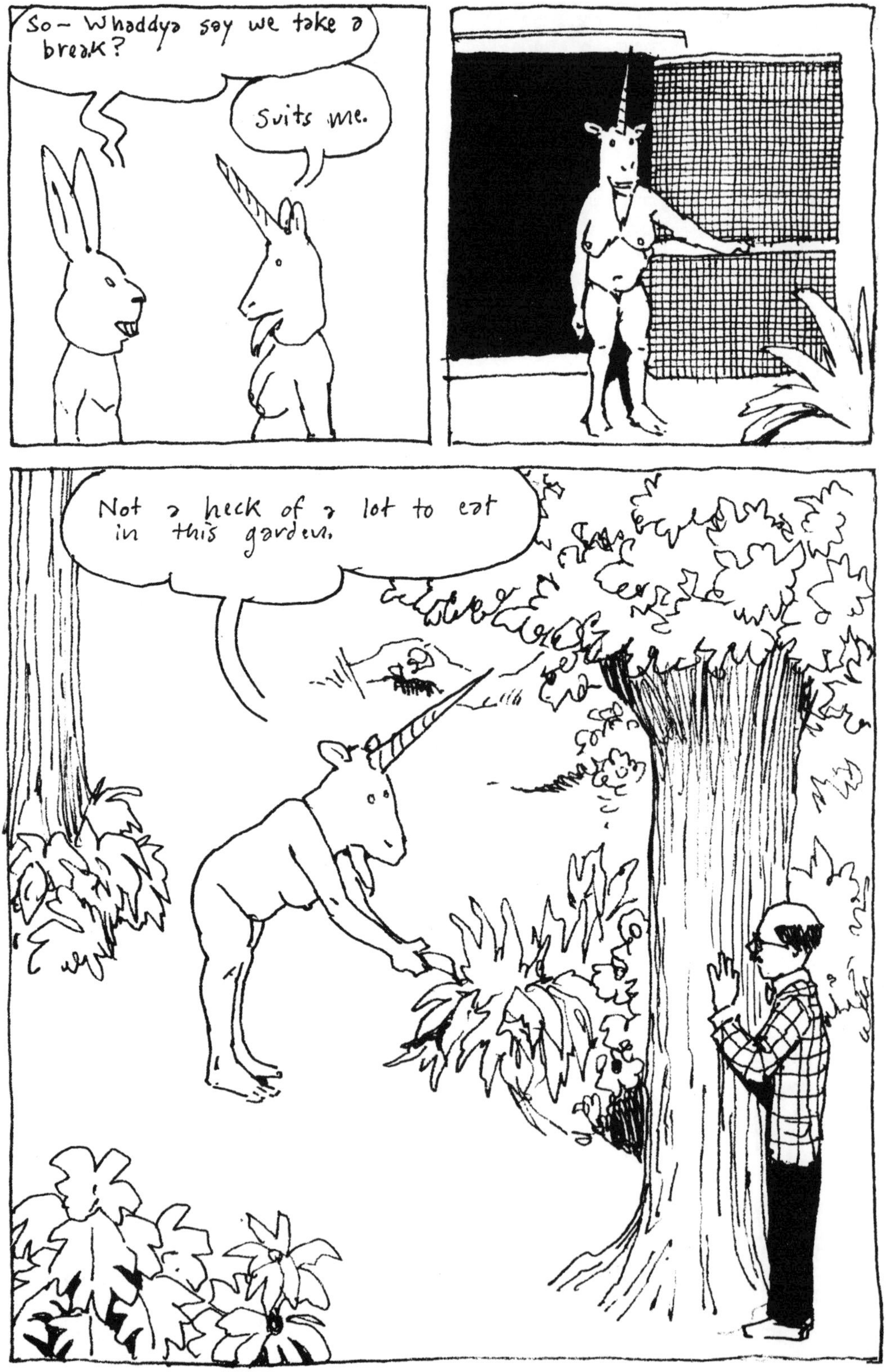
So- Whaddya say we take a break?
Suits me.
Not a heck of a lot to eat in this garden.

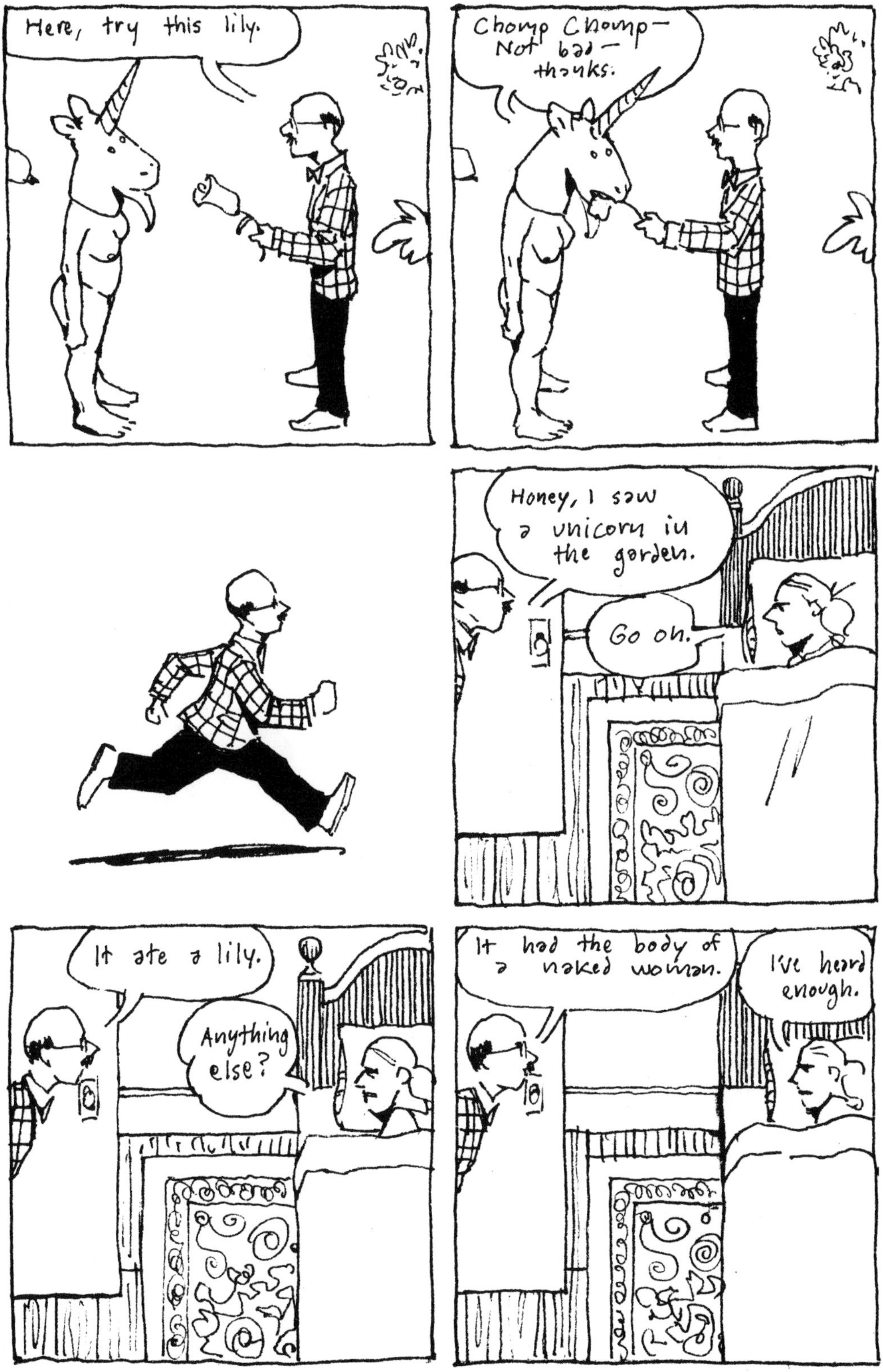
Here, try this lily.
Chomp Chomp— Not bad— thanks.
Honey, I saw a unicorn in the garden.
Go on.
It ate a lily.
Anything else?
It had the body of a naked woman.
I've heard enough.

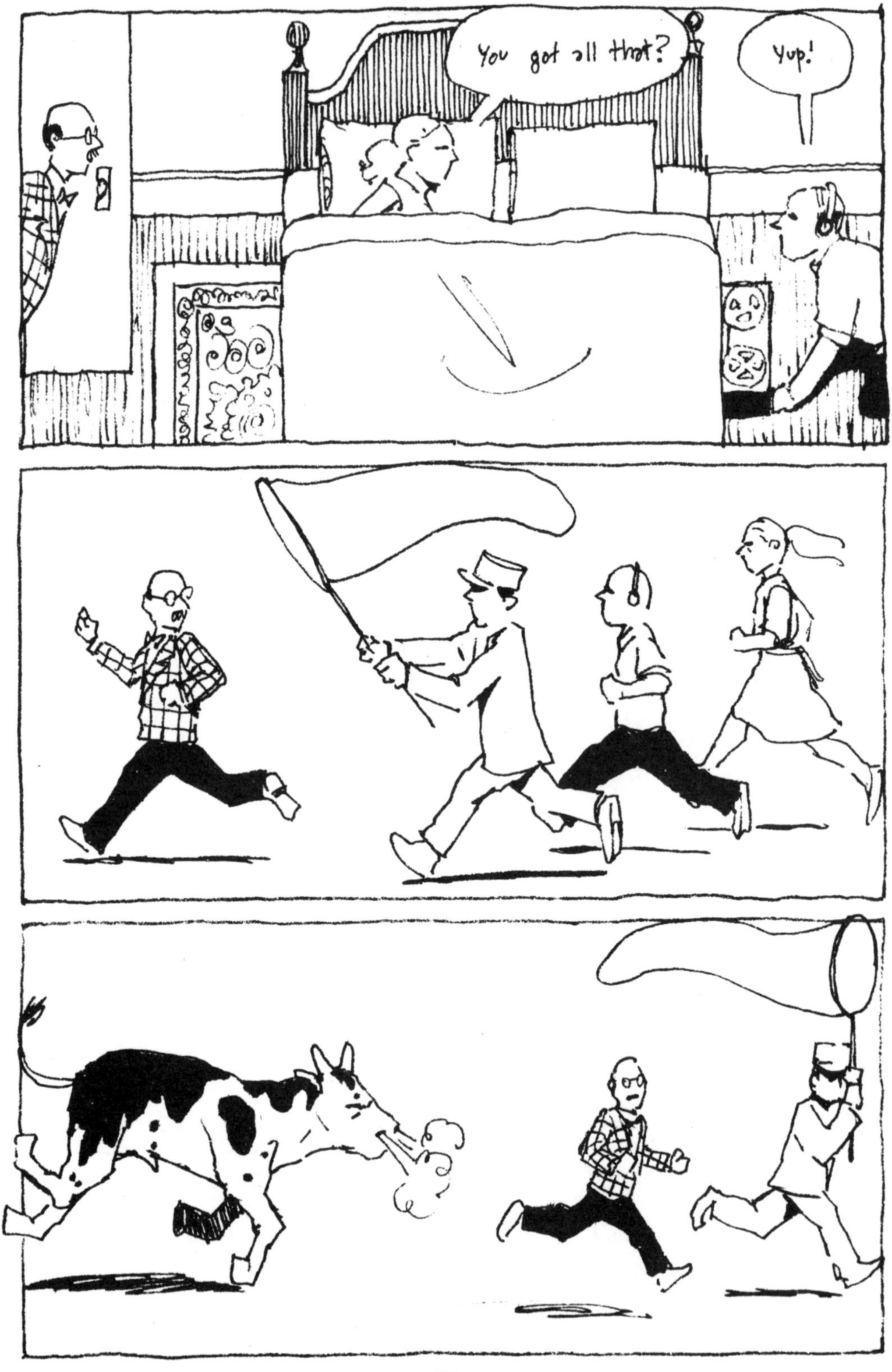
You got all that?
Yup!

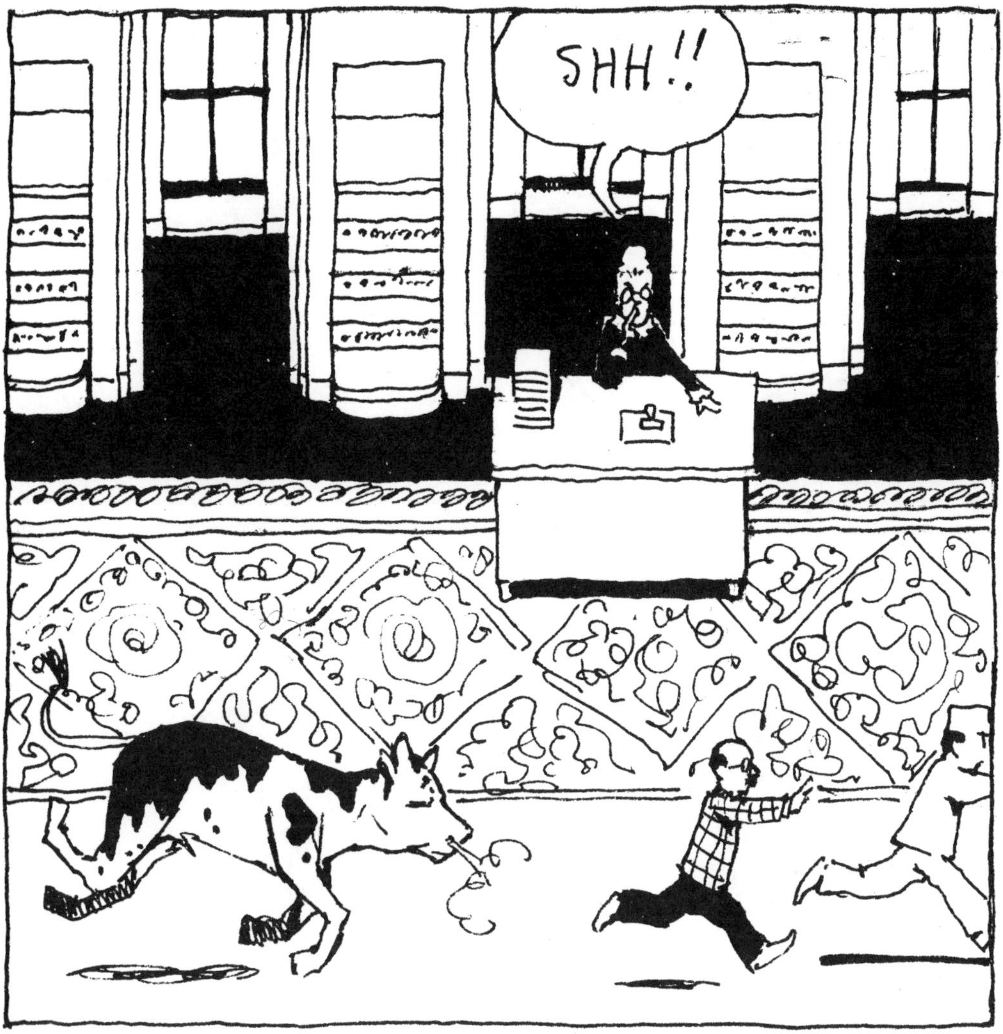
SHH!!

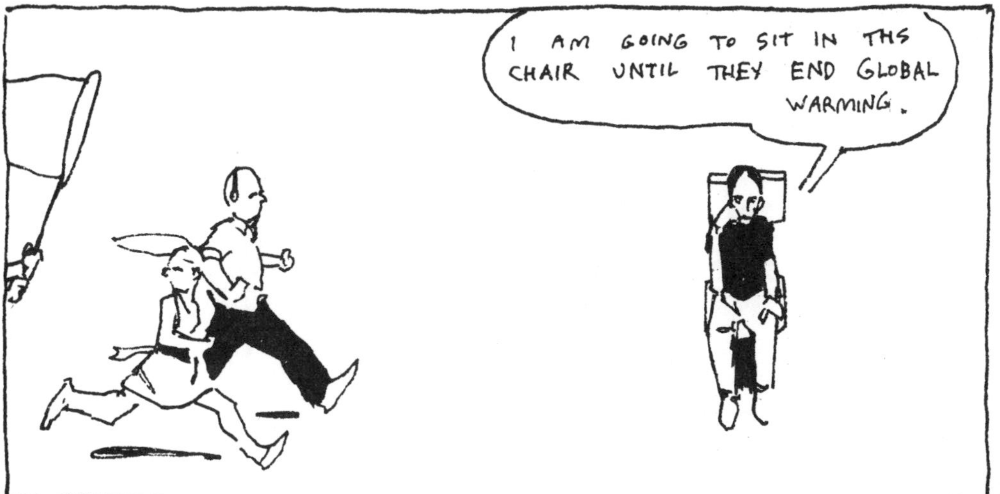
I AM GOING TO SIT IN THIS CHAIR UNTIL THEY END GLOBAL WARMING.

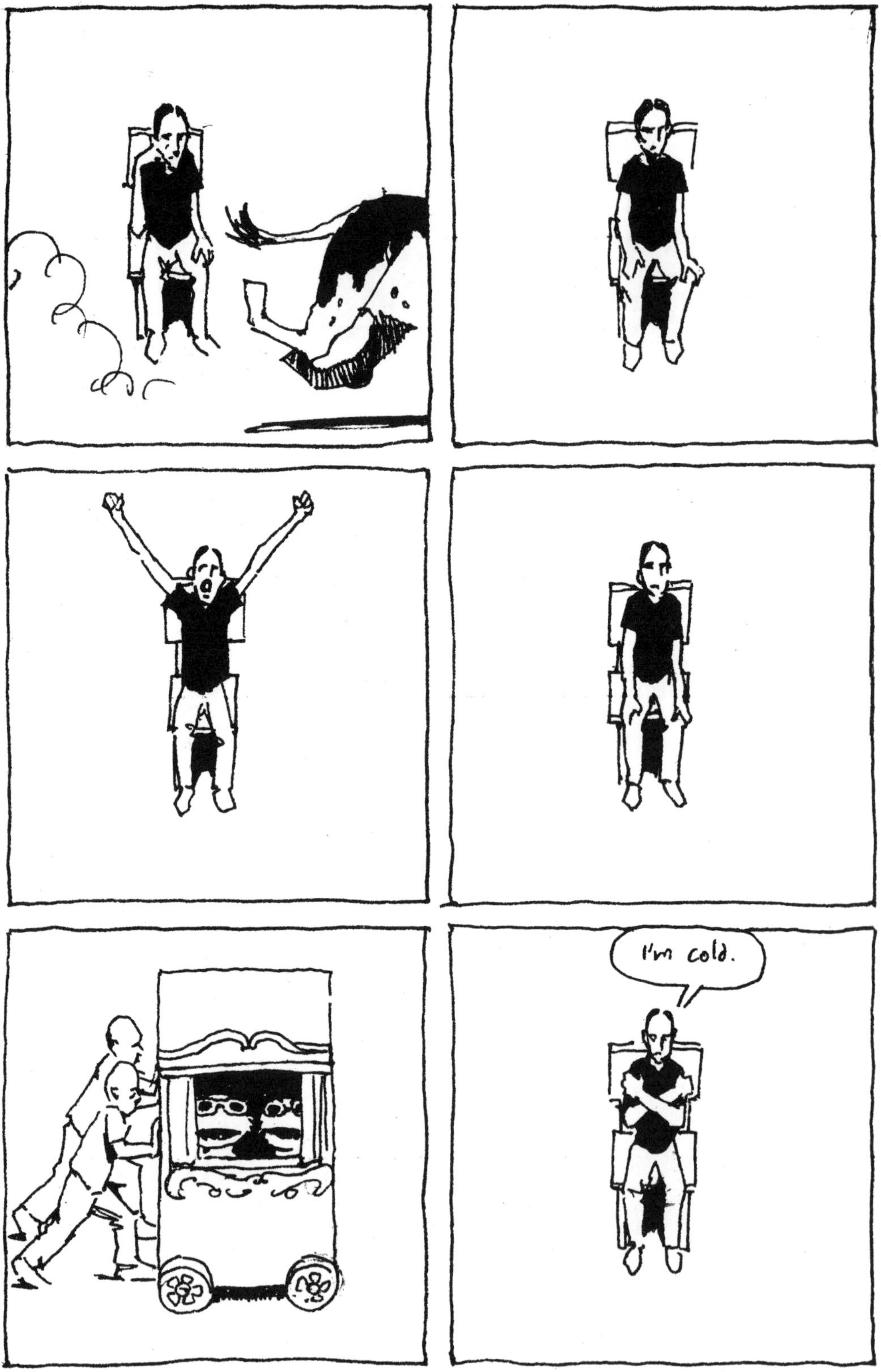
I'm cold.

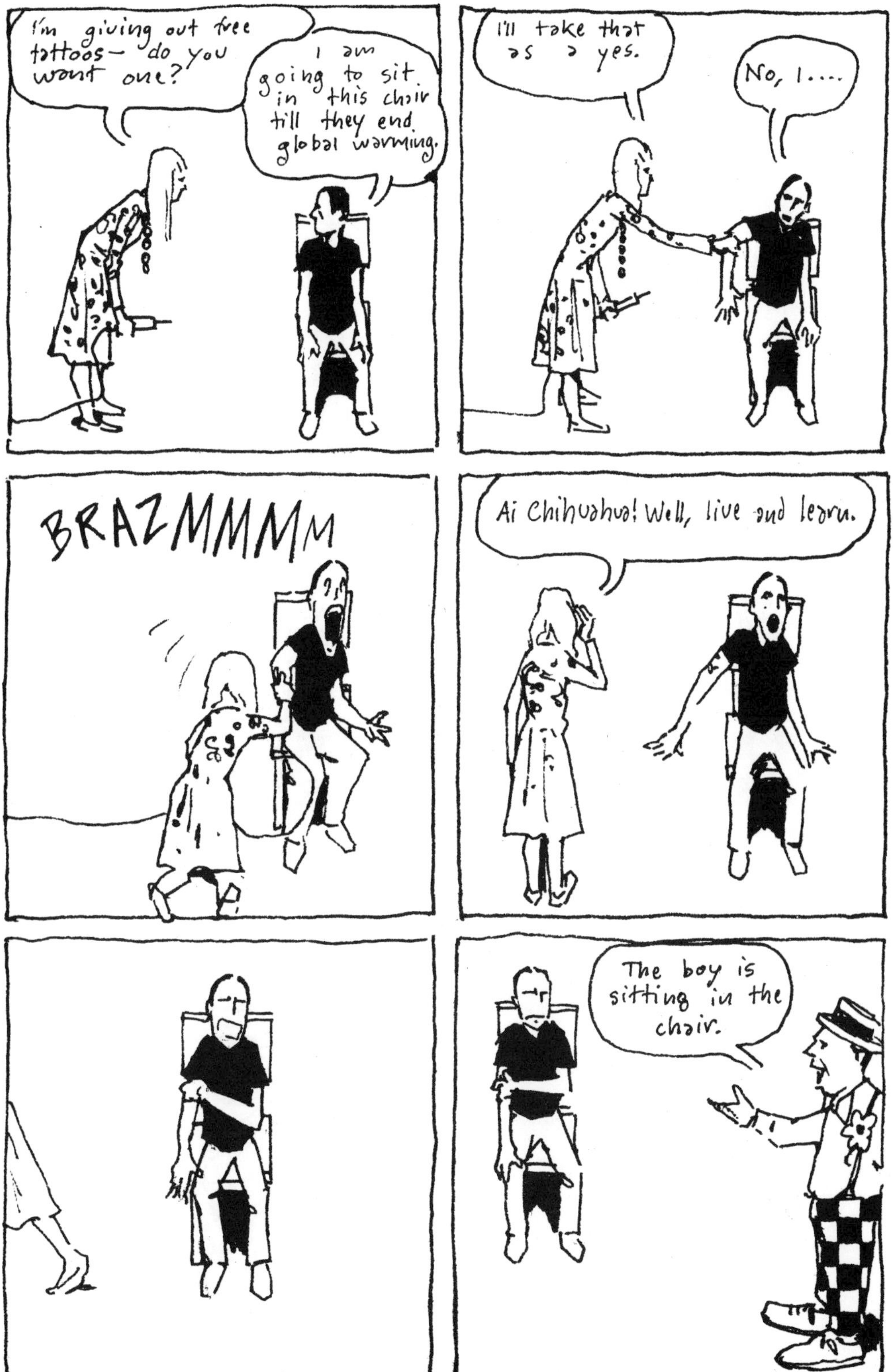
I'm giving out free tattoos— do you want one?
I am going to sit in this chair till they end global warming.
I'll take that as a yes.
No, I....
BRAZMMMM
Ai Chihuahua! Well, live and learn.
The boy is sitting in the chair.

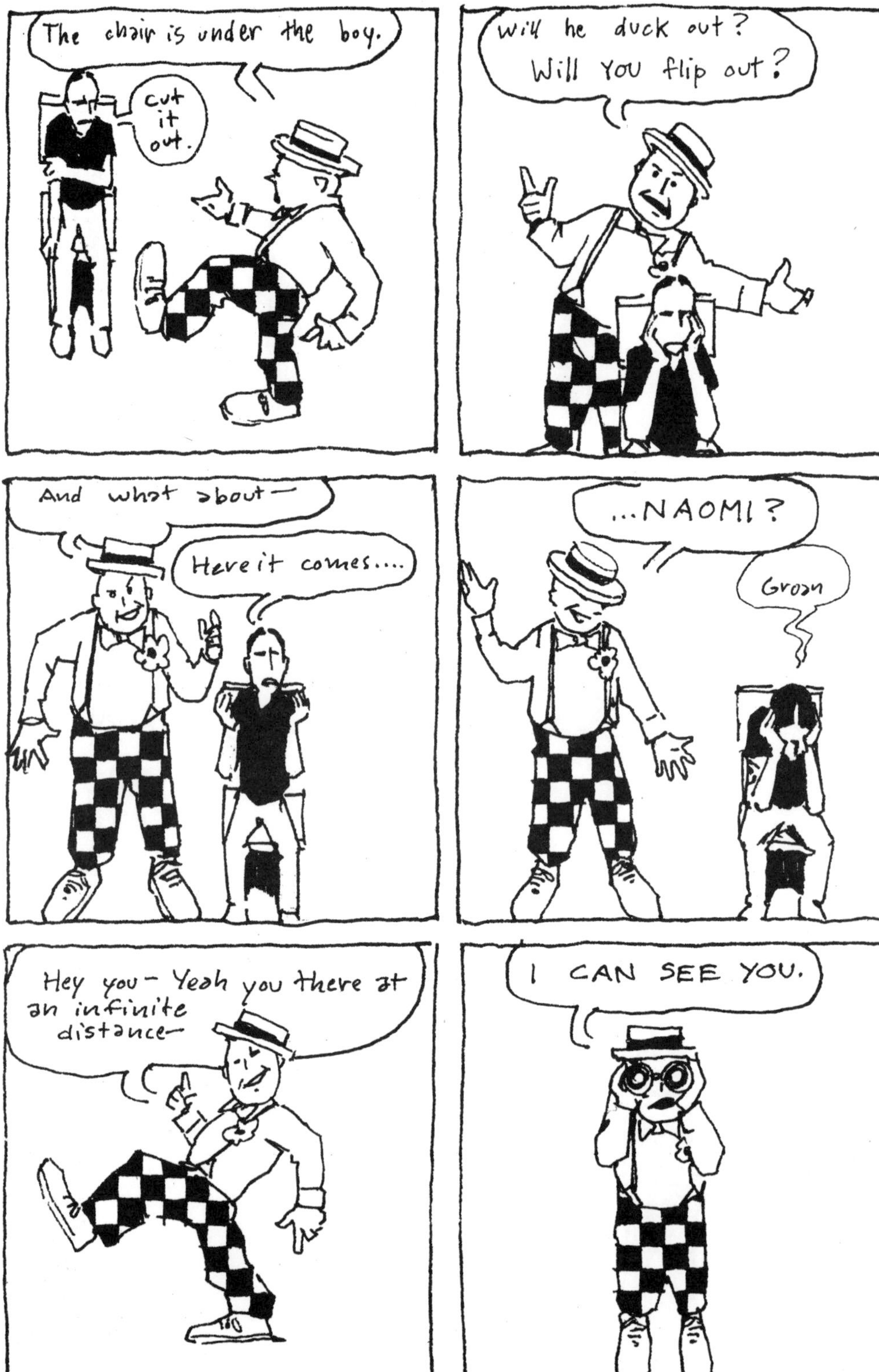
The chair is under the boy.
Cut it out.
Will he duck out? Will you flip out?
And what about—
Here it comes....
...NAOMI?
Groan
Hey you— Yeah you there at an infinite distance—
I CAN SEE YOU.

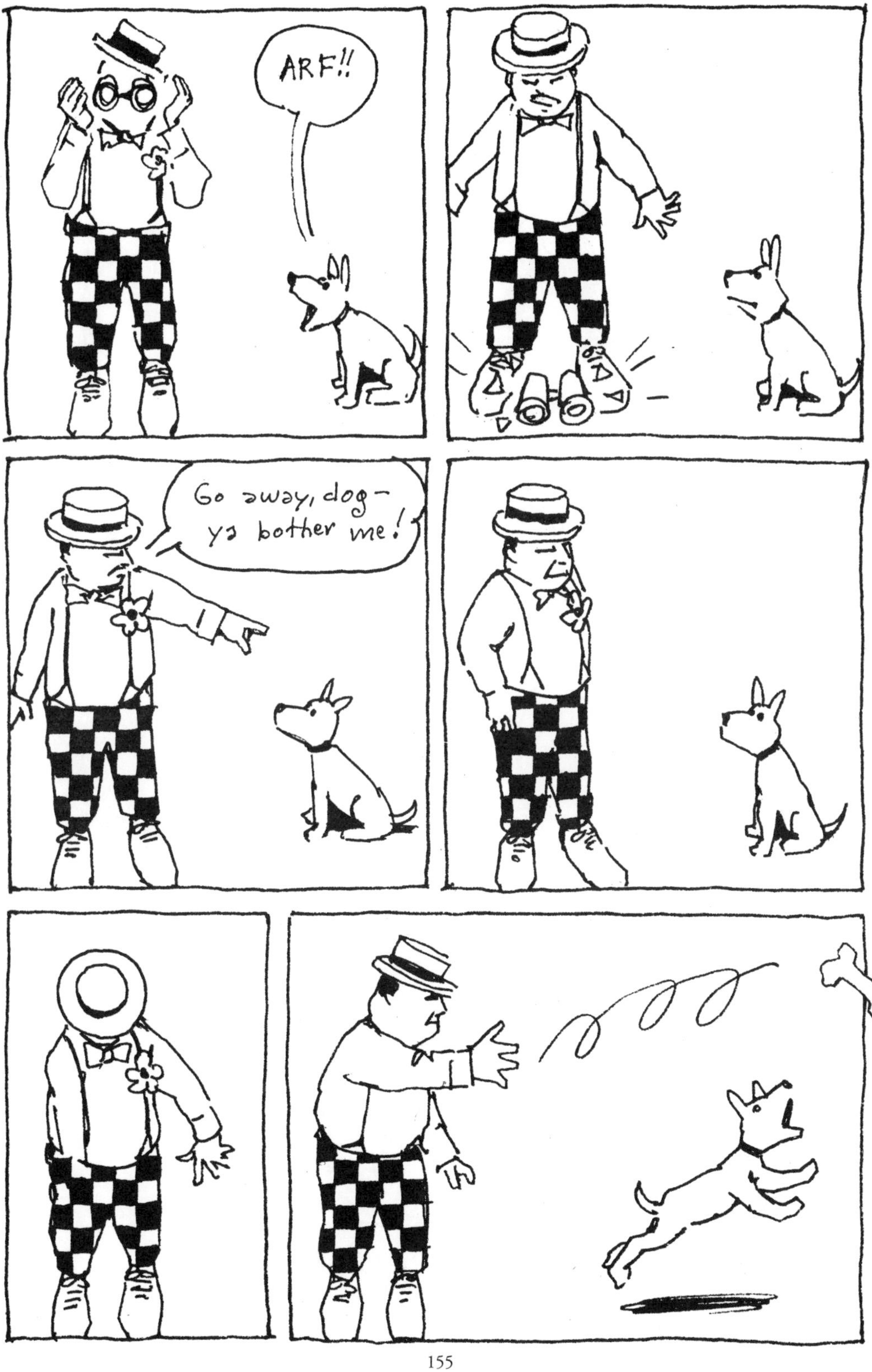
ARF!!
Go away, dog—
ya bother me!

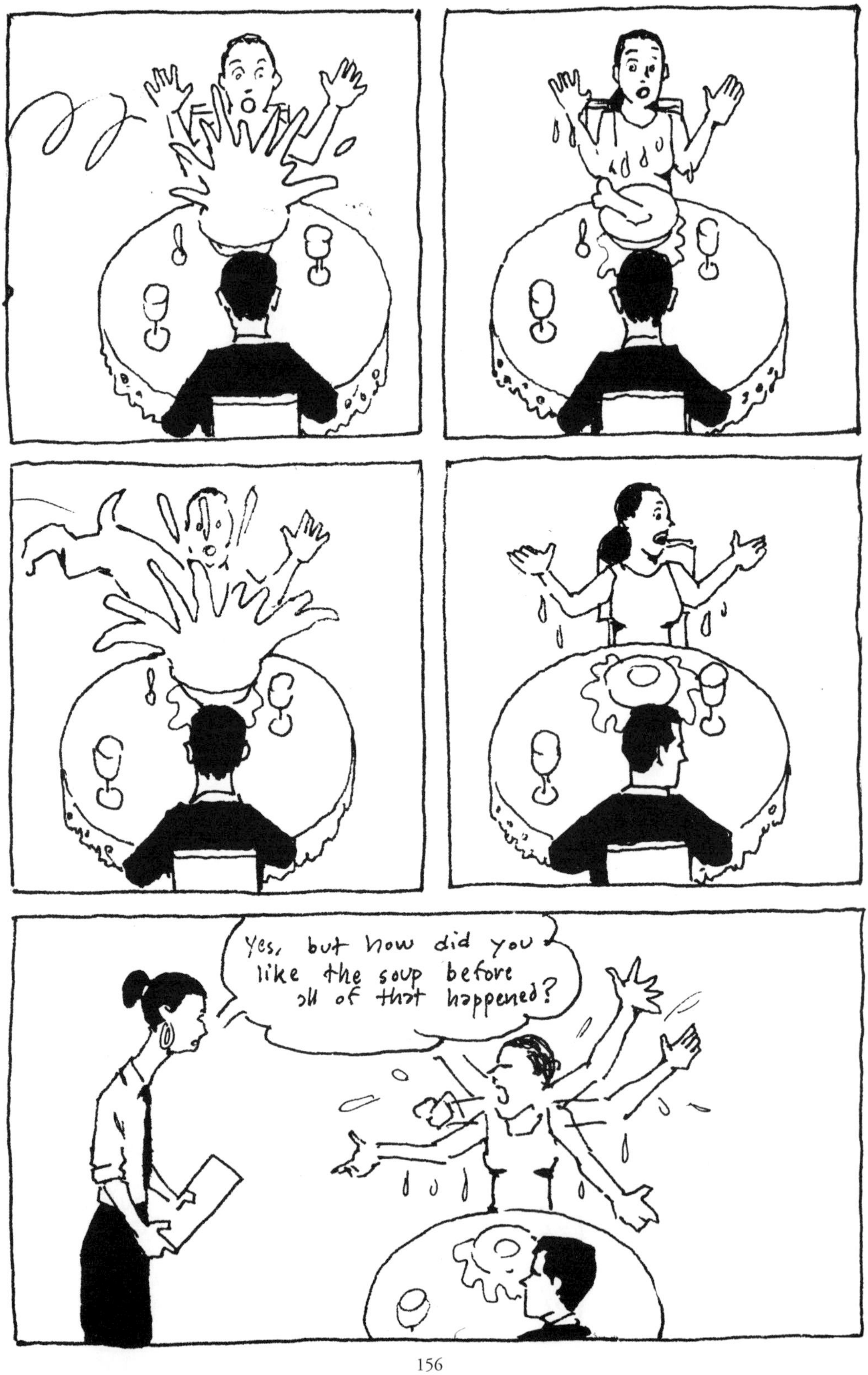
Yes, but how did you like the soup before all of that happened?

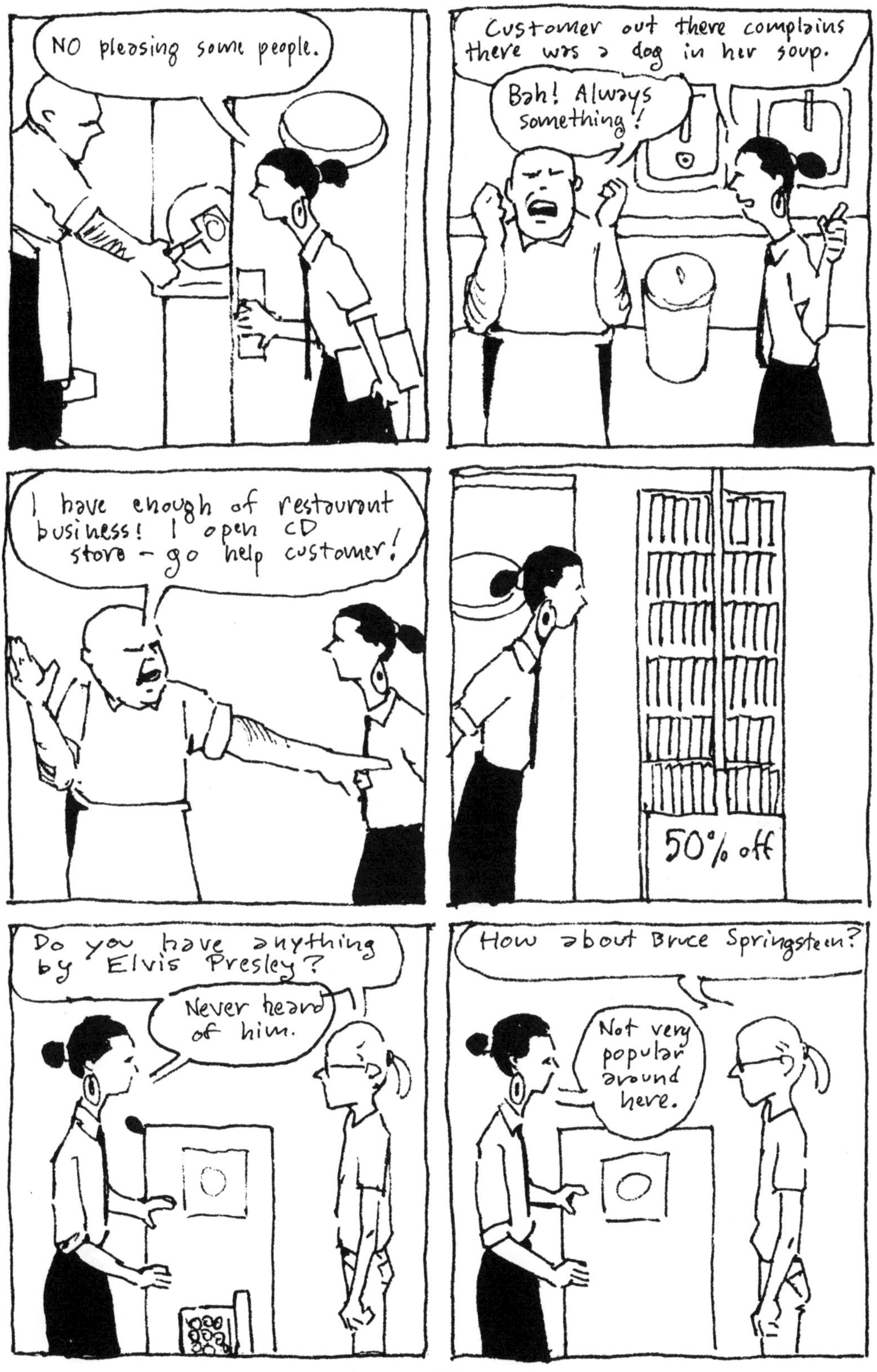
NO pleasing some people.
Customer out there complains there was a dog in her soup.
Bah! Always something!
I have enough of restaurant business! I open CD store - go help customer!
50% off
Do you have anything by Elvis Presley?
Never heard of him.
How about Bruce Springsteen?
Not very popular around here.

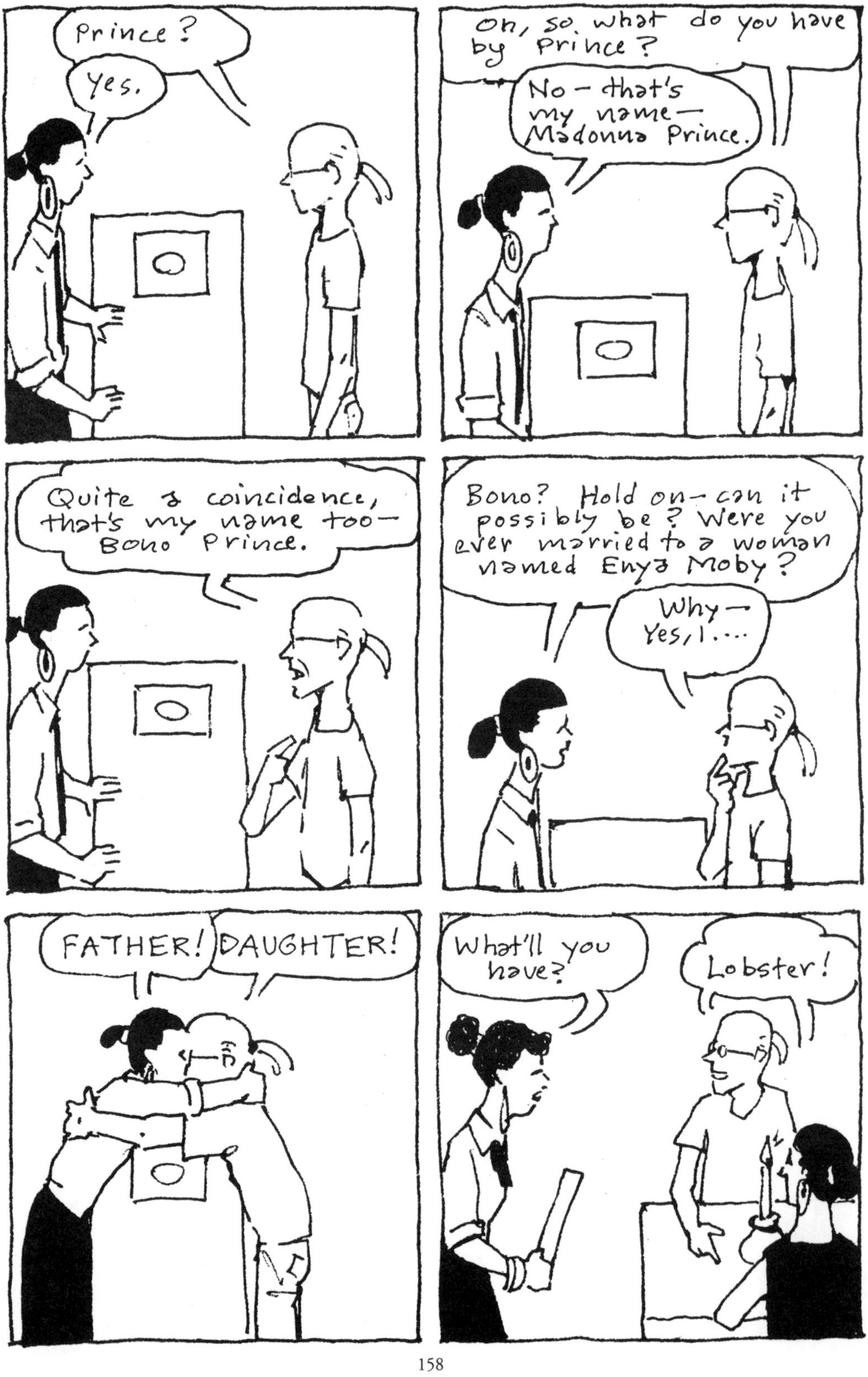
Prince?
Yes.
Oh, so what do you have by Prince?
No—that's my name—Madonna Prince.
Quite a coincidence, that's my name too—Bono Prince.
Bono? Hold on—can it possibly be? Were you ever married to a woman named Enya Moby?
Why—Yes, I...
FATHER!
DAUGHTER!
What'll you have?
Lobster!

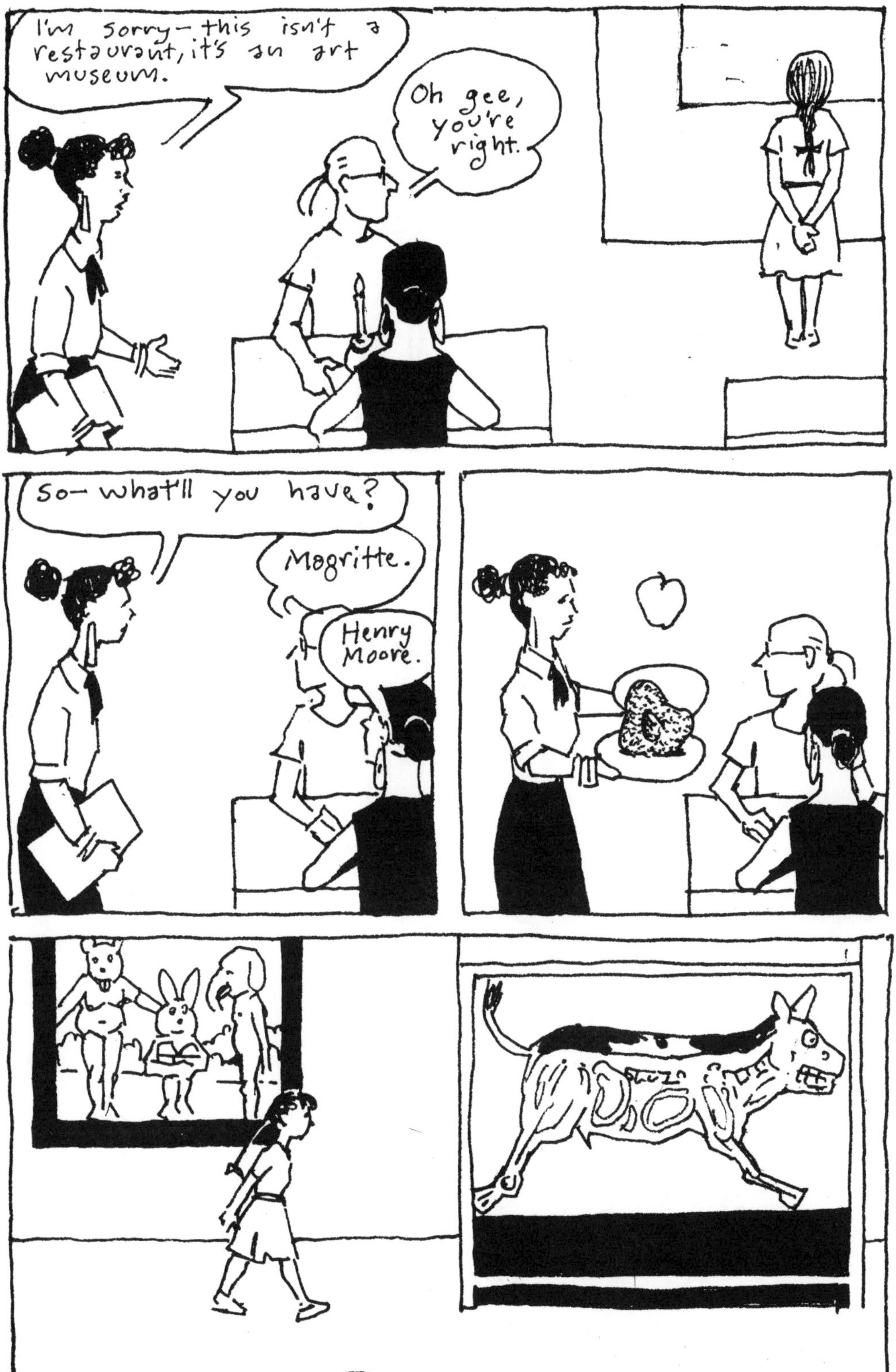
I'm sorry—this isn't a restaurant, it's an art museum.
Oh gee, you're right.
So—what'll you have?
Magritte.
Henry Moore.

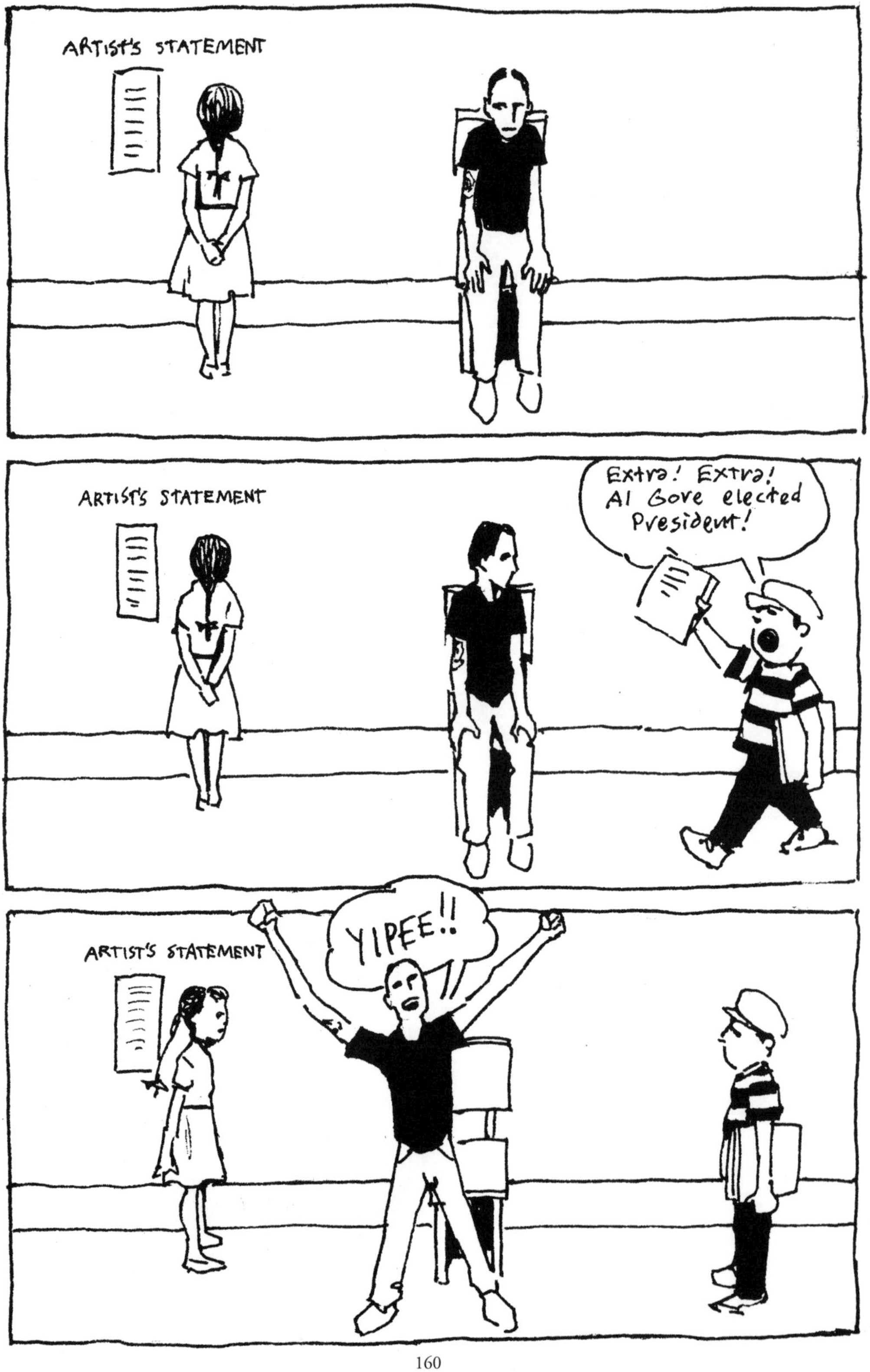
ARTIST'S STATEMENT
ARTIST'S STATEMENT
Extra! Extra! Al Gore elected President!
ARTIST'S STATEMENT
YIPEE!!

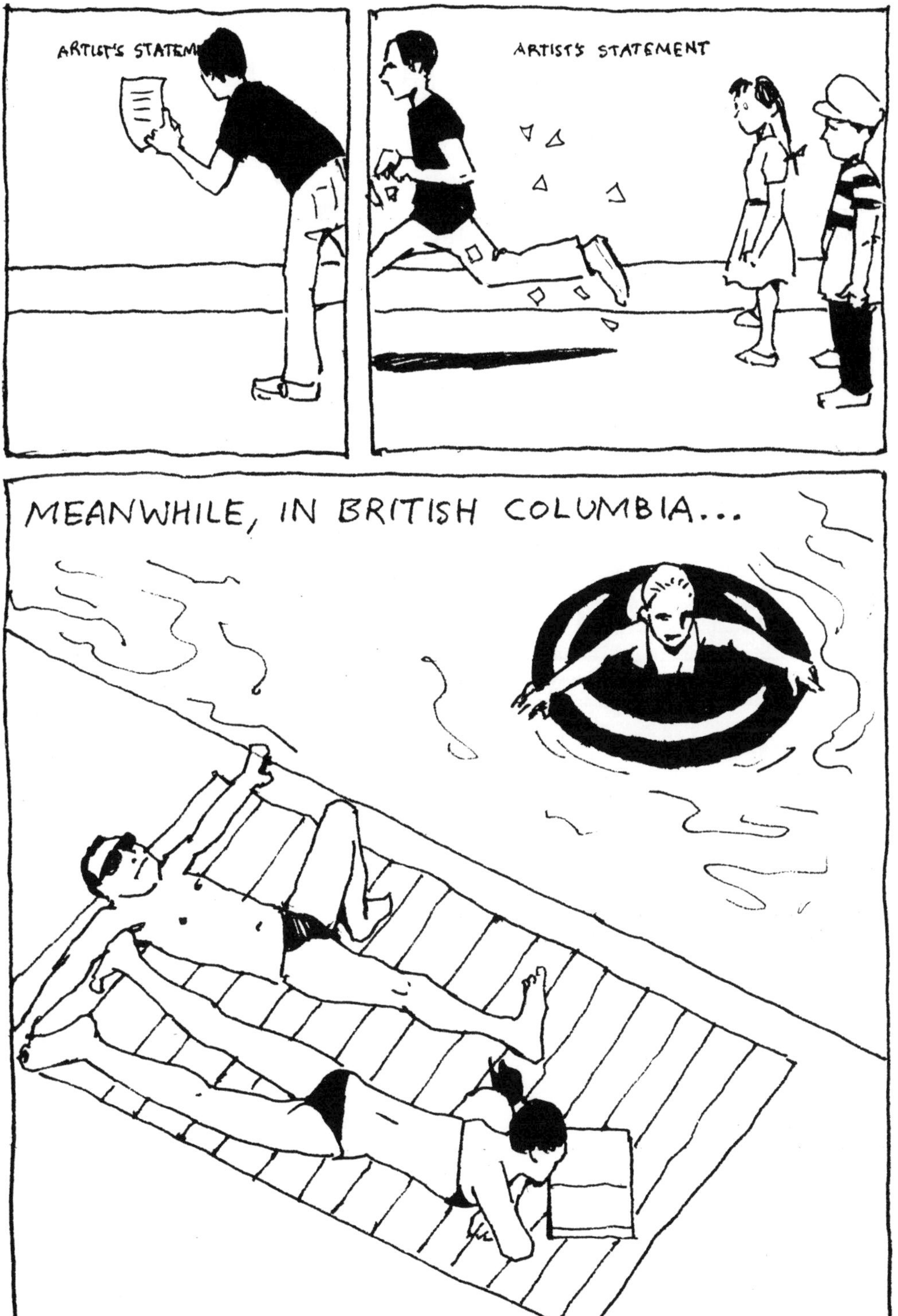
ARTIST'S STATEM
ARTIST'S STATEMENT
MEANWHILE, IN BRITISH COLUMBIA...

Brrr— I'm starting to get goosebumps!
Hey— it's startin' to snow, eh?
Don't look now, but we've got company!
END

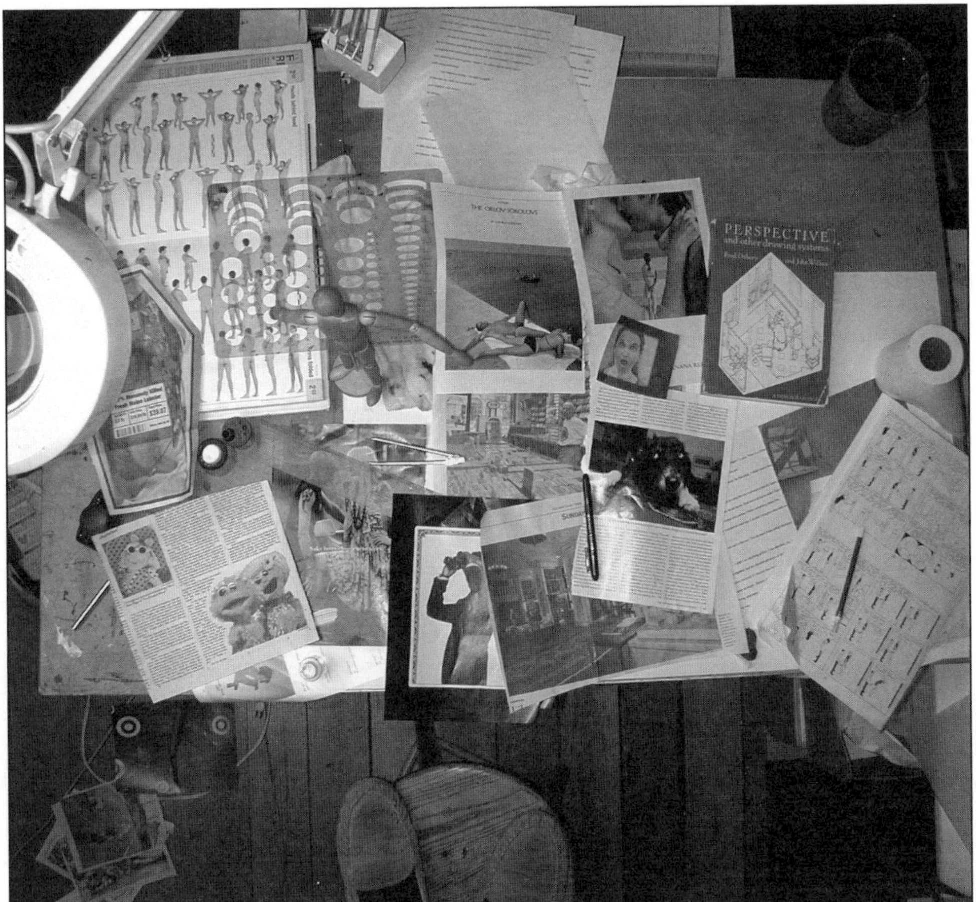
PERSPECTIVE
and other drawing systems

David Chelsea's drawing table during his "From an Infinite Distance" session. Photo by the artist.

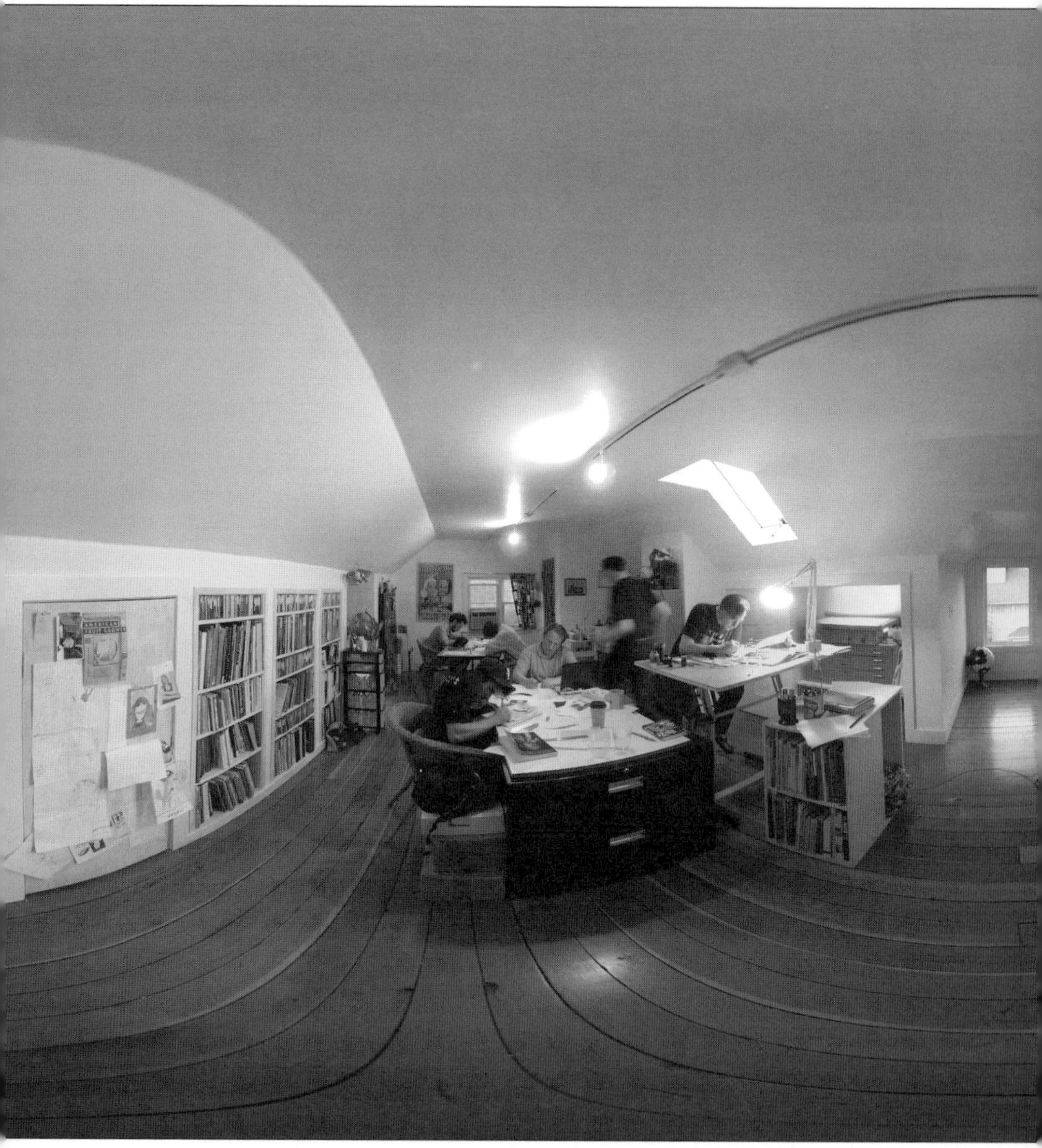

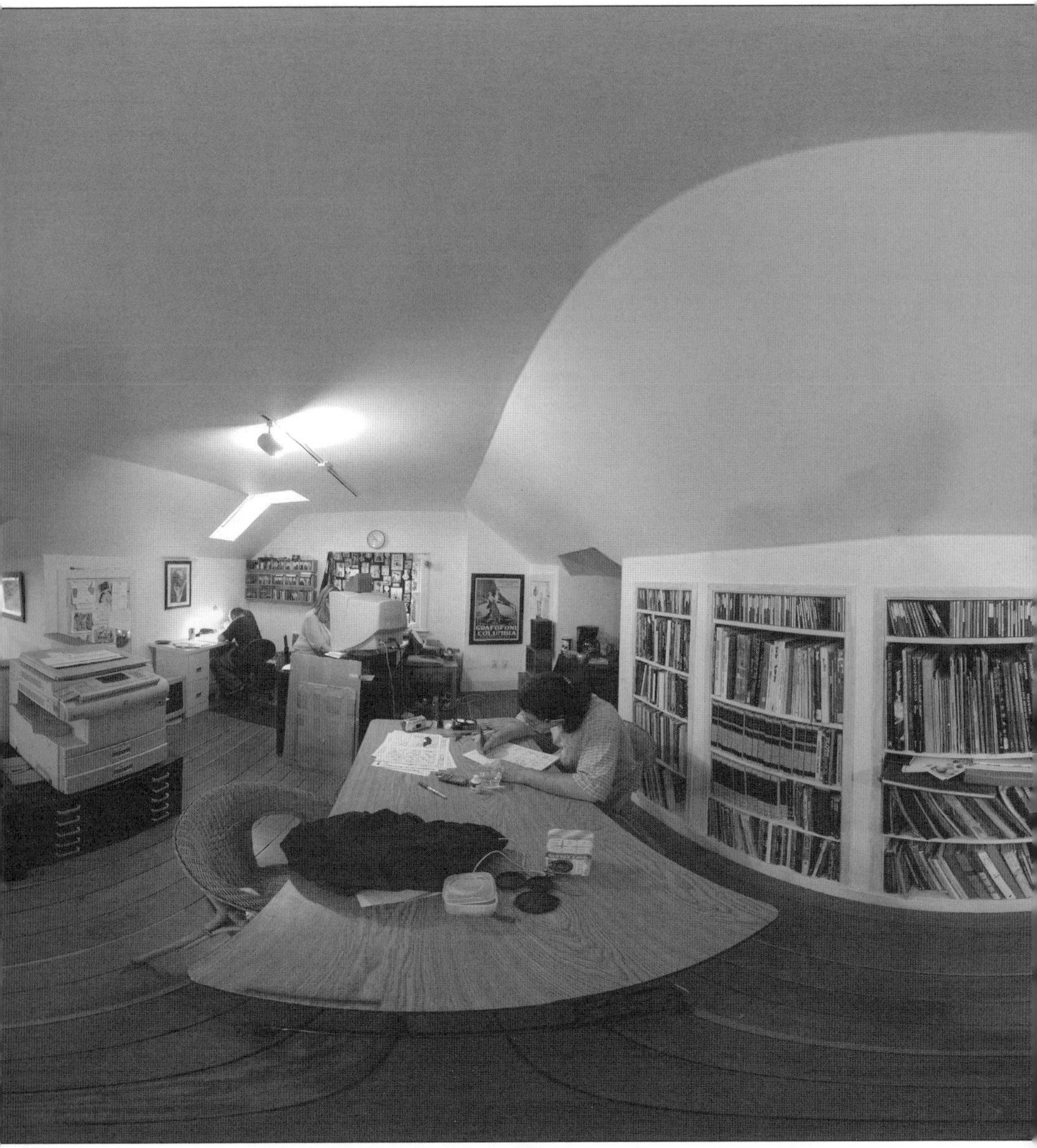
GRAFOFONI
COLUMBIA

David Chelsea and other artists working in David's studio. Taken in July 2006 by photographer Tom Lechner, during the "Bingo the Cat" session. Used with permission. A full-color, immersive look into this panoramic photo can be found at Mr. Lechner's website, TomLechner.com. A direct link to the panoramic photo is: http://www.tomlechner.com/spheres/index.php#spheres.

The 24-Hour Comic Book

A **"CulturePulp"** journalism comic by Mike Russell • grey-tones by Chad Essley

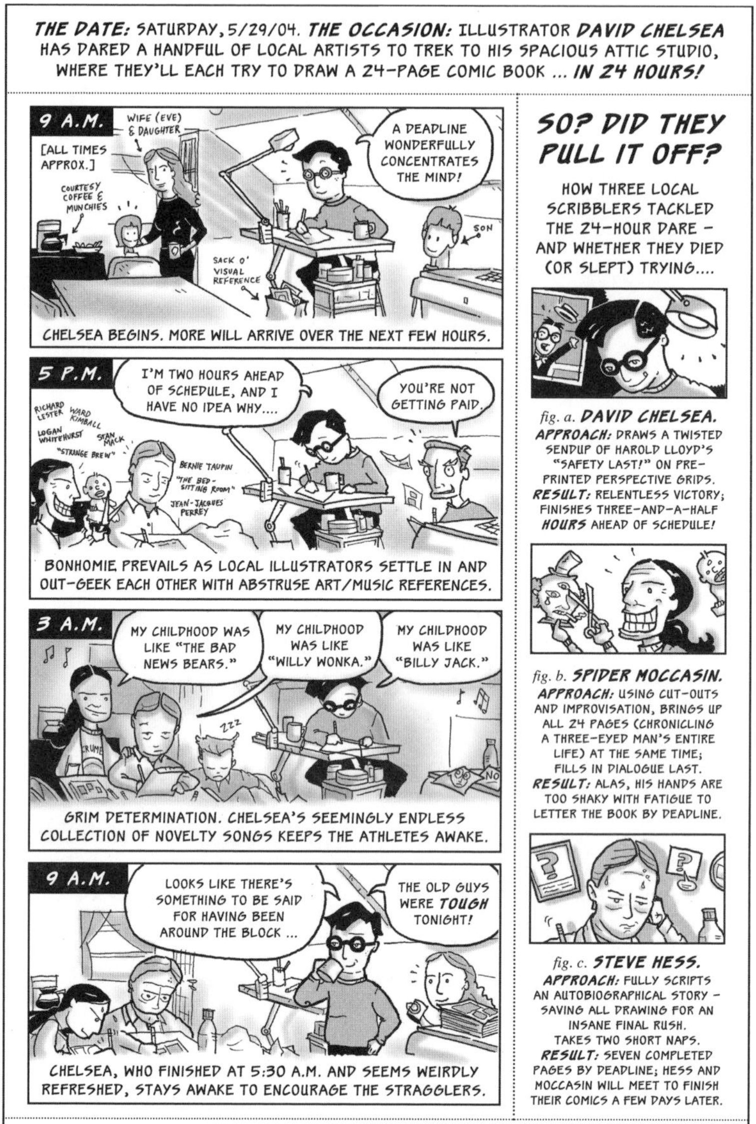

THE DATE: SATURDAY, 5/29/04. THE OCCASION: ILLUSTRATOR DAVID CHELSEA HAS DARED A HANDFUL OF LOCAL ARTISTS TO TREK TO HIS SPACIOUS ATTIC STUDIO, WHERE THEY'LL EACH TRY TO DRAW A 24-PAGE COMIC BOOK ... IN 24 HOURS!
9 A.M.
[ALL TIMES APPROX.]
WIFE (EVE) & DAUGHTER
COURTESY COFFEE & MUNCHIES
A DEADLINE WONDERFULLY CONCENTRATES THE MIND!
SACK O' VISUAL REFERENCE
SON
CHELSEA BEGINS. MORE WILL ARRIVE OVER THE NEXT FEW HOURS.
5 P.M.
I'M TWO HOURS AHEAD OF SCHEDULE, AND I HAVE NO IDEA WHY....
YOU'RE NOT GETTING PAID.
RICHARD LESTER
WARD KIMBALL
LOGAN WHITEHURST
STAN MACK
"STRANGE BREW"
BERNIE TAUPIN
"THE BED-SITTING ROOM"
JEAN-JACQUES PERREY
BONHOMIE PREVAILS AS LOCAL ILLUSTRATORS SETTLE IN AND OUT-GEEK EACH OTHER WITH ABSTRUSE ART/MUSIC REFERENCES.
3 A.M.
MY CHILDHOOD WAS LIKE "THE BAD NEWS BEARS."
MY CHILDHOOD WAS LIKE "WILLY WONKA."
MY CHILDHOOD WAS LIKE "BILLY JACK."
ZZZ
GRIM DETERMINATION. CHELSEA'S SEEMINGLY ENDLESS COLLECTION OF NOVELTY SONGS KEEPS THE ATHLETES AWAKE.
9 A.M.
LOOKS LIKE THERE'S SOMETHING TO BE SAID FOR HAVING BEEN AROUND THE BLOCK ...
THE OLD GUYS WERE TOUGH TONIGHT!
CHELSEA, WHO FINISHED AT 5:30 A.M. AND SEEMS WEIRDLY REFRESHED, STAYS AWAKE TO ENCOURAGE THE STRAGGLERS.
SO? DID THEY PULL IT OFF?
HOW THREE LOCAL SCRIBBLERS TACKLED THE 24-HOUR DARE – AND WHETHER THEY DIED (OR SLEPT) TRYING....
fig. a. DAVID CHELSEA.
APPROACH: DRAWS A TWISTED SENDUP OF HAROLD LLOYD'S "SAFETY LAST!" ON PRE-PRINTED PERSPECTIVE GRIDS.
RESULT: RELENTLESS VICTORY; FINISHES THREE-AND-A-HALF HOURS AHEAD OF SCHEDULE!
fig. b. SPIDER MOCCASIN.
APPROACH: USING CUT-OUTS AND IMPROVISATION, BRINGS UP ALL 24 PAGES (CHRONICLING A THREE-EYED MAN'S ENTIRE LIFE) AT THE SAME TIME; FILLS IN DIALOGUE LAST.
RESULT: ALAS, HIS HANDS ARE TOO SHAKY WITH FATIGUE TO LETTER THE BOOK BY DEADLINE.
fig. c. STEVE HESS.
APPROACH: FULLY SCRIPTS AN AUTOBIOGRAPHICAL STORY – SAVING ALL DRAWING FOR AN INSANE FINAL RUSH. TAKES TWO SHORT NAPS.
RESULT: SEVEN COMPLETED PAGES BY DEADLINE; HESS AND MOCCASIN WILL MEET TO FINISH THEIR COMICS A FEW DAYS LATER.

ENDNOTES AND DIGRESSIONS: **1.** For the sake of narrative tightness, we sort of ... lied when we called the 24-hour challenge "Chelsea's dare"; said challenge was actually thrown down a while back, online, by comics guru Scott McCloud. (Mr. Chelsea just had the idea to make a party out of it.) You can read McCloud's original "dare" online at *www.scottmccloud.com/inventions/24hr/24hr.html*. **2.** In addition to his excellent, autobiographical "David Chelsea in Love," our host has also written "Perspective! for Comic Book Artists," available now at your local art store. **3.** CulturePulp's own Chad Essley and Mike Russell both attended the challenge -- and stayed awake most (or, in Chad's case, all) of the night — though neither seriously undertook a 24-page comic book.

WWW.CULTUREPULP.COM

David Chelsea's first 24-hour comics session was a bit of a media event. Cartoon journalist Michael "Mike" Russell was present and drew this strip for the *Oregonian*, as a part of his ongoing *Culture Pulp* strip. Reprinted with permission.

David Chelsea working during his "Jesusland" session. Photo by Eve Harris Celsi. Used with permission.

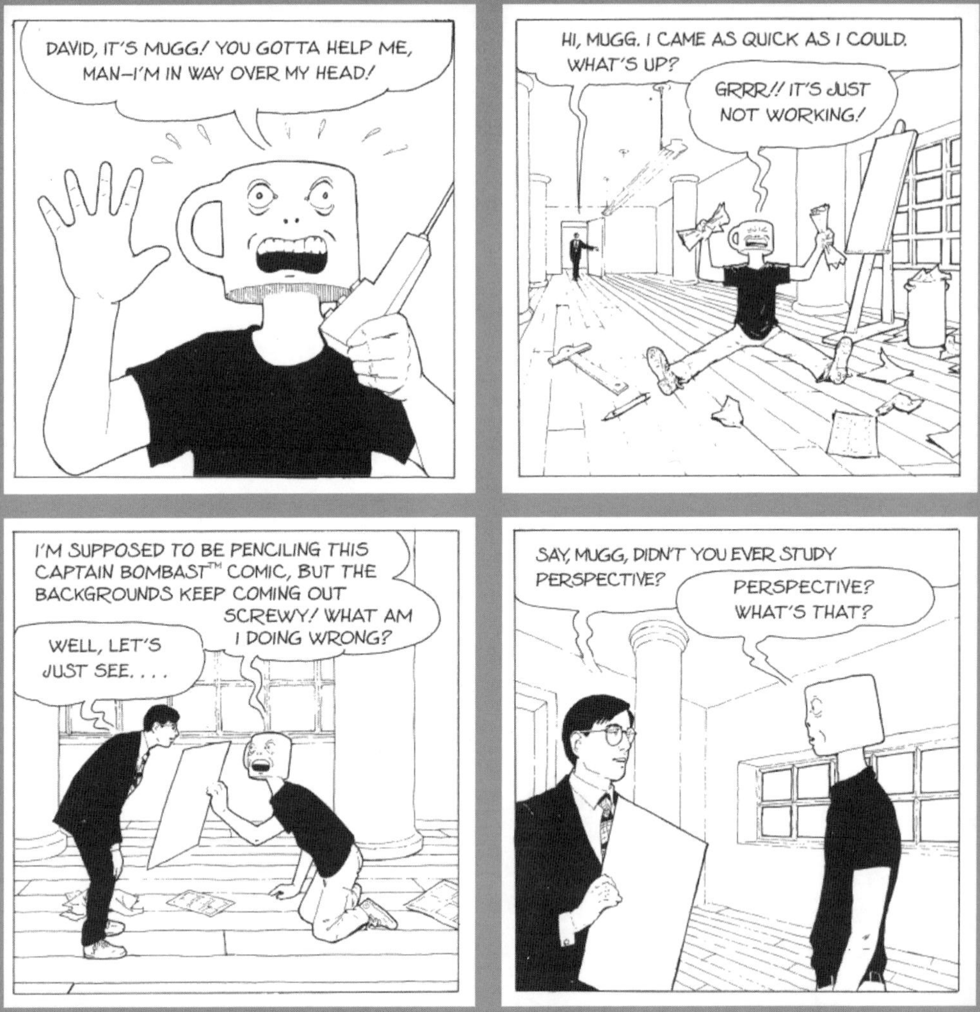
DAVID, IT'S MUGG! YOU GOTTA HELP ME, MAN—I'M IN WAY OVER MY HEAD!
HI, MUGG. I CAME AS QUICK AS I COULD. WHAT'S UP?
GRRR!! IT'S JUST NOT WORKING!
I'M SUPPOSED TO BE PENCILING THIS CAPTAIN BOMBAST™ COMIC, BUT THE BACKGROUNDS KEEP COMING OUT SCREWY! WHAT AM I DOING WRONG?
WELL, LET'S JUST SEE. . . .
SAY, MUGG, DIDN'T YOU EVER STUDY PERSPECTIVE?
PERSPECTIVE? WHAT'S THAT?

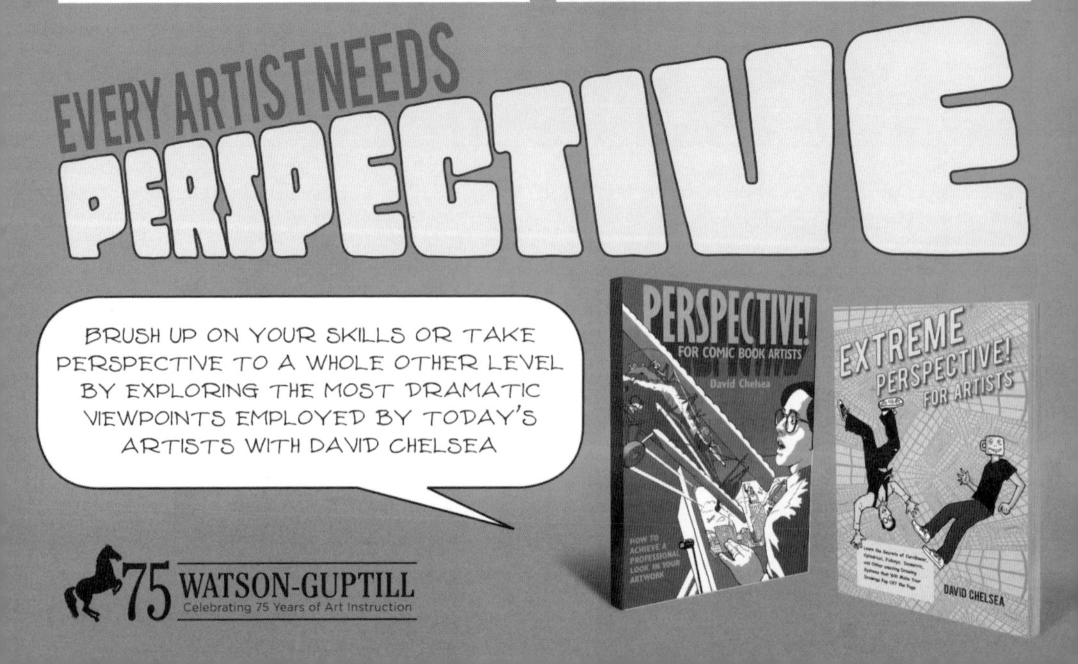
PERSPECTIVE!
FOR COMIC BOOK ARTISTS
David Chelsea
HOW TO ACHIEVE A PROFESSIONAL LOOK IN YOUR ARTWORK
EXTREME PERSPECTIVE! FOR ARTISTS
DAVID CHELSEA

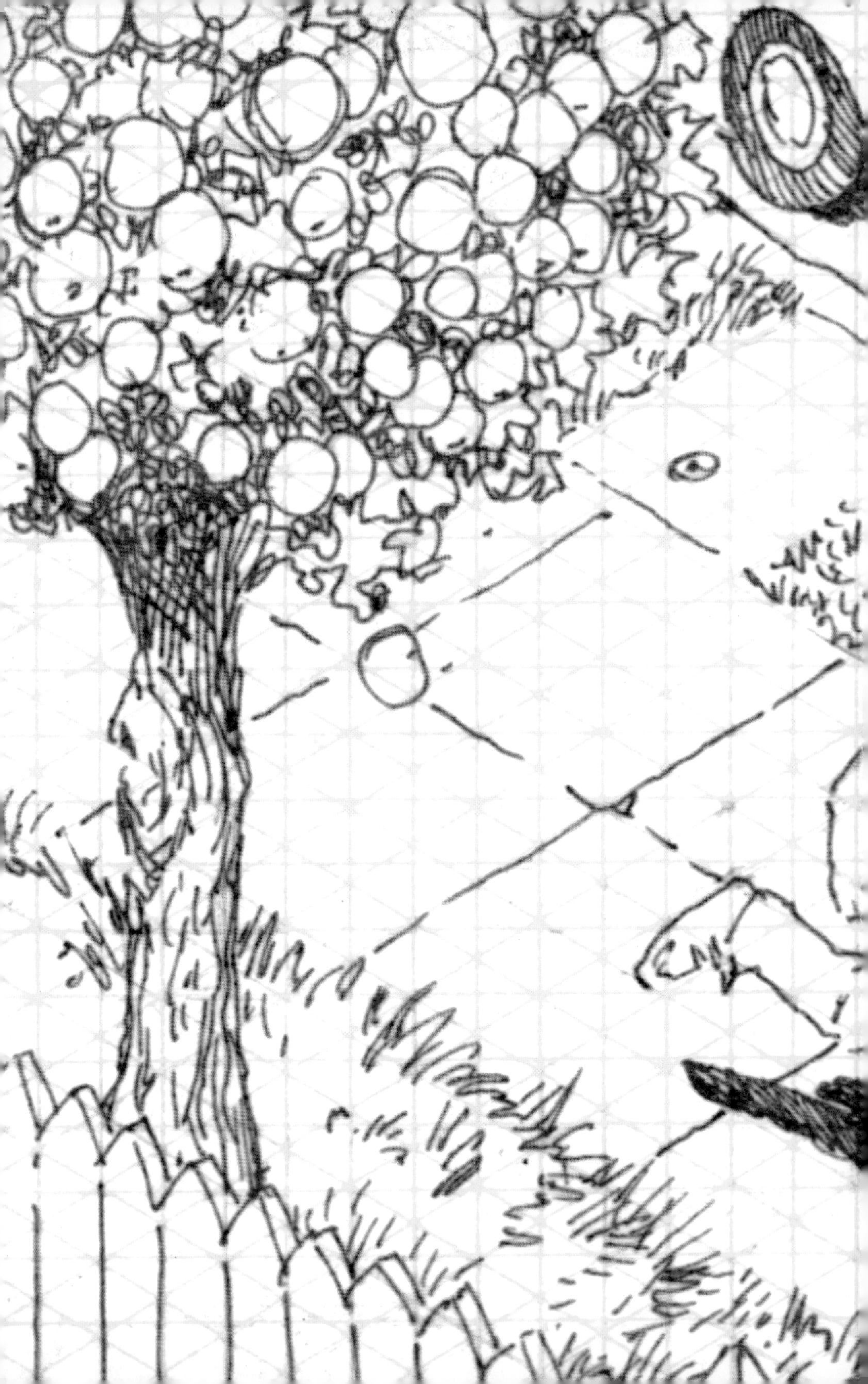